THE PASSIONATE EYE

Impressionist and Other Master Paintings from the Collection of Emil G. Bührle, Zurich

Catalogue of the exhibition in commemoration of the 100th birthday
of the collector Emil G. Bührle

This catalogue has been made possible by the
INDUSTRIAL AND COMMERCIAL BANK ZURICH LTD.

RIZZOLI INTERNATIONAL PUBLICATIONS, INC.

Exhibition dates

National Gallery of Art, Washington
6 May – 15 July 1990

The Montreal Museum of Fine Arts
3 August – 14 October 1990

Yokohama Museum of Art
2 November 1990 – 13 January 1991

Royal Academy of Arts, London
1 February – 9 April 1991

This exhibition has been organized by the Foundation Emil G. Bührle Collection,
Zurich, Switzerland, and the National Gallery of Art, Washington

Published by Artemis Verlag Zurich

For the English edition:
Editors Office, National Gallery of Art, Washington
Translation of German texts by Ulrike Mills, National Gallery of Art, Washington,
Luci Collings, editor, Royal Academy of Arts, London, and Henry A. Frey, Zurich
Conception: Hortense Anda-Bührle, Margrit Hahnloser-Ingold, Charles S. Moffett
Design: Peter Rüfenacht, Artemis Zurich
Production: Franz Ebner, Artemis Zurich
Printed by Imprimeries Réunies Lausanne S. A., Renens, Switzerland

Cover: Camille Pissarro, *Road from Versailles to Louveciennes* (cat. 19, detail)

Contents

Authors

Christian Bührle (CB), *Foundation Emil G. Bührle Collection, Zurich, cats. 7, 8, 9, 85*

Ann Dumas (AD), *cats. 29, 30, 31, 32, 33, 45, 46, 47, 48*

Frederik J. Duparc (FJD), *Chief Curator, The Montreal Museum of Fine Arts, cats. 1, 2, 3, 4, 5, 6*

Margrit Hahnloser-Ingold (MH), *Foundation Emil G. Bührle Collection, Zurich, cats. 69, 70, 71, 72, 73, 74, 75, 76, 77, 78, 79, 80, 81, 82, 83, 84*

Charles S. Moffett (CSM), *Senior Curator of Paintings, National Gallery of Art, cats. 21, 22, 23, 24, 25, 26, 27, 28, 38, 39, 40, 41, 42, 43, 44, 49, 50, 51, 52, 58, 59, 60, 61, 62, 63*

Marla Prather (MP), *Assistant Curator, National Gallery of Art, cats. 53, 54, 55, 56, 57*

Margaret Denton Smith (MDS), *cats. 10, 12, 13, 14, 15, 17, 18, 34, 35*

MaryAnne Stevens (MAS), *Librarian and Head of Education, Royal Academy of Arts, cats. 16, 19, 20, 36, 37, 64, 65, 66, 67, 68*

Janis A. Tomlinson (JAT), *Assistant Professor, Columbia University, cat. 11*

This exhibition has been made possible by

Martin Marietta Corporation
for the National Gallery of Art, Washington, D. C.

American Express Canada, Inc.
Swissair Canada
Martin Marietta Canada, Ltd.
The Government of Canada
for the Montreal Museum of Fine Arts, Montreal

Yomiuri Shimbun
for the Yokohama Museum of Art, Yokohama

Glaxo Holdings p.l.c.
for the Royal Academy of Arts, London

Bally Japan, Ltd.

Industrial and Commercial Bank Zurich Ltd.

Foreword

"When you throw a stone into calm water," wrote Emil Georg Bührle, "a circle appears on the surface, which generates a second, concentric one, then a third, and so on, depending on the force of the initial impact." Beginning with his first purchase in 1925, Bührle's art collection has followed since 1934 a similar pattern, ever widening, with one acquisition growing out of another. He might purchase several works by a single artist—as he did, most notably, with Cézanne, van Gogh, and Manet. Or he might pursue the connection between one artist, style, or period and another. In all of his collecting, he bought with a sophisticated and informed eye, and he formed a collection that is recognized throughout the world as one of the best created during this century.

Organized to commemorate the centennial of Bührle's birth, and responding to an initiative of the National Gallery of Art and the enthusiasm of all of us, *The Passionate Eye* is yet another circle in the calm water. In twenty-five years of collecting Bührle acquired more than three hundred works of art, including painting, sculpture, and works on paper. The present exhibition focuses on his paintings, which were his greatest love. Its selection of eighty-five works, lent by both the Foundation Emil G. Bührle Collection in Zurich and the Bührle family, represents the full spectrum of his collection and offers a rare opportunity to see works that remain in private hands in the context of the broader collection.

What unites Emil Bührle's collection is the superb quality of the works of art. Whether acquiring works by Cuyp, Cézanne, or Picasso, he selected premier examples. He could appreciate the beauty of paintings as diverse as a religious procession by Goya, a capriccio of Venice's Grand Canal by Canaletto, an intimate still life by Manet, or an analytical cubist portrait by Braque. Some of Bührle's acquisitions are art-historical icons, among them van Gogh's *The Sower*. But he displayed the same discernment and sensitivity in choosing a seventeenth-century Dutch landscape or an early twentieth-century still life. Of all the portraits of young women that Renoir painted, Bührle chose one that is exceptional in its technical virtuosity, elegance, and sympathetic rendering of the sitter. Of the landscapes by Renoir, he chose one of the artist's finest "high" or "classic" impressionist works of the early 1870s, which also happens to have played an important role in the first impressionist group show in 1874.

Bührle's acquisitions were made with a passionate commitment to works of art that are inviting, engaging, and stylistically significant. His paintings give enormous pleasure and, in many cases, have contributed substantially to the history of art. Equally important, in the history of collecting they bespeak the eye and mind of a great connoisseur, whose discriminating acquisitions have withstood the test of time.

We are most grateful for the opportunity to share Emil G. Bührle's extraordinary achievement with audiences in the United States of America, Canada, Japan, and Great Britain, and we would like to extend our sincerest and deepest thanks to Hortense Anda-Bührle, Dieter Bührle, and the Trustees of the Foundation Emil G. Bührle Collection for their generosity in lending to this exhibition. In addition, we would like to express our gratitude to the many people who participated in the organization and selection of the exhibition and in the publication of the catalogue, especially Hortense Anda-Bührle, Margrit Hahnloser-Ingold, Jürg Wille, and Christian Bührle of the Foundation Emil G. Bührle Collection; and Franz Ebner, Fritz Hofer, and Peter Rüfenacht of Artemis Verlag, Zurich.

At the National Gallery preparations have been overseen by Charles S. Moffett, Senior Curator of Paintings, D. Dodge Thompson, Chief of Exhibition Programs, Elizabeth Driscoll Pochter, Exhibitions Officer, Mary Suzor, Registrar, Elizabeth A. Croog, Associate Secretary-General Counsel, Elizabeth A. C. Weil, Corporate Relations Officer, Gaillard F. Ravenel and Mark A. Leithauser, Chief and Deputy Chief of Design and Installation, Frances Smyth, Editor-in-Chief, Tam Curry, Editor, Florence E. Coman, Assistant Curator, and Elizabeth P. Streicher, Associate Research Curator. Alice Whelihan, Indemnity Administrator for the Federal Council on the Arts and the Humanities, coordinated the indemnity for the Washington venue.

The exhibition's showing at the Montreal Museum of Fine Arts was organized by Frederik J. Duparc, Chief Curator. Pierre Archambault, Claude Pardis, and Simon Labrie were in charge of transportation, security, and installation. Danielle Sauvage, Director of Communications, was responsible for promotion and publicity. We would also like to acknowledge Sylvie Brousseau for revision of some of the catalogue texts and Natalie Vanier.

Yosoji Kobayashi, President of the Yomiuri Shimbun, Minoru Horiuchi, Director of the Culture and Sports Promotions Department, Akihiko Itoh, General Manager of the Cultural Promotion Department, Hiroomi Osada, Assistant General Manager of the Cultural Promotion Department of the Yomiuri Shimbun, Tokyo, and Kyoko Imazu, Cultural Correspondent of the Yomiuri Shimbun, Paris, and Akihiro Nanjo, Director of Art Yomiuri France, as well as François Daulte, President of the Hermitage Foundation, Lausanne, made arrangements for the exhibition at the Yokohama Museum of Art.

Jiro Enjoji, Chairman of Board of Directors of the Yokohama Art Foundation, and Atsushi Takeda, Curator in chief, contributed to the organization of the exhibition's showing.

Preparations for the exhibition at the Royal Academy of Arts were made by Piers Rodgers, Secretary, Norman Rosenthal, Exhibitions Secretary, and MaryAnne Stevens, Librarian and Head of Education. These members of the staff were ably supported by Annette Bradshaw, Deputy Exhibitions Secretary, Sue Thompson, Exhibitions Assistant, and Jennifer Taylor, Manager, Sponsorship and Corporate Membership Scheme of the Royal Academy Trust. Supplementary editing of catalogue texts was expertly handled by Luci Collings.

We would like to take this opportunity to express our profound gratitude to our sponsors.

Special thanks must go to Martin Marietta Corporation, whose generous financial support has made possible the initial organizational stages of this exhibition and its presentation at the National Gallery of Art. We wish to thank in particular Norman R. Augustine, Chairman and Chief Executive Officer, Caleb B. Hurtt, President and Chief Operating Officer, and William B. Harwood, Vice President.

The Montreal Museum of Fine Arts would like to thank American Express Canada, Ltd., for their generous contribution. We also wish to thank Swissair, and in particular Josef Waegeli, Swissair's General Manager for Canada, who was sensitive to the needs of the museum. We are grateful to Martin Marietta Canada Ltd. and President William Griffin, for contributing to the presentation in Montreal. Moreover, the exhibition enjoyed the support of La Presse and CKAC, two longtime friends of the museum, as well as the support from the Government of Canada through the Insurance Programme for Travelling Exhibitions.

We are also deeply grateful to Glaxo Holdings p. l. c., and particularly the Chairman, Sir Peter Girolami, who once again have expressed their support of the Royal Academy by sponsoring the exhibition in London.

Finally, we would like to express our warmest thanks to the scores of other colleagues in Zurich, Washington, D. C., Montreal, Yokohama, and London, who have worked so diligently to bring this project to completion.

J. CARTER BROWN

Director
National Gallery of Art

PIERRE THÉBERGE

Director
The Montreal Museum of Fine Arts

MICHIAKI KAWAKITA

General Director
Yokohama Museum of Art

ROGER DE GREY

President
Royal Academy of Arts

Preface

Emil Georg Bührle was born on 31 August 1890. On the occasion of the centenary of his birth, his family feels it is fitting to honor his memory.

Throughout his life, painting was my father's greatest passion and one to which he owed countless hours of joy and happiness. It therefore seemed appropriate to commemorate this anniversary with an exhibition that brings together the greatest works from his collection, works which reflect both his love of impressionist and postimpressionist paintings and also his wider interests, ranging from the Dutch and Venetian schools to the masters of the twentieth century.

Emil Bührle had himself for many years wanted to mount an exhibition of the collection in its entirety, but had always regarded it as being far from complete. In 1956 he saw the opportunity for such a show, having funded the addition of a new wing to the Zurich Kunsthaus, a gift to the city of Zurich. However, this new wing was still under construction when, in November 1956, and still in his prime, he suddenly died. The inaugural exhibition, in 1958, was held in memory of the Donor and comprised 273 paintings, 30 medieval sculptures and 18 works of ancient art. Several further exhibitions of the collection then followed: Charlottenburg Palace, Berlin (1958); Haus der Kunst, Munich (1958–1959); Royal Scottish Academy, Edinburgh (1961), and the National Gallery, London (1961).

Many paintings from the Bührle Collection are, and have been, in constant demand for exhibitions all over the world, and the administrators of the estate have been torn between an awareness of the need for conservation and a desire to contribute to and promote the study of art history. The Foundation E. G. Bührle, controlling the greater part of the collection, was established by the family after my father's death in order to make the works available to the public. However, the constant flow of loan requests, particularly in the last decade, has made it difficult to honor our initial undertaking to keep the art on display locally. Consequently, in addition to this exhibition's main purpose as an homage to E. G. Bührle, it also brings to an end the current lending activities of the Foundation.

We are profoundly grateful to the museums that have shown such spontaneous interest in this exhibition, in particular the National Gallery of Art, Washington, D. C., and its Director, J. Carter Brown; the Museum of Fine Arts (Musée des beaux-arts) in Montreal and its Director, Pierre Théberge;

the Yokohama Museum of Art and its General Director, Michiaki Kawakita, as well as Akihiro Nanjo and François Daulte; and the Royal Academy of Arts, London, and its President, Roger de Grey. We greatly appreciate the understanding and considerate cooperation shown by these institutions and their staff, especially the National Gallery of Art, Washington, and its Senior Curator of Paintings, Charles S. Moffett; Norman Rosenthal, Exhibitions Secretary, and MaryAnne Stevens, Librarian and Head of Education from The Royal Academy, and Frederik J. Duparc, Chief Curator of the Montreal Museum of Fine Arts.

We should also like to thank the scholars who have contributed to the catalogue as well as the Swiss staff who helped with the organization of this exhibition, most significantly our friends and colleagues Dr. Margrit Hahnloser and Dr. Jürg Wille, and also Christian Bührle Jr., Paul Pfister, our conservator, and Franz Ebner, Director of Artemis Publishers, and his team.

The exhibition *The Passionate Eye / Un Regard passionné* would not have been possible without the most generous support of the sponsors Martin Marietta Corporation for Washington, D. C.; American Express Canada, Ltd., Swissair Canada, Martin Marietta Canada, Ltd., La Presse and CKAC, and the Government of Canada through the "Insurance Programme for Travelling Exhibitions" for Montreal; Yomiuri Shimbun, and Bally Japan, Ltd., for Yokohama; and Glaxo Holdings p. l. c. for London. Neither the catalogue nor the exhibition would have been possible without the splendid assistance provided by the Industrial & Commercial Bank Zurich Ltd. It is a privilege to record here our deep appreciation of all these contributions.

We hope that those visiting this exhibition, its organizers, and all those involved in its realization can experience something of the joy felt by Emil Bührle throughout his life as he strove to bring to fruition the dream of his youth.

HORTENSE ANDA-BÜHRLE

President, Foundation Emil G. Bührle Collection

The bust *Emil G. Bührle* by Otto Charles Bänninger, 1956.

Emil Georg Bührle in his picture gallery in Zurich, 1953.

Emil Georg Bührle

A Student of Art History Turned Industrialist and Art Collector

MARGRIT HAHNLOSER-INGOLD

The story of Emil Georg Bührle the collector is an extraordinary one. Born in southern Germany into a middle-class family, the young Bührle studied literature and art history and dreamt of paintings. These dreams were temporarily cast aside when he was called to serve as an officer in the First World War. After the war he pursued a career that was closer to reality, and met with overwhelming success as an industrialist. But later, remembering his earlier dream, he began to collect, surrounding himself with exquisite works of art.

Oskar Kokoschka, who had painted Bührle's portrait in 1952, four years before his death, offered these impressions in a commemorative essay: "He was a lonely man [who] often stayed at his office until dawn, unless he happened to be host to a chief of state, or a government minister or emissary... and they would come from all over the world. Every once in a while he would invite me, almost shyly, to walk over to the neighboring building with him and look at his collection, even though it could only be viewed under artificial light. . . . We would contemplate this or that painting which he had just acquired. His brown eyes could truly see, which is not generally the case with collectors. Was it then that his innermost being was brought alive, when he felt the magical touch of art?"[1]

Kokoschka's question preoccupies anyone who makes a study of Bührle's life. This man assembled a spectacular collection of impressionist and postimpressionist paintings, and created it almost secretively, entirely in his spare time. The treasures not only adorned his house but were piled up in a vacant apartment on the second floor of a nearby building (now occupied by the Foundation)—the so-called gallery. He was able to retreat here during the few leisure hours at his disposal—usually late in the evening or on Sundays—in order to nurture his passion for art and to spend time in silent contemplation of his paintings. This passion was vividly described by René Wehrli, at that time Director of the Zurich Kunsthaus: "How great Emil Bührle's love of art was, could be felt especially strongly when one visited him. Then, it was quite likely that—even if it was late at night—he would get up, take a bunch of keys and invite one to go with him into the annex, where his paintings were hanging. One would then go through the unlit garden, climb up a flight of stairs and enter an apartment bare of furniture, where the masterpieces were ranged along the walls, as if in a museum storeroom. Even if one had come there for a specific purpose, to inspect a new acquisition, let us say, the collector never failed to make a tour of the entire collection and to linger before this or that painting, depending on the particular mood of the moment. Little was ever said, for Bührle was a man who thought and acted constructively and was not prone to analysis. It was more as if these paintings were living beings or thoroughbred creatures, which one would stroke and to which one would utter an encouraging word, believing that they would somehow understand. This pure, almost childlike, and simple delight in the beauty of these objects was expressed more with gestures than in words, and the guest realized that here was a refuge, a place where the 'spinning globe' stood still and where, in these unembellished rooms, containing objects of the highest rank and value, the important thing was not mere display or discussion, but reflection."[2]

Unlike the great Swiss collector, Oskar Reinhart, from Winterthur (a slightly older man), Emil Bührle had not the means to devote himself entirely to his art and the pursuit of his dream, for at an early age he had determined to restore to profitability a debt-ridden company. The two collectors, though profoundly different personalities, remained for many years on friendly terms.

In 1919, at the end of the First World War, Bührle (now aged twenty-nine) decided to abandon his academic and military life and to make his way in a new sphere, in the world of industry. He was, in his own words, "firmly resolved to achieve something in this field."[3] When, after a long period of successful industrial activity—which was not without its occasional ups and downs—he could once more devote himself to this urge to collect works of art, he came to the following realization: "The true entrepreneur is related to the artist, only he does not create with a pen, a brush, or a chisel, he creates with what already exists. It is not by chance that all great industrial leaders derive a special pleasure from building and that many of them also collect paintings or sculptures, if indeed they are not themselves painters or sculptors. This creative instinct cannot be acquired, it must be innate. The intuition of the creative entrepreneur cannot be learned in schools or from books."[4] Bührle knew that one could neither acquire the passion for collecting nor a creative imagination; such qualities were innate in a person. As a former art student, Bührle was singularly fortunate in being able to call on his earlier knowledge when he sought to make his boyhood dreams come true.

Both as a collector and as an industrial entrepreneur Bührle possessed a highly developed creative intuition that was to shape his life and determine his success. It also brought him closer to art itself, although he modestly observed: "My knowledge of art history has, of course, assisted me greatly as a collector, even though I regard myself as a mere amateur in this field. A philologist is no more predestined to be a poet than is an art historian to be a collector. I would say, rather, that the true collector is a frustrated artist."[5] In Bührle's case, the felicitous combination of an entrepreneurial instinct, openmindedness, and a thirst for culture drew him toward creative activity. Everything that he turned his hand to prospered, in the spheres of both business and collecting.

It is interesting to note that the initial inspiration for the formation of the Foundation Emil G. Bührle Collection after the death of the collector almost certainly came from the United States rather than from Europe. Owing, possibly, to his business relations with that country, he could well have drawn upon the examples of such self-made tycoons as Frick and Albert C. Barnes, whose collections were transformed into public museums or foundations.

Industrialist and Collector

Within a European context Bührle's biography is unusual. The collector himself has described his early years as follows: "Born in 1890 in Pforzheim in Baden, I attended school there until I was thirteen, then graduated, in 1909, in Freiburg im Breisgau. Between the ages of sixteen and seventeen I was very interested in technical matters, prompting my classmates to call me 'electric Jake'.[6] But through the study of poetry, inspired by a certain Elisabeth, I decided to pursue a course of literature and art history. In 1910, in the third semester, I went to the University of Munich. Unfortunately for me the renowned Swiss art historian, Heinrich Wölfflin, had just left to take up a post in Berlin. The beginning of the war in August 1914 tore me away from my dissertation [on the novelist Jean Paul] and swept me up into the conflict. Four years served on the front, in France, Russia, Rumania, and again in France, turned an unworldly aesthete and philosopher into a man accustomed to looking reality squarely in the eye, making quick decisions, acting upon them, and taking responsibility for others."[7]

In 1919–1920, at the end of the war, Bührle was a volunteer, later becoming manager at the Machine-Tool Factory Magdeburg. His marriage to Charlotte Schalk, the artistically gifted daughter of a prominent banker in Magdeburg, was of considerable importance for his future career.

It was at this point that the contemplative man also possibly came under the influence of the postwar philosopher, Oswald Spengler, whose ideas were quoted by Bührle in later years, "Harshness, Roman severity are now the dominant forces in this world. For anything else there will soon be no room. Art, yes, but in concrete and steel. Poetry, yes, but written by men with iron nerves and relentless vision. Religion, yes, but use your prayer

The art student Emil Georg Bührle before the First World War.

book, not Confucius printed on parchment—and go to church. Politics, yes, but by statesmen, not utopians."[8]

In 1924 the young businessman was sent by his company to Zurich, where it had taken over the stock of the debt-ridden Swiss Machine-Tool Works in Oerlikon near Zurich. He was to stay there for the rest of his life, reorganizing the company, becoming director, then owner, and achieving considerable success. His experiences in the war combined with his entrepreneurial spirit led him to develop prototypes of air defense and anti-tank weapons. To undertake such re-organization of a company in the 1920s, a time of worldwide crisis, took vision and courage. Bührle's main consideration no doubt remained investment in new technology but, despite a large number of international orders, he had no wish to encourage expansion for its own sake, thereby risking falling into debt. His wise management caused the firm to prosper. It is not surprising, therefore, that his collecting activity got under way at much the same time; prior to this success he had had neither the time nor the means for such pursuits. The outbreak of the Second World War in 1939 led to economic recession in Switzerland and heavy losses for the firm in 1940, when Bührle was anxious to prevent the threat of possible redundancies. This once again hampered the collector's initial enthusiasm. The inner flame, however, could not be extinguished and was rekindled so vigorously after the war had passed that in a relatively short time, between 1946 and Bührle's death in 1956, the greater part of the collection was assembled. During this time, according to his secretary, Hans Bänninger, Bührle's fervor for collecting often moved him to buy works of art by the dozen. Adding up the cost of his purchases, he would heavily sigh, "I need a guardian, don't you think?"

Bührle did not buy art according to established guidelines, but chose to follow his personal preferences, as he described in a lecture of 1954: "In the fall of 1913, at the Nationalgalerie [in Berlin], I saw for the first time the marvelous French paintings that the brilliant Swiss Director of the Nationalgalerie, Hugo von Tschudi, had acquired—to the chagrin of the Emperor [Wilhelm II]. The atmospheric quality of these paintings, especially the lyricism of a Vétheuil landscape by Claude Monet, overwhelmed me completely. At that time I had not yet been to Paris and could therefore not yet judge with what degree of truth to nature these radiantly charming landscape paintings had captured the essence of the countryside around Paris."[9] This was a decisive moment in determining the direction Bührle would pursue in his collecting, and he later offered this metaphor to describe how he worked: "When you throw a stone into calm water, a circle appears on the surface, which generates a second concentric one, then a third, and so on, depending on the force of the initial impact."[10] The "stone" first made its impact for Bührle in 1913 when he was confronted by the paintings of Manet, Monet, Renoir, Degas, Cézanne, and van Gogh. Twenty years later they became the core of his collection, as he recalled: "Only in 1934 did the first circle define itself, though the stone had struck the water in 1913. This took place when—in the enthusiastic company of my wife, as always—I purchased my first Degas drawing and a still life by Renoir. This first circle, reaching from Corot to Cézanne and van Gogh, filled out rapidly and always remained the heart of my collection."[11]

Bührle left scarcely any essays or letters for posterity, although all the writings by him that we do possess show he had great literary skills. He was an industrialist, and the time needed for what was close to his heart had to be found in the evening or at night, a fact confirmed by Oskar Kokoschka and by his family. Bührle was evidently a mystery to his friends and associates, for he appeared to require no sleep, spending his nights reading, or contemplating his paintings. If we seek to discover the precise nature of his understanding of and relationship to art, and the method behind his purchases, we find very little written evidence to assist us.

In the meantime the company had grown substantially and now included the textile, welding, and airplane industries as well as activities in high vacuum thin film and coating technology. In those years the first step into the hotel business was also taken. It seems therefore that in the 1940s Bührle became increasingly aware that he could not do full justice to either his cultural interests, or to his collector's passion, without assistance. "You'll have to continue lending me a hand", he said to his young assistant, the art historian Walter Drack, whom he had taken on in 1948 as curator of the collection.

Whenever he could, Bührle visited local art galleries. Lists of his purchases show that he often bought from Aktuaryus in Zurich, then the city's most progressive art gallery. There he found his first paintings by Corot, Courbet, Pissarro, and Daubigny, as well as the landscape by Monet, *Field of Poppies.* That same year he bought his first, small Cézanne and a flower still life by van Gogh. These quiet, unassuming works were testimony to his first great love, the impressionists, and began to define the inner core of the collection. At the end of 1937 the collection gained a magnificent late Cézanne, *Mont Sainte-Victoire,* Manet's *Rue Mosnier with Flags,* van Gogh's *Olive Orchard* (see cats. 44, 25, 61), and an early Brittany landscape by Gauguin. Bührle found these paintings in Lucerne at the gallery of Siegfried Rosengart, who was the first expert to advise the passionate collector, and who is said to have warned him: "The expensive thing about this picture, Mr. Bührle, is not the sum you have just paid for it, but the fact that from now on you will only be able to buy pieces of equal rank."[12] How right Rosengart was. Emil Bührle had taken the first great step toward assembling a collection of masterpieces, and the stunning group of works that entered his house in 1937–1938 was a bold harbinger of the glories to come. From then on, he was ceaseless in the pursuit of his dream.

Portrait of the collector, 1956.

Bührle's purchases seem to have been made in sporadic bursts. During the early years of the war, owing to the uncertainty of world affairs and Bührle's own business losses, few works were added to the collection, but, as the war neared its end, he succumbed once more to the urge to buy. Through the agency of the Aktuaryus Gallery, the resolute collector discovered *The Dinner* by Monet (see cat. 46), and—thanks to Paul Rosenberg—further important works: *Madame Camus at the Piano* by Degas (see cat. 29); *Roses and Tulips in a Vase* by Manet (see cat. 28); *A Girl Reading* by Corot (see cat. 13); and five Italian landscapes by Karl Blechen, which appealed to his romantic, literary nature, and were a reminder of his German origins. The spreading circle, however, began to extend even further, reaching forward into the twentieth century, to the Nabis and the Fauves, and back to Delacroix and the beginnings of the nineteenth century. It should be mentioned at this point that in 1925, in the Wolfsberg Gallery in Zurich, Bührle picked out a landscape by Vlaminck, done in the 1920s, entitled *House by the Water,* to hang in his own house. In 1929 he had persuaded his father-in-law to purchase in Magdeburg two watercolors by Heckel. Although his first love remained the painting of the impressionists and postimpressionists, he was receptive to quality and beauty in all periods and schools—an openness of spirit which also awakened his curiosity about modern art.

A brief note of 1944 (preserved by chance) informs us that in a relatively short time Bührle had purchased twelve paintings by artists from Corot to Matisse. This magnificent group documents his voracious appetite for painting and his need to experience works of art at first hand. Daily struggles with his company business may have increased his desire to escape into the world of art and to associate with like-minded people who could advise him on his collecting. From 1943 onward, Bührle worked closely with the art dealer Fritz Nathan, whose love of music and literature further strengthened their relationship. "I am very pleased that our business association has developed into a good friendship," Bührle told him. "My trust has been betrayed too often not to value your thoroughly honest character."[13] Nathan, who had also cultivated a relationship of mutual trust with Oskar Reinhart, not only became an esteemed purchasing agent but also a partner in night-time discussions, a companion for art excursions, and an eager participant on musical outings. Several superb works joined Bührle's collection through Nathan's good offices: van Gogh's *Wheat Field with Cypresses, Blossoming Chestnut Branches,* and *The Sower;* Daumier's *The Free Performance;* Renoir's *Harvesters;* and Vlaminck's *Banks of the Seine at Chatou* (see cats. 62, 63, 12, 16, 50, and 76).

Through Fritz Nathan, Bührle was reunited with a war-time comrade, Arthur Kauffmann, who then lived in London and who recalled their first meeting: "It was the year 1917. We were in the middle of the First World

War, not far from Gulianca, a small town in the barren, sandy landscape of the Moldau in eastern Rumania. On the horizon appeared the lonely figure of a tall, slim officer of the dragoons. He walked toward me. We continued the journey together. I had my first discussions with Emil Bührle about poets and painters, books and pictures, talks that we continued in the East or in France, wherever our division happened to end up."[14] Kauffmann knew a great deal about art and became Bührle's closest confidant in such matters. When Bührle had difficulty in making a decision about various offers, Kauffmann's opinion often settled the matter. The successful negotiations for Manet's *Port of Bordeaux,* Cézanne's *Thaw in L'Estaque,* Monet's *Camille Monet, Son, and Nurse in a Garden,* and Gauguin's *Idyll in Tahiti* (see cats. 22, 38, 47, and 56) can be credited to his influence.

Following the war, news spread quickly in the West of this avid and enthusiastic collector at work in Zurich, and offers began to come from around the world. On business trips to Paris, London, or New York, Bührle visited, among others, the galleries of Wildenstein and Kaganovitch, Marlborough, Rosenberg, Seligmann, and Knoedler. In his more immediate circle his contacts soon included such dealers as Feilchenfeldt, Beyeler, Heilbronner, and Griebert. Such was his progress that when Walter Drack took an inventory in 1949, he counted fifty works of art; by 1956 the collection had increased dramatically.

Bührle's choices were occasionally influenced by a passing mood. Attending an exhibition of works by Picasso with Arthur Kauffmann, Bührle paused to admire a flower still life. "This picture was once offered to you but you turned it down," said Kauffmann, to which Bührle replied, "Where were my eyes?"[15] As a collector, he relied primarily on his eyes, yet was also led by his recognition of quality. If he did not take an immediate liking to a work of art, he would often take it home and examine it on a broad shelf in his library that he called "the bench for the accused." There a work might have to stay for a week or more before a decision was made as to whether it should join the collection. Silent study of the work, opinions solicited from the family, and late-night discussions with knowledgeable friends would finally lead him to a verdict. Bührle was a patient and attentive listener, an attribute that was confirmed by all who knew him. He possessed the rare gift of really paying attention to what was being said, although he allowed few to know what was going on in his mind or what motivated him. He listened willingly to the views of others on art, but then, as in his business dealings, he made his decision alone, frequently in an unexpected, surprising way. If he was taken by a painting not even the most vigorous protestations from his daughter Hortense could make him change his mind. This is reported to have been the case with his purchase in 1952 of Franz Marc's great painting *The Dog in Front of the World* (see cat. 79). Bührle refused to

give in, and his daughter subsequently learned to recognize the artistic merit of the work. Only very rarely—and then usually for other than artistic reasons—did Bührle change his mind concerning a work of art. When during the 1940s Courbet's great painting of the *Two Sleeping Women* was standing on the "bench for the accused" and Bührle wanted keenly to acquire it, he acceded most reluctantly to his wife's wishes; she dismissed it as a "museum piece" and did not want it hanging in her home. If, however, his family pressed him to purchase beautiful objects, he was open to suggestions, although he himself lived a life of almost spartan simplicity. It was only his hunger for paintings that seemed to know no limits. Paintings revealed to him the mysteries and fundamental truths of human existence and conjured up worlds whose great communicative power rested on each individual artist's ability to inspire. He saw in them not only the achievements of craftsmen but images of man and inexhaustible fields for interpretation. It was probably not by chance that a surprisingly large number of portraits found a place in his collection. In these representations of people he was not so much fascinated by the narrative and psychological aspects as by the artist's total vision of life, a vision which he was able to detect in a Frans Hals or in a self-portrait by Cézanne, but which he also discovered in a field of poppies or a pond of waterlilies by Monet.

Emil Bührle never lost sight of his aim to collect the works of the impressionists. According to Walter Drack, he could ruthlessly reject a splendid Rubens or a Cranach with the words: "I do not want anything baroque or Renaissance." He often felt as if he had been duped, and prices could terrify him, since, given what he had endured and achieved during his lifetime, he never allowed himself to forget the real value of things. He did not buy art as an investment; he bought it as a companion. He could defiantly reject overpriced offers, even though he fully realized when he was letting something special slip out of his grasp. At the Cognac auction in Paris 14 May, 1952, for example, he did not venture to outbid Madame Walter-Guillaume for Cézanne's small masterpiece *Apples and Biscuits.* He was convinced that "I, after all, am the blockhead who pays the highest price." Such things often happened at the same time as his business worries, which always preyed heavily on his mind. It was, however, a vicious circle, for it was precisely at these times that he most needed this intense contact with art, which served for him as a great emotional release.

At the end of 1953 when he was in the United States on business, he persuaded the young art historian Peter Nathan, then in New York, to provide him with daily information about works of art and galleries, regardless of the time of day or night. Despite his business losses in the States (his company in Asheville, North Carolina, was in financial difficulties owing to a change in the political situation), he felt compelled to buy works of art, mainly by the Fauves—Braque, Dufy, Matisse, Vlaminck—but also an important portrait by Ingres of *Monsieur Devillers* (see cat. 12). If we run

The collector with his daughter Hortense on a trip to America, 1947.

The collector with his wife Charlotte in the loggia of their residence in Zurich, 1941. The mural painting is by Alfred Mez, a former fellow student of Emil Georg Bührle.

through the list of purchases for 1953, we see that the catch was an incredibly rich one: two large Canalettos (see cats. 8 and 9); several Dutch masters (Hobbema, Pieter de Hooch, Ruysdael); works by Chardin, Chassériau, Delacroix, Géricault, and Puvis de Chavannes; Manet's *The Swallows* (see cat. 24); Monet's *Camille Monet with Dog* (see cat. 45); Pissarro's *Road from Osny to Pontoise—Hoar Frost* (see cat. 20); Cézanne's *The Thaw in L'Estaque or The Red Roofs* (see cat. 38) and *Factory near Sainte-Victoire;* Mary Cassatt's *Mother and Child;* Toulouse-Lautrec's *Napoleon;* Gauguin's *Pape moe* (see cat. 54) and *Still Life with Fruit, Basket, and Knife* (see cat. 57); Vuillard's *The Visitor* (see cat. 73); a number of Picassos; Rouault's portrait of Guy de Charentonay (see cat. 75); and many more. At this point the growth of the circle became conspicuous. Did Bührle wish to establish new connections between paintings, to provide a context for and to extend and define the actual core of the collection? Did he already have at this time a public exhibition in mind? He was to enlighten us a year later: "The first circle, roughly defined by Corot, van Gogh, and Cézanne, filled up rapidly, and always remained the heart of the collection. Soon, nevertheless, the next circle began to take shape, extending forward to the Fauves, and backward to Delacroix and Daumier. Finally, Daumier led back to Rembrandt, and Manet to Frans Hals. Once the seventeenth century was reached, a certain expansion of the Dutch and Flemish schools was inevitable. A further spreading circle took me back to the French painters of the eighteenth century and then forward into the immediate present. The pronounced similarity between the atmospheric gravities of the impressionists proper and the Venetians of the eighteenth century finally brought me to Canaletto, Guardi, and Tiepolo."[16]

No one knew exactly what the collector had in mind, but steadily there grew within him a desire to display what he had assembled over the years on neutral walls, in a general exhibition, to try out the collection, as it were, by subjecting it to spatial constraints. He knew from experience that everything that is created and published must one day be exposed to criticism. Sadly, however, he did not live to experience the visual and intellectual adventure of a public exhibition of his works, for in November 1956 a heart attack abruptly ended his intensely active life. Bührle would definitely have gone on to change many things, to complement his collection or to discard items, for he stated in 1954 "that I myself by no means regard this collection as in any way complete. If a collection can ever reach a state of completion, mine is still very far from reaching that stage. What's more, in the course of time the original boundaries have been shifted several times, which has certainly enriched my task but has also made it correspondingly more difficult."[17]

His great mission may have remained unaccomplished, but shortly before his untimely death he confided to the diplomat and historian Carl J. Burckhardt: "I was ceaselessly determined—throughout my life—to gather such paintings around me; Monet's enchantment has held me in thrall and I wanted to have Cézanne, Degas, Manet, Renoir, close to me on my own walls. And I have succeeded, for now they are here. Any time spent with them had to be stolen, but this time was returned to me richly. Each of the moments was infinite. . . . I myself am convinced that the sights of the world are inexhaustible and that in the vision inspired by them in successive generations of artists there can be expressed, now as always, everything that is latent within us, everything and more."[18]

Bührle formed an art collection that today is world-renowned, but his contributions as a benefactor are less well known, for he shunned publicity and gave most of his support to Swiss cultural causes. In 1944 he established the Goethe Foundation to provide funds in the areas of science, theater, music and the maintenance of important monuments, and he created a second foundation to encourage Swiss literary ventures. Concerts and the Lucerne Festival too could count on his financial backing over the years. The Zurich Kunsthaus meant a great deal to him and in 1944 the passionate collector was persuaded to become a member of the museum's Acquisitions Committee. From 1953 until his death, he held the position of Vice-President of the Zürcher Kunstgesellschaft. The instance of a collector also being interested in public art institutions, participating actively in their affairs and thus directly inspiring new cultural activities, is well known, especially in America. There, art museums have often been the result of private initiatives, with donors of the collections working closely with museum staff.

The Zurich Kunsthaus, and the Zürcher Kunstgesellschaft, are also the products of private initiatives. It was not until 1954 that these institutions received an increased contribution from the municipality to cover their operating costs. Only very small sums were available for purchases so that without additional private donations it was scarcely possible to acquire significant works. In the minutes of a meeting in 1954 the following appears: "Emil Bührle welcomes the new members of the Sammlungskommission and regrets that he can do so only now. It is two years since any meetings have been held. Lack of funds has not permitted any new acquisitions."[19] Not surprisingly, the industrialist often supplemented existing funds to facilitate acquisition. This is again evident from the minutes of a meeting in 1953: "Mr. Bührle, with great understanding, repeatedly steps in when there is a possibility of acquiring a picture for the collection and when it is not possible for the museum, for financial reasons, to do so."[20]

So it was that in 1951, with a group delegated by the Kunsthaus, he made a journey to Giverny, to the former studio of Monet, to obtain paintings of waterlilies by the master and to prepare for the great Monet exhibition planned in Zurich for 1952. The generous patron immediately bought two works by Monet, one of which, *Waterlilies and Iris,* he gave to the museum. During the Monet exhibition he succumbed once more to the temptation to buy and acquired yet another splendid work for his own collection. According to the minutes: "Mr. Bührle has secured yet another great painting, which, we trust, will later find a place in the new annex of the Kunsthaus."[21] However, the painting in question, over four meters wide, became one of the jewels of his Foundation.

Library in the residence in Zurich with *Port-Marly* by Sisley, *Wheat Field with Cypresses* by van Gogh, and with medieval wood sculptures on the mantel.

Music room of the residence in Zurich with a Madonna by Tilman Riemenschneider, with *Woman in Red Shawl* by Degas, *The Port of Bordeaux* by Manet. In distant background: *Still Life with Fruit, Basket, and Knife* by Gauguin.

Dining room of the residence in Zurich with *Harvesters* by Renoir, and *Camille Monet with Dog* by Monet.

He also generously underwrote the cost of a new exhibition wing for the Kunsthaus. When negotiations with the municipality became protracted, he came up with judicious counter-demands, as we can see from the minutes: "Mr. Bührle has declared his readiness to finance the entire new project, on condition that the municipality for its part guarantees an annual contribution toward the running of the Kunsthaus."[22] Bührle did not live to see the dedication of the building in 1958, but in his memory the new wing opened with an exhibition of his own collection. The simple, yet versatile, exhibition gallery, seventy meters long and eighteen meters wide, is still proving itself to be an ideal, flexible display area.

Emil Bührle exerted a wide-ranging influence as a patron, not only because of his constant financial help but also because of the intellectual acumen and clear-headedness with which he sought to resolve problems. "He saw things with clarity and simplicity, and defined any steps to be taken," said Franz Meyer, then President of the Zürcher Kunstgesellschaft, of his colleague.[23] René Wehrli, the former acting Director, recalls that despite his great business commitments, Bührle could suddenly turn up in the Kunsthaus on a Sunday morning: "The collector… would have a look at the rooms being reconstructed, get caught up in the excitement of arranging pictures, offer suggestions, and would work for an entire morning, carrying pictures, as a modest member of a team."[24]

Despite the pressures of work, Bührle was keenly involved in anything to do with art. In this environment he found inspiration and, perhaps even more importantly, he acquired knowledge. He learned to assess the many offers that came to him from all countries and centuries. These led to discoveries, trained his vision, and also paved the way for his appreciation of the abstract art of the twentieth century, including Mondrian. The growing number of exhibitions of modern international art after the war were also greatly influential and served to guide him in his private purchases. As early in 1945 in Zurich there were exhibitions of expressionist, cubist, and futurist art; in 1946 of Braque, Kandinsky, and Picasso; in 1947 of Kokoschka; and in 1948 of Rouault and Klee. In 1949 Bührle lent many works to the great impressionist exhibition held in the Kunsthalle in Basel, and in 1952 there was an important Monet exhibition in Zurich, followed by one of van Gogh in 1954, and of Cézanne in 1956.

Regular exhibitions of art from earlier centuries also inspired the tireless collector to add to his collection. We all too easily forget that a creative spirit is constantly in need of nourishment. Bührle never lost his liking for medieval wood sculpture and altarpieces, and between 1952 and 1956 he amassed a number of extraordinary works. If a church needed funds he would again step in; he was behind the building of the Old Catholic Christ Church and had it decorated with expensive wood carvings and stained glass. He rescued from the art market a valuable fourteenth-century Pietà of

Swiss origin, which had been sold in Germany during the Second World War by Professor Heribert Reiners. In 1950, for the exhibition at the Kunsthaus, "European Art from the Thirteenth to the Twentieth Century taken from Collections in Zurich," he lent fifty-eight works by artists from Multscher to Utrillo. He was always especially delighted to see his own works exhibited in shows because he liked to compare them with their "rivals."

Direct contact and friendship with artists were not a deeply felt need of his, and he had dealings with only a few artists. He did not seek the company of the artist himself, but of his works, which he could contemplate at leisure. His cool, disciplined courtesy certainly had its charm, but it did not easily encourage people to relax in his presence. Despite this, he did support contemporary Swiss artists, most notably during the Second World War, when many of them were compelled to return penniless from abroad. Furthermore, from the start of his collecting activity, he maintained an interest in Swiss art, and he planned to display only these works on the premises of his firm. As early as 1937 he purchased his first works by Hodler, two views of Lake Geneva, from Aktuaryus in Zurich. They adorned his office for years. These were soon followed by a *Warrior* and a sketch for the Marignano frescoes, also by Hodler. By 1947 his collection of Swiss works, from Hodler to Hubacher, already amounted to more than one hundred items. During the war, in the large rooms of the newly built staff cafeteria, Bührle commissioned mural paintings by Walter Clénin, Karl Hügin, Ernst Georg Rüegg, and Max Truninger. In the company newsletter he explained his motives thus: "We spend most of our lives at our place of work. Our environment, whether we are aware of this or not, has a marked influence on the way we feel and think. A harmonious environment, combining practicality and beauty, motivates us and helps us more easily to overcome many of the stresses and strains of the daily routine. In offices especially, an artistic display of works of art can improve the working climate and induce employees to take an increased interest in their tasks. Thus we have tried to brighten the offices and, in particular, the rooms of our recreation building, where we spend many a leisure hour, with pictures of proven quality. In this way we hope not only to awaken and promote an understanding of art and of the harmonies of form and color but also to provide employees with a certain imaginative compensation for the 'matter-of-factness' of their bare, industrial environment."[25] Bührle clearly wanted his employees to share something of his own experience of art, but he was also perfectly aware that he could not ask too much of them in terms of their aesthetic tastes. He therefore selected figurative, non-abstract works as being more readily accessible to the man-in-the-street. Today, his son Dieter Bührle continues to collect for the firm.

In 1941, he generously financed an art prize in Zurich known as the

Emil Georg Bührle with his son Dieter in the conference room of his firm, 1956. In the background, the painting *The Warrior* by Ferdinand Hodler.

Dedication of the new construction in the Kunsthaus Zurich, 1958. From left to right: Dieter Bührle, Franz Meyer, Charlotte Bührle, Federal Council Member Streuli, Hortense Anda-Bührle before the bust of Emil Georg Bührle.

"Swiss Award for Painting" (the current title is "Award for Swiss Painting"). The first ceremony took place in 1941 at the Galerie Beaux-Arts on Bleicherweg and then, from 1944 on, at the Zurich Kunsthaus. The prize was subsequently awarded in 1943, 1945, and 1949. The panel of judges included the donor and the Director of the Kunsthaus, Wilhelm Wartmann, as well as such well-known Swiss artists as, in 1942, Cuno Amiet and Ernst Morgenthaler, and enthusiastic collectors such as Oskar Reinhart, Hedy Hahnloser, and Hans Mayenfisch. Up to thirty artists participated at any one time, and this small and lively forum, helped to create a market for the exhibiting artists. Bührle was always open-minded and without prejudice in his approach, an attitude born out by the spectator's award, instituted by him at the same time. This, again, gave added publicity to the artists involved.

Bührle, the patron, constantly strove to make art accessible to those who could least afford it. He pioneered a new kind of patronage, bringing art not only into private houses and museums but also into the offices of an industrial firm. He expressed the belief that "Obviously the artist and the technician live in very different worlds. What they have in common is their starting-point: Creativity."[26] He thereby pronounced what was undoubtedly the central force in his own nature, that which drove forward both his industrial enterprise, and his activity as a collector and patron. It is best described in his own words: "The activity of the collector consists in a personal selection and particular arrangement of specific works of art. The most important thing for the collector is quality. The artist develops a certain style, which is, as a rule, detected at once by the connoisseur of his work; in the same way the collector is led by his temperament—to which

Mural painting by Karl Otto Hügin, *The Ages of Man,* 1949, recreation building of the Machine Tool Works, Oerlikon-Bührle Ltd., staff cafeteria.

Mural painting by Walter Clénin, *Agriculture,* 1943–1953, recreation building of the Machine Tool Works, Oerlikon-Bührle Ltd., staff cafeteria.

Mural painting by Ernst Georg Rüegg, *The Life of the Peasant,* 1942–1946, recreation building of the Machine Tool Works, Oerlikon-Bührle Ltd., staff cafeteria.

certain works strongly appeal, others less so, and some not at all—to develop a kind of style, which determines the character of the collection. The more distinctly such a style is expressed in a collection, the more it becomes a kind of creation, and justifies the labor and the financial resources that the collector has devoted to it."[27]

Aware that his collection had by no means attained a definitive shape (insofar as this was at all possible) Bührle nevertheless had a vision of a rounded and self-contained entity that he did not want broken up and which, unfortunately, he was unable to complete. The idea of setting up a foundation was therefore an obvious one, and one which was realized by his heirs.

[1] "Emil Georg Bührle 1890–1956," *Neujahrsblatt der Zürcher Kunstgesellschaft* (1957), 18. / [2] "Bührle," 1957, 5–6. / [3] "Bührle," 1957, 43. / [4] "Bührle," 1957, 37. / [5] "Bührle," 1957, 44. / [6] Designation at that time for an amateur constructor. / [7] *Werkmitteilungen der Werkzeugmaschinenfabrik Oerlikon Bührle & Co., Zürich-Oerlikon,* 4 (1944): 3. / [8] "Bührle," 1957, 22. / [9] "Bührle," 1957, 42. / [10] "Bührle," 1957, 40. / [11] "Bührle," 1957, 43. / [12] *Von Matisse bis Picasso; Hommage an Siegfried Rosengart* [exh. cat., Kunstmuseum] (Lucerne, 1988), 21–22. / [13] Letter from Bührle to Fritz Nathan, 4 January 1944. Excerpts taken from Fritz Nathan, *Erinnerungen aus meinem Leben* (Zurich, 1965). / [14] Arnold Kübler, "Aus der Sammlung Emil Georg Bührle," *DU,* December 1957, 47. / [15] Urs Schwarz, "Zürcher Kunstsammler neuester Zeit: Fünf Portraits," *Neujahrsblatt der Chorherrenstube* 198 (Zurich, 1977), 52. / [16] "Bührle," 1957, 43. / [17] "Bührle," 1957, 40. / [18] Carl J. Burckhardt, "Begegnung mit Emil Bührle," *Sammlung Emil G. Bührle* [exh. cat., Kunsthaus] (Zurich, 1958), 21. / [19] Minutes of the Collections Commission, Zurich Kunsthaus, 23 November 1954. / [20] Minutes of the Executive Committee, Zurich Kunsthaus, 29 May 1953. / [21] Minutes of the Collections Commission, Zurich Kunsthaus, 10 June 1952. / [22] Minutes of the Executive Committee, Zurich Kunsthaus, 9 December 1952. / [23] "Bührle," 1957, 2. / [24] "Bührle," 1957, 8. / [25] *Werkmitteilungen* 7, no. 2 (May 1947), 23. / [26] *Werkmitteilungen* 7, no. 2 (May 1947), 22. / [27] "Bührle," 1957, 44.

Unfortunately the author was not personally acquainted with the collector and industrialist Emil G. Bührle. She owes a debt of particular gratitude to Mrs. Hortense Anda-Bührle and Dr. Dieter Bührle for furnishing her with valuable information, for their patience in replying to questions and for their candor and friendliness in conversation. The following have also contributed substantially to the success of this portrait of a collector: Dr. Hans Bänninger, Dr. Walter Drack, Dr. Alfred Gerber, Dr. Peter Nathan, Dr. René Wehrli—people who were in close touch with the collector during his lifetime.

Foundation E. G. Bührle Collection

CHRISTIAN BÜHRLE

Emil Georg Bührle's primary concern in his final years, in addition to augmenting his collection and planning its first comprehensive exhibition, was the preservation of his treasures for the future. A large number of paintings for which there was no room in his home had been rather unsatisfactorily displayed in the cramped conditions of some unfurnished rooms in an adjacent house. His collection of medieval sculpture was also housed there, in similarly crowded circumstances.

My grandfather rejected the idea of giving his collection to a museum, fearing that this might lead to dispersal of the works through various of its departments and the loss of the collection's unique character. He was much more taken—despite initial resistance—by the idea of setting up a foundation, open to the public, which would preserve the collection as an integral whole. Everything, however, was still at the planning stage when he died in November 1956.

Following Bührle's death and the sudden curtailment of his plans for the future of the collection—he had acquired some 150 works after 1951, now in the possession of the Foundation—his heirs thought it appropriate to carry on the work which he had begun.

The collection, comprising 320 items, was shown at the opening in 1958 of the new wing of the Zurich Kunsthaus, which Bührle had donated to the city. In accordance with his plans, his heirs, Frau Charlotte Bührle-Schalk, Frau Hortense Anda-Bührle, and Dr. Dieter Bührle, resolved to set up a foundation to administer the major portion of the collection. Thus in a deed dated 24 February 1960, the Foundation received 168 paintings and 30 sculptures as a permanent gift, with the stipulation that they be put on public display.

These works reflect the essence of my grandfather's collection: the impressionists and postimpressionists (including Manet, Cézanne, van Gogh, Gauguin, Monet, Renoir, Degas, and Toulouse-Lautrec) are all represented by major works. A highlight of the collection—my grandfather's pride and joy—are the three portraits by Cézanne, purchased between 1948 and 1953. Ingres, Delacroix, Canaletto, Guardi, Hals, and Rembrandt are all prominent in the collection, as are the masters of the twentieth century.

A number of less important works were subsequently removed, the sale

The Foundation E. G. Bührle Collection, Zollikerstrasse 172, Zurich.

Interior.

of which financed various operating expenses and made possible the purchase, in the early 1960s, of two works that superbly complement the existing holdings; Braque's *Ship at Le Havre* of 1905, and an early Gauguin portrait of his wife, painted in 1878.

Since its inauguration thirty years ago, the Foundation E. G. Bührle Collection has been housed in that same building on the outskirts of Zurich that once served the collector as a repository. Its extensive gardens and distinctive furnishings give it the feel of a private home, where the visitor finds a collection bearing the imprint of Bührle's personality. The collection's international reputation is based on not only the artistic quality but also on the superb condition of the works of art.

While this exhibition commemorating the centenary of Bührle's birth is touring Washington, Montreal, Yokohama, and London, the Foundation is mounting an exhibition of Swiss painters of the nineteenth and twentieth century taken from the Collection. This show is a selection of 56 paintings from the Romantic period up to the present day, including works by Alexandre Calame, Johann Gottfried Steffan, Ferdinand Hodler, Felix Vallotton, Giovanni Giacometti, Cuno Amiet, Max Gubler, and Albert Schnyder, and will be on display at the Foundation.

Catalogue

Frans Hals   c. 1581/1585–1666

1   Portrait of a Man, 1660s

Aside from Rembrandt, Frans Hals was undoubtedly the greatest portraitist of the Dutch golden age. His powerful and effective brushstroke, so apparent in the Bührle portrait, was inimitable.

Hals was probably born in Antwerp, but while he was still very young, his family moved to Haarlem, where he lived for the rest of his life. He was trained by the mannerist painter Carel van Mander before becoming a member of the Haarlem guild in 1610. Although Hals had many portrait commissions throughout his career, he suffered ever worsening financial difficulties and eventually came to live in extreme poverty. In 1661, toward the end of his life, he was exempted from the guild dues, and the following year he was granted a modest pension from the Haarlem burgomasters.

Hals continued to paint during the last years of his life, and the present work along with other late portraits in Cambridge, Munich, Amiens, and Haarlem make clear that his artistic vision and masterly technique did not diminish but only gained richness and strength. The sitter for this portrait has not been identified, and the lack of a coat of arms, date, or early history of the painting make it highly improbable that the identity of the young man will ever be known. The somewhat unusual absence of Hals' monogram on the painting had led earlier in the century to unjustified doubts as to the authorship. In fact, the painting is a characteristic and brilliant example of Hals' late style. The absence of dated pictures from his last years make it impossible to determine an exact date, but we can safely assume that it originated during the 1660s at the same time as his celebrated group portraits of the regents and regentesses of the Old Men's Alms House in Haarlem. The Bührle portrait shares their concentrated power and bold brushstroke, which eliminate all but the most essential features of the sitter. A few touches of bright red in the man's right eye, on his face, and on the nail of his thumb, and the slightly paler red of his lips, further animate the portrait.   FJD

Oil on canvas
70.5 × 58.5 (27¾ × 23)
Foundation E. G. Bührle Collection

Jan van Goyen   1596–1656

2   *The Castle Montfoort, 1648*

2a. Van Goyen, *The Castle of IJsselstein,* 1648, National Gallery of Canada, Ottawa.

Jan van Goyen was one of the most important Dutch landscape artists of the seventeenth century, and probably the most prolific. More than twelve hundred paintings bear his name, and he made more than a thousand drawings. Many of these sketches were done during the artist's numerous trips through the Netherlands, and Van Goyen would often base his paintings on the sketches, taking great liberties with the topography.

The preparatory sketch for the Castle Montfoort in the Bührle painting is not known, although the accurate rendering of the building suggests that Van Goyen made use of a sketch done on the site. A black chalk drawing of the castle seen from the other side, preserved in the Bibliothèque Nationale in Paris, is evidence that the artist visited the area. That drawing belongs to a series of nine dating from the early 1640s, all in the same technique and same format, done during one of Van Goyen's journeys. Perhaps the lost preparatory drawing for the Bührle painting belonged to the same series. Alternatively, the painting may have been based on a much earlier drawing, for the castle, seen from the same angle, also appears in two winter scenes by Van Goyen from around 1624 and 1634.

The setting for the castle in this painting is topographically inaccurate. The bastion with the windmill and the other buildings to the right of the square tower that protects the bridge are imaginary, or at least bear no relation to the actual site, as is clear when we compare this painting with a drawing by Roelant Roghman of the Castle Montfoort. The buildings recur, moreover, in a painting by Van Goyen that depicts the castle of IJsselstein (see fig. 2a). The two panels not only share the same dimensions and date but both employ a diagonal recession and a repoussoir boat. The preparatory sketch for the Ottawa painting belongs to the series of nine drawings mentioned above.[1]

The compositional scheme in the Bührle painting must have been very successful, for in addition to the landscape in Ottawa, Van Goyen used the same composition for a number of other large panels dating from the second half of the 1640s. Common features include a large building on the bank of a river to the right and a distant view to the left. Examples may be found in Schwerin and Minneapolis museums[2] and in various private collections.

The present work originated at a time when the artist was slowly moving away from the strongly monochromatic color scheme that had dominated not only his own landscapes of the 1630s and early 1640s but Dutch painting of that period in general. Touches of strong local colors lend the painting a decidedly lively character.

FJD

Oil on panel
65.5 × 98 (25¾ × 38⅝)
Signed and dated at lower left: VG 1648
Private collection

3   *Interior of the St. Bavo Church, Haarlem, 1636*

3a. Saenredam, cartoon for *Interior of the St. Bavo Church, Haarlem,* Staatliche Museen Preussischer Kulturbesitz, Berlin-Dahlem.

Pieter Jansz. Saenredam, son of the well-known engraver Jan Saenredam, moved at age twelve to Haarlem, where he served his apprenticeship with the portraitist Frans de Grebber. In his teacher's studio he met the architect and painter Jacob van Campen, who became his life-long friend and probably also introduced him to the principles of perspective that were to play a dominant role in Saenredam's career.

Probably as late as 1627 Saenredam began to draw and paint church interiors (and occasionally exteriors), soon establishing himself as the master of the genre. With his knowledge of architecture and perspective, he produced impressive works of art that are at the same time highly accurate architectural representations. They document a number of important Dutch buildings, some of which have since disappeared.

It is the still-extant Grote Kerk (St. Bavo) in Haarlem that is represented in Saenredam's works more often than any other church.[1] Between 1627 and 1636 alone Saenredam made more than twenty sketches, drawings, and cartoons of the interior of this late Gothic church, on which he based ten paintings that date from the same period. The Bührle painting is from this series. It shows the view from the Kerstkapel (Christmas chapel) looking from the northwest toward the northern ambulatory, choir, and south transept.

The genesis of this small panel is fully documented. A small sketch of the same view is dated 1634/1635, while the construction drawing or cartoon in Berlin is dated 22 December 1635 (see fig. 3a). An autograph inscription on the latter also provides the date 9 May 1635 for the completion of the present painting.

The overall impression of serenity in the almost monochromatic setting is enlivened by a genre-like family group on the left, a few other figures on the right, and a memorial hatchment in the middle. The signature and date from part of the red chalk graffiti on the foreground pillar to the right.   FJD

Oil on panel
43 × 37.5 (16⅞ × 14¾)
Signed and dated on pillar at right:
P. Saenredam fecit / 1636.
Foundation E. G. Bührle Collection

Aelbert Cuyp   1620–1691

4   *Thunderstorm over Dordrecht, c. 1645*

Views of Cuyp's native city of Dordrecht not only occur frequently in the artist's paintings and drawings but are among the best-known topographical subjects in Dutch seventeenth-century art. One of the oldest cities in the province of Holland, Dordrecht was strategically situated at a junction of rivers, its harbor guaranteeing the city steady commercial activity over the centuries.

Unlike most of the paintings by Cuyp and artists such as Jan van Goyen, this work depicts Dordrecht from the landside. The city is dominated by the impressive Grote Kerk, a cross-shaped basilica with an incompleted tower dating from the fourteenth century. Left of center is the Gevangenpoort, one of the gates that form part of the ramparts of the city.

The painting was probably executed shortly before 1645, when Cuyp was still influenced by the work of Jan van Goyen but had already started to develop his own style. *Thunderstorm over Dordrecht* is rightly considered one of Cuyp's early masterpieces. The subject matter is quite unusual in Dutch art. Apart from Cuyp, who painted another thunderstorm over Dordrecht in the early 1650s, it was Van Goyen, in particular, who was very much attracted by this phenomenon.

Cuyp's landscape paintings became immensely popular during his lifetime—and even more so in the eighteenth and nineteenth centuries—and he was praised as "the Dutch Claude." The present work, like most of Cuyp's paintings, was acquired by British collectors, his most ardent admirers during the last quarter of the seventeenth and the first half of the eighteenth centuries. Cuyp's paintings strongly influenced British landscape painters such as Wilson and Gainsborough and later Turner and Constable. On 6 September 1834 the latter wrote about this painting:

I am going tomorrow to Ham (House). ... It has ... on its walls ... also a truly sublime Cuyp, a tempest, still mild, and tranquil. The village of Dort, is seen with its solemn tower and windmills under an insidious gleam of a faint watery sun, the cattle lying and ruminating in the foreground, while a horrid rent in the sky, almost frightens one, and the lightning descends to the earth over some poor cottage with a *glide,* that is so much like nature, that I wish I had seen it before I sent my "Salisbury" away. ...[1]

It is a clear testimony of Constable's admiration for Aelbert Cuyp.   FJD

Oil on panel
77.5 × 107 (30½ × 42⅛)
Signed at bottom right: A. cuÿp.
Foundation E. G. Bührle Collection

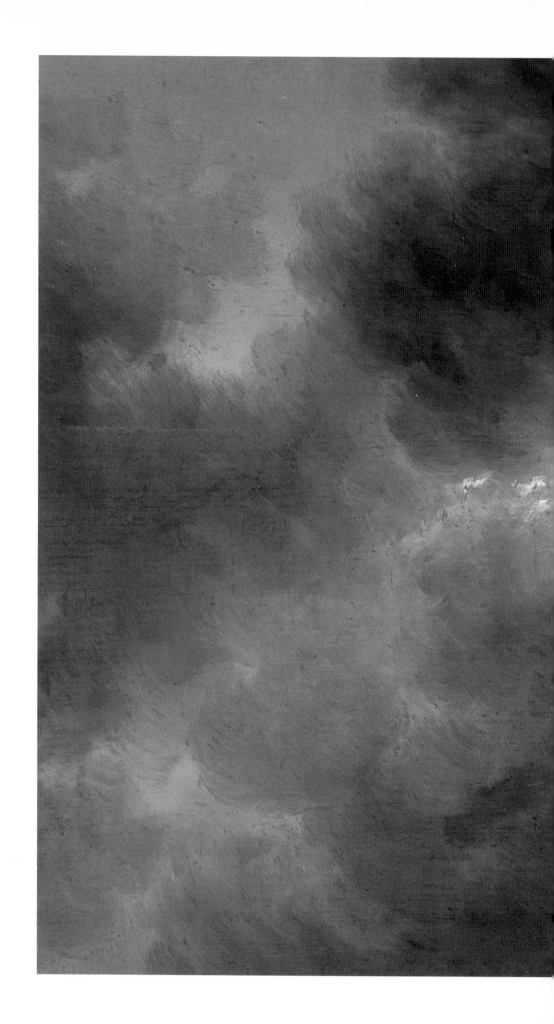

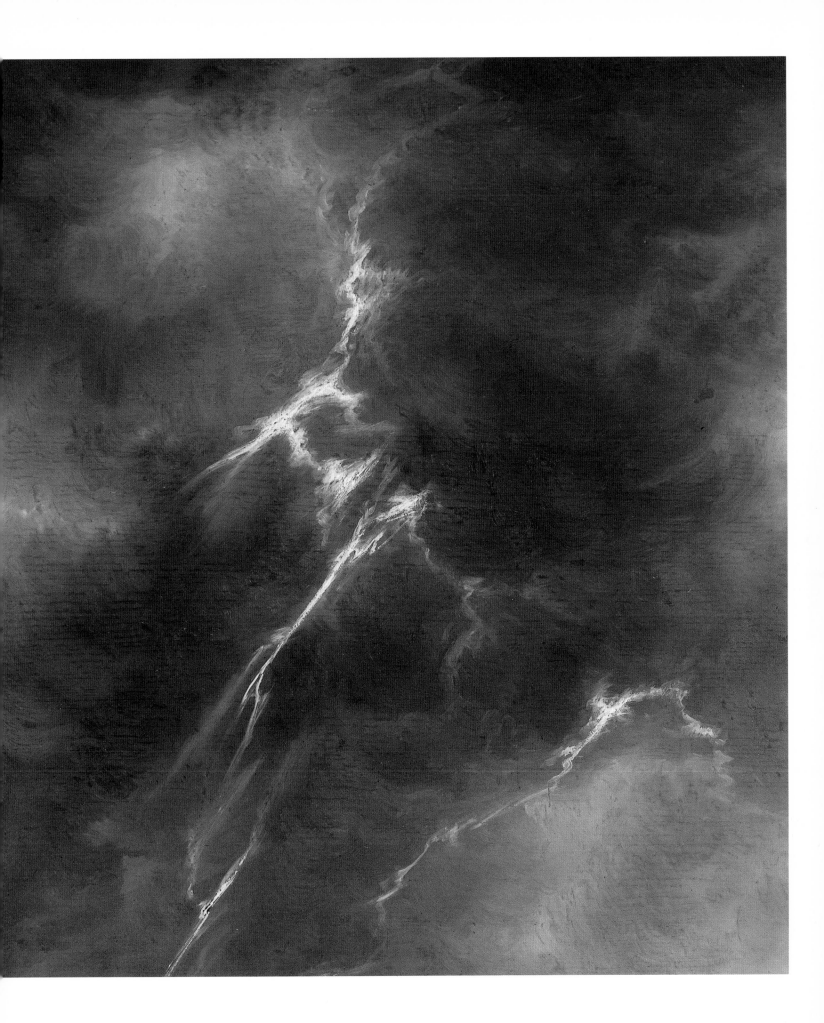

Willem van Aelst   1627–c. 1683

5   Hunting Still Life with Dead Partridge, 1676

Willem van Aelst is considered one of the leading Dutch still-life painters of the second half of the seventeenth century. His talent was recognized early, and he joined the St. Lucas Guild in his native city of Delft at age seventeen. In 1645 he left for France, where he stayed until 1649 and then traveled to Italy. He worked for the grand duke of Tuscany, Ferdinand II de Medici, in Florence until 1656. The Italian form of his name, used in the signature for this picture, which was painted almost twenty years after Van Aelst's return to Holland, testifies to the impact of his Italian sojourn.

Van Aelst's elegant and balanced compositions, painted in a most refined technique, are characteristic of Dutch painting around 1675. His œuvre is devoted exclusively to still lifes, depicting flowers, fruit, game, or so-called breakfast pieces *(ontbijtjes)*. The present composition, with its various hunting attributes, is predominantly monochromatic, accented with a few bright colors. Yellow ocher and azure blue are present in the feathers of the kingfisher on the right, and the same blue appears in a fly on the throat of the dead partridge. The red of the hawk's hood stands out against the dark background.

The diversity of the objects in the painting demonstrates the artist's virtuosity in rendering different textures: the soft, feathered bodies of the dead birds set against the chilly marble slab. The table top rests on a relief that depicts Silenus, a rural Greek god who is a follower of Bacchus, as a fat old drunkard supported on either side by satyrs. A similar relief is found in Van Aelst's hunting still life of 1681, formerly in the collection of James Simon, Berlin.   FJD

Oil on canvas
58 × 46 (22⅞ × 18⅛)
Signed and dated at upper left:
Guill.mo. van. Aelst. 1676.
Private collection

Pieter de Hooch   1629–c. 1684

6   *The Cardplayers, c. 1658*

6a. Johannes Vermeer, *Officer and Laughing Girl,*
The Frick Collection, New York.

Born in Rotterdam, De Hooch moved to Delft in 1655 after an apprenticeship with
the landscape artist Nicolaes Berchem in Haarlem. Although he lived in Delft only
until 1661, when he moved to Amsterdam, his Delft years constitute the most important period in his career.

During the late 1640s and 1650s Delft must have been one of the most stimulat-
ing artistic milieus for a young artist in the Netherlands. The local St. Lucas Guild
counted among its members some of the most innovative artists of the time. Gerard
Houckgeest and Emanuel de Witte, who both specialized in painting church interiors, settled there in 1635 and 1641. Rembrandt's most gifted pupil, Carel Fabritius, moved to Delft in 1652. And Johannes Vermeer, born in the same city in
1632, spent all of his life there. The works of each of these artists reveal a lively interest in the rendering of interior spaces or secluded courtyards inhabited by common
people.

More than almost any other picture by De Hooch, *The Cardplayers* shows the
artist's close relationship to Vermeer, and in particular to the latter's *Officer and
Laughing Girl* (fig. 6a). Thoré-Bürger, the French critic who rediscovered Vermeer
in the 1880s, even attributed the present picture to the master. The exact relationship between the two pictures is unclear, but it is believed that they originated in
Delft around 1658. Their compositions strongly resemble each other, and an exceptionally subtle rendering of the modulations of natural light is common to both. It
has long been assumed that Vermeer's picture was the source of inspiration for De
Hooch; but we should not rule out the reverse.

The painting depicted in the upper right corner of the interior represents *Christ
and the Adulteress,* which suggests a moralizing intent, especially in connection
with the card in the soldier's hand, as cards often allude to fidelity.   FJD

Oil on panel
50 × 45.5 (19⅝ × 17⅞)
Signed on the chair at the left: P D H
Private collection

7   *Diana Bathing, c. 1755–1760*

7a. Tintoretto, *Mercury and the Three Graces,* 1577–1578, Palazzo Ducale, Venice.

This work originally belonged to Count Francesco Algarotti (1712–1764) and was described in detail in the catalogue of his collection, published in Venice in 1779.[1] It shows the mythological scene of Diana being surprised by Actaeon while bathing, depicted many times from the High Renaissance on, especially in Venetian painting. According to Ovid's *Metamorphoses,* the most important literary source for the story, Diana, the goddess of wild animals, was in the habit of resting at a spring in a sacred valley when she tired of hunting.[2] One day the Theban prince Actaeon arrived at the spring and happened upon Diana refreshing herself. So that he would not boast of having seen the virgin goddess nude, she turned him into a stag, and he was torn to pieces by his own dogs.

Tiepolo painted the story of Diana and Actaeon at least four times. One of these works, also listed in the catalogue of the Algarotti collection, is today thought to be lost. The Bührle painting differs from the two extant versions[3] by representing the hunter Actaeon not at the moment of transformation but as a stag leaping in the background. The dramatic event of the metamorphosis has been glossed over here in favor of an idyllic, though interrupted, bathing scene, allowing Tiepolo the opportunity to paint "the quintessential Venetian theme of the nude female body in rich abundance."[4]

The composition is defined by two groups of figures backed by stands of trees, which form blocks of color that frame the landscape in the distance. Particular emphasis is given to Diana through the intense colors of the fabrics surrounding her and objects arranged as still lifes beside her. Her figure, seen from the back, is reminiscent of images from the Venetian cinquecento, among them Tintoretto's *Mercury and the Three Graces* (fig. 7a), 1577–1578 (Venice, Palazzo Ducale, Sala dell'Anticollegio). The same is true of the nymph antithetically opposite her, who recalls the reclining figure in Titian's *Bacchanal* of 1518/1519 (Museo del Prado, Madrid). This conspicuously placed nymph is most likely Diana's favorite companion, Callisto, who, according to Ovid, had been robbed of her virginity by Jupiter and had been transformed into a bear by the jealous Juno.[5]

Despite its theatrical effects, the painting presents a calm, balanced composition and a relatively cool palette dominated by subtle pastel tones, which can also be observed in frescos from 1757 in the Villa Valmarana in Vicenza. Classical stylistic elements in the treatment of the nude and the predominance of cameo-like profiles, which are more pronounced in the painting, can be explained by the Francophile tastes of Algarotti. As the one who commissioned the painting, he had probably expressed his desires that the painting correspond to classical artistic ideals.   CB

Oil on canvas
79 × 90 (31⅛ × 35⅜)
Foundation E. G. Bührle Collection

8   *Santa Maria della Salute, c. 1738–1742*

8a. Canaletto, *Grand Canal with Santa Maria della Salute Looking Eastward,* c. 1735–1740, private collection.

This panorama is shown from a heightened, imaginary vantage point above the Grand Canal looking eastward. Beginning at the right, it depicts the baroque church of Santa Maria della Salute, built between 1631 and 1681 after plans by Baldassarre Longhena in gratitude for the end of the plague. From this architectural monument, represented in minute detail, the view proceeds along the façade of the Patriarchal Seminary to the Customhouse, set apart by its tower, then crosses the canal to the Riva degli Schiavoni. From the far left, reflected in the water, the buildings along the Molo (quai) include the Zecca (mint) built by Jacopo Sansovino with the Ponte della Pescaria, the Library of San Marco, also built by Sansovino, and the famous Doge's Palace with the column of the lion of Saint Mark, and beyond the Molo, the prison behind the Ponte della Paglia.

The view is a topographically rearranged composition. These structures are not in fact opposite Santa Maria della Salute on the Grand Canal but are farther to the east along the Basin of San Marco. Yet the buildings are rendered with a precision that is astonishing even for Canaletto. This clarity of conception, which is rooted in the rationalism of the Enlightenment, is not seen in his earlier paintings. The air is crystalline, perhaps in the calm after a storm, and an intense light falls from high in the southern sky on Salute's magnificent northern portal. With colorful figures scattered across the plaza, the church assumes a stagelike character. The picture is enlivened by the rippled surface of the canal's dark greenish blue water and by windtorn clouds. The cloud in the upper left corner is almost equal in chromatic value to the plaza in front of the Salute, establishing a strong diagonal axis.

Like the Grand Canal itself, Santa Maria della Salute, especially its north entrance, was among the preferred motifs in paintings of Venice. It has continued to be represented in more recent times by such artists as Turner, Boudin, Monet, Signac, and Kokoschka. Canaletto himself painted the same view no fewer than a dozen times. This version, whose background may have been finished by assistants, is nearly identical to one in a Geneva (?) private collection (fig. 8a).[1] Together with the Bührle collection's *Grand Canal* (cat. 9), the *Salute* belongs to a series of six or seven views of Venice, which Canaletto perhaps executed on commission from the collector, art dealer, and ambassador to Venice, Joseph Smith, for the duke of Buccleuch.[2] On the basis of its style and topographic layout, this series has been dated between 1738 and 1742.[3]   CB

Oil on canvas
121,5 × 152 (47⅞ × 59⅞)
Foundation E. G. Bührle Collection

9   *The Grand Canal, c. 1738–1742*

9a. Canaletto, *The Grand Canal Looking Southwest from Ponte Rialto to Ca' Foscari,* c. 1733–1735, Galleria Nazionale d'Arte Antica, Rome.

Seen from the height of the Rialto bridge, partly in view at the lower left, this panorama shows a stretch of Venice's Grand Canal looking southwest toward the gothic Ca' Foscari. The latter closes off the composition in the distance, where the canal turns south in a wide loop toward the Basin of San Marco. The viewer's eye is directed down the dark greenish blue waterway past myriad buildings once witness to Venice's past glories. Most notable on the left bank are the Dolfin-Manin Palace by Jacopo Sansovino (behind the wooden shed on the Campo di San Bartolomeo), the gothic Bembo Palace, the Loredan Palace, and the Grimani Palace by Michele Sammicheli. The latter is bathed in sunlight on one side and because of its height constitutes a break in the row of buildings. Opposite these palaces are the simpler houses of the Riva del Vin, which once served as the marketplace for the wine trade. Today many of these shops have been converted into cafés and restaurants, protected from rain and heat by the small overhanging roofs; they convey an impression of everyday life in mid-eighteenth-century Venice.

Like Canaletto's *Santa Maria della Salute* in the Bührle collection (cat. 8), this painting is a very precise rendering of the unique cityscape of Venice. Despite the accuracy of its representation, however, it is not pedantic or boring. Lively impastoed figures, gondolas that ply the canal, and cloud formations in a breezy morning sky establish an easy play of accents without interfering with the tranquil mood. Light from the southeast fills the scene with a quiet luminosity, emphasizing the house fronts of the Riva del Vin, subtly differentiated in color. Canaletto's primary interest seems to have been to offer a typical scene in his hometown.

Canaletto painted many views of the Grand Canal, which is among the most popular subjects in paintings of Venice. He chose various "ideal" vantage points, but he painted at least seven versions of the section from the Rialto to the Ca' Foscari, all very similar to each other. The Bührle version, along with its companion here, *Santa Maria della Salute* (cat. 8), belonged to a series of six or seven views of the Grand Canal created between 1738 and 1742 for the duke of Buccleuch.[1] It is nearly identical in form and palette to a work of a few years earlier in the Galleria Nazionale d'Arte Antica in Rome (fig. 9a),[2] differing only in its distribution of ships and accessory figures.

CB

Oil on canvas
121 × 152 (47⅝ × 59⅞)
Foundation E. G. Bührle Collection

10   *Portrait of the Painter Laurent Pécheux, 1756–1757*

Laurent Pécheux was born and trained in Lyon, then moved to Rome in 1752 to further his artistic studies.[1] He met success in Italy, becoming a member of several academies and eventually court painter in Turin. But despite the official recognition, Pécheux was an unremarkable artist, whose ambitious history paintings were characterized by a tepid neoclassicism and whose portraits lacked both grace and incisiveness.

When Greuze met Pécheux during his visit to Rome from January 1756 to April 1757, Pécheux had not yet lapsed into mediocrity but was beginning to be recognized and to receive important commissions. Greuze, too, was on the brink of success. Before leaving for Italy, he had been elected an associate member of the French Royal Academy, and his submissions to the 1755 Salon (his first) had been very well received. Pécheux and Greuze were also about the same age and came from similar backgrounds; both were from the provinces and both began their artistic training in Lyon. We sense these shared experiences and ambitions in the direct way Greuze painted Pécheux and in the frank manner in which Pécheux presented himself. He is casually and soberly dressed, unassuming, yet confident in his gaze and in the way he holds himself erect.

Because the background and areas of the face have been painted over in the Bührle painting, it is difficult to render an accurate assessment of the work. Nevertheless, the overpainting does not obscure the poise and assuredness of either the painter or his subject.   MDS

Oil on canvas
73 × 59.5 (28¾ × 23⅜)
Foundation E. G. Bührle Collection

11   Procession in Valencia, 1810–1812

11 a. Goya, *The Bullfight,* 1922, The Metropolitan Museum of Art, Wolfe Fund, Catherine Lorillard Collection.

Perhaps to be identified with a work listed as *Una procession* in an 1828 inventory of Goya's studio, this painting was given its present title in the 1867 sale catalogue of the Salamanca Collection.[1] It was there described as pendant to a bullfight scene now in The Metropolitan Museum of Art (see fig. 11a), but sold for 1,100 francs less, perhaps due to the popularity of the bullfight theme in mid-nineteenth-century France.[2] In both paintings Goya sketches his figures broadly in black strokes, subsequently applying color accents to control and lead the viewer through the composition. The marking "x + 1" in the lower right corner suggests that the *Procession in Valencia* was one of the paintings inventoried in 1812 upon the death of Goya's wife, Josefa Bayeu.[3]

Goya first depicted a religious procession in 1787, as one in a series of cabinet paintings commissioned by the duke and duchess of Osuna. He returned to the theme in the *Procession of Flagellants* of c. 1816 (Royal Academy of San Fernando, Madrid) and in the *Pilgrimage of Saint Isidore,* one of the series of "black" paintings executed on the walls of Goya's suburban house, the Quinta del Sordo, between 1819 and 1824 (Museo del Prado, Madrid).[4] Formally, the processional theme allowed Goya to experiment with a protean form, masterfully exploited in the *Procession in Valencia* where the procession snakes through the landscape to create the illusion of space, anticipating the processions seen in the later black painting.

The theme probably held more than a merely formal interest for Goya, however. These rituals had been criticized by enlightened reformers during the late eighteenth century, and several of their more popular (and less religious) elements, such as huge puppets and "little devils," were outlawed in 1780.[5] Goya may reveal his disdain for such popular ritual by including an ass in the lower left corner, interpreted alternatively as an image of false devotion or an illustration of a fable in which the ass takes himself to be the object of veneration.[6] In *Procession in Valencia* the animal stubbornly refuses to move, stopping to urinate and thus providing an indecorous introit for what follows. Members of various religious orders begin the procession proper, and spectators include two gentlemen and a boy in dress that would, by Goya's time, have been long outdated. Previously, the artist had used such anachronisms to underscore the backward nature of provincials.[7] One might wonder if that is his intent here.

JAT

Oil on canvas
105.5 × 126 (41½ × 49⅝)
Foundation E. G. Bührle Collection

12   *Portrait of Monsieur Devillers, 1811*

When Ingres' tenure as a *pensionnaire* at the French Academy in Rome ended in 1810, he decided not to return to Paris but to remain in Rome. Fortunately for Ingres, who needed to support himself, Rome, having been annexed by Napoleon in 1809, was full of imperial bureaucrats eager to have their portraits painted by this talented young artist. Among those seeking Ingres' services was the director of probate and estates, Hippolyte-François Devillers.

In contrast to other French officials, such as Marcotte and Cordier, who sat for Ingres in civilian clothes, Devillers chose to be painted in official uniform. In this portrait he wears a black *frac,* or dress coat, with ears of wheat embroidered in silver on the high standing collar, cuffs, and pockets.[1] The jacket is worn over a white embroidered vest and creamy white knee breeches. Devillers stands with his right hand in his vest, a fashionable pose favored by Napoleon, and holds under his left arm a black *bicorne.* A ceremonial sword hangs at his hip.

It is Devillers' face, however, rather than the stunning ensemble of black, white, and silver, that is the focus of Ingres' painting. Here, as in his best portraits, Ingres penetrates surface description to reveal the personality of his sitter. Devillers was a man of the new, postrevolutionary age, born to middle-class parents in the provinces and promoted because of service to the State, not ancestral claims to privilege. Ingres portrays Devillers, dressed in the elegant uniform of his office, as a man proud of his position, but not arrogant or affected. In fact, the forty-five-year-old bureaucrat here has an amiable demeanor, with intelligent eyes and a thin but sensual mouth. The slight puffiness under his eyes suggests the long hours of a dedicated administrator but also hints at the full life of a bachelor, a *bon vivant.* Ingres includes one detail that alludes to the private pleasure of Devillers: the gold octagonal snuff box in his left hand.

Also in 1811 Ingres made a drawing of Devillers in civilian dress, seated and clutching his snuff box.[2] A year later the artist did another graphite drawing of Devillers, standing (half-length) with books and an inkwell in the background.[3]   MDS

Oil on canvas
96.5 × 78.5 (38 × 30⅞)
Signed and dated at lower left:
Ingres à Rome / 1811.
Foundation E. G. Bührle Collection

Camille Corot 1796–1875

13 *A Girl Reading, c. 1845–1850*

A Girl Reading represents the private side of Corot's œuvre, a work unencumbered by the demands of the Salons or his clients, for Corot exhibited primarily landscapes, keeping his small figure paintings to himself. Free from public and critical expectations, these works retain the informality of the study and the intimacy of the studio.

Corot began to concentrate on figure studies after returning from his third trip to Italy in 1843. He relished the times when he would hire a model, often from his neighborhood, dress her up in an Italian costume, and then paint her picture, usually with a book, holding a mandolin, or simply deep in reverie. These simple studies evoked nostalgic memories for Corot of his trips to Italy. At the same time they mirrored Corot's own solitary existence.

The model in *A Girl Reading* wears a red jacket trimmed in gold at the cuffs and a red ribbon in her hair, a costume that reappears in later figure paintings such as *The Studio* of 1865–1870 (Musée du Louvre, Paris). Characteristic of Corot's early figure studies, the model retains the specificity of a portrait, which all but disappears after 1850.[1]

This painting is one of the first Corot did of the figure reading, a theme he returned to throughout his life. No doubt he selected such poses of self-absorption because they conveyed his own introspective nature. But just as important, they allowed him to concentrate on painting. As a visitor to Corot's studio in 1851 noted, Corot's object in painting the figures was to try to achieve the tonal harmony he had developed in his landscapes.[2] The book in *A Girl Reading* is not simply the vehicle of her quiet but is also, with her white blouse and the white edging in the background, essential to the painting's cohesiveness.

A Girl Reading is striking for its freshness and simplicity. In this work Corot managed to effectively balance the mood of the picture whith pictorial concerns, a balance that would elude him in later figure pieces when sentiment became more weighty than art.   MDS

Oil on canvas
42.5 × 32.5 (16¾ × 12¾)
Signed at lower left: COROT
Foundation E. G. Bührle Collection

14   *A Turkish Officer Killed in the Mountains*
or *The Death of Hassan, 1825–1826*

Delacroix painted this exotic jewel, rich and mysterious, when inspired by the fierce passions of Byron's poetry and stirred by the suffering of the Greeks at the hands of the Turks as they fought for independence from the Ottoman empire. This overlapping of the artist's interests has led to confusion concerning the subject of the painting. Traditionally called *The Death of Hassan* after a scene in Byron's "The Giaour" (first published in 1813), it has recently been identified as *A Turkish Officer Killed in the Mountains,* a painting that was included in the 1826 Galerie Lebrun exhibition to aid the Greeks.[1]

That it could represent either says much for Delacroix's ability to produce something original, while taking inspiration from the poet, for even those who are convinced that the painting is of *A Turkish Officer* admit that it is clearly related to and dependent on Byron's poem. Set in seventeenth-century Greece, "The Giaour" centers on a nameless Venetian, the *giaour* (a non-Mussulman), who kills the Turk Hassan to avenge the death of his beloved Leila. Hassan had his beautiful slave drowned upon learning that she was not only unfaithful but consorting with an infidel. The giaour gets revenge with Hassan's death, but he remains tormented by his lost love until he dies.

Reading "The Giaour" in 1824, Delacroix immediately recognized episodes that lent themselves to pictorial composition,[2] and he portrayed the death of Hassan in a watercolor, a small oil, a lithograph,[3] and indirectly in the Bührle oil. This painting, unlike the other works, leaves out a crucial element in the narrative: the giaour confronting his mortally wounded enemy. It is this omission and the fire in the background (read as a sign of battle) that has led Johnson to decide that the painting does not represent the death of Hassan. There is a very strong relationship, however, between Delacroix's image and Byron's verses as well as with earlier pictorial interpretations.

Delacroix depicts the figure here just as Byron describes the slain Hassan, "His back to earth, his face to heaven," with "His turban far behind him roll'd."[4] He dresses the figure in the flowered *palampore* that Byron specifies, brilliantly confounding the red in the pattern with Hassan's blood. The strongest visual link between this painting and Byron's poem is Géricault's 1823 lithograph of the giaour on his horse staring down at his hated enemy, which shows Hassan in the same pose as does Delacroix: crumpled over a rocky mound that supports his head and contorts his left shoulder and arm.[5] Delacroix's genius was to forego the climatic moment chosen by Géricault and others and find power in the moment after.[6]   MDS

Oil on canvas
32.5 × 41 (12¾ × 16⅛)
Signed at lower left: Eug. Delacroix
Private collection

15   *Arab Musicians, 1836*

"This place is made for painters," Delacroix wrote his friend Frédéric Villot from Tangier. "If you ever have a few months to spare, come to Barbary and there you will see those natural qualities that are always disguised in our countries, and you'll feel moreover the rare and precious influence of the sun, which gives intense life to everything. I shall doubtless bring back some sketches, but they will convey very little of the impression that all this makes on one."[1] When Delacroix returned to Paris in June 1832 after several months in North Africa, he brought with him several albums of sketches, some hand-colored, with notes that were intended to serve as *aides-mémoires* for future works.

Delacroix painted *Arab Musicians* four years after his trip to Morocco, recalling the strong impressions made upon him by the landscape, the light, and the people. Culling individual figures from his reference sketches, many of which are extant, Delacroix constructed a scene of the spontaneous entertainment by two musicians. The composition, however, is anything but spontaneous. The figures, which seem scattered haphazardly across the page, are carefully placed to achieve a balance between the right and left sides of the picture. The two musicians and the squatting figures next to them anchor the center of the composition. Two figures in the foreground with their backs to us—a hooded man on the left, a young man in blue on the right—and the crouched figures next to them bracket the scene at the sides. A more subtle series of echoes are found in the crowd: for instance, the Jewess in red and gold on the left and her counterpart in white on the right.

Although painted in Paris, the Bührle watercolor conveys Delacroix's delight in the lively, exotic customs of Morocco and his appreciation of both the people and the intense colors of the landscape—"black green" meadows and "raw blue" mountains. He particularly admired the natural ease with which the people carried themselves, crouched, and reclined, as compared with the restricted movements of Europeans. Delacroix saw in these "sublime children of nature," in the way they richly draped their simple garments, a classical nobility truer than had ever been painted by the neoclassical artist Jacques-Louis David.[2]

Delacroix used this watercolor as the basis for the oil painting *Arab Players* that he exhibited at the Salon of 1848 (Musée des Beaux-Arts, Tours).[3] The oil differs only slightly from the watercolor in overall composition, but it lacks the clarity and freshness of the earlier work.   MDS

Watercolor
42.5 × 58.5 (16¾ × 23)
Signed and dated at lower right:
Eug. Delacroix. 1836.
Private collection

Honoré Daumier   1808–1879

16   *The Free Performance, c. 1843–1845*

Daumier was probably best known during his lifetime as the creator of caustic political and social satires, widely disseminated in lithographs published in the French daily and weekly newspapers. Yet he prized most highly his work as a painter. In fact, his paintings, including *The Free Performance,* explore many of the same subjects and display the same handling of media as his lithographs.

The Bührle painting was probably executed fairly early in Daumier's career, possibly before 1845.[1] Any attempt to give the work a precise date, however, is made very difficult by the major restoration that the picture appears to have undergone, involving extensive retouching of almost all figures except the head in the center at the back.

In both paintings and lithographs Daumier had been interested as much in the physical character of a crowd as in the characteristic gesture or facial expression that defined the social position or political affiliation of individual subjects. The crowd was a manifestation of the collective life, whether on the street, in the law courts, in a domestic setting, or at the theater. When observing such gatherings of humanity at the theater, Daumier recorded both the action seen across the footlights and the reaction within the audience. Among the spectators he captured responses that ranged from the polite, restrained expressions of the wealthy occupants of stalls and grand tier boxes (e. g., *La Loge,* 1845–1857[2]) to the uncouth excitement of the public in the cheap parts of the upper house.

In the Bührle painting a crowd of common people leans eagerly over a railing to glimpse the drama being played out beyond the lower left edge of the composition. Daumier's ability to capture within a confined area so rich a range of reactions has been well summarized by critic Philippe Burty: "No word could give an exact idea of the diversity of physiognomies which the play on the stage enthralls, lights up, excites, frightens, amuses. A stance, taut or limp, the play of muscles, the direction of a glance, the light in the irises of the eye, all that make a body react and a mind think is caught in an infinite moment of action, fixed with an incomparable art based upon moral observation and physiological conditions..."[3] Daumier explored the subject of audiences engrossed in theatrical performances in many of his lithographs.[4] Two drawings also appear to be related to the composition and emotional character of this painting.[5]

MAS

Oil on panel
55.5 × 44.5 (21⅞ × 17½)
Signed at lower right corner: h. Daumier
Foundation E. G. Bührle Collection

17   *Portrait of a Hunter, probably 1849–1850*

This is an odd, compelling work. There is a tension in it between Courbet's realism—the frank portrayal of the world around him—and his use of an archaic artistic convention to present that world. He forces the burly hunter, with his large hat and rifle, into a format characteristic of fifteenth- and sixteenth-century portraits. These bust-length portraits show the sitter in profile against a neutral background; the space is very cramped, often circumscribed by a painted frame or ledge at the bottom bearing an inscription. But Courbet rejects the clarity that is a hallmark of these portraits in favor of his interpretation of Rembrandt: golden amber light imbedded in dark shadow.

Courbet admitted to studying the art of both the "ancients" and the "moderns" in order to discover his own individuality.[1] He frequently took over earlier art forms and transformed, even subverted, them. The fifteenth- and sixteenth-century portraits Courbet would have seen were certainly portraits of kings and nobles, not ordinary hunters.

Opinions as to the date of this work vary from 1846 to 1849–1850.[2] It seems most reasonable to date the work around 1849, because it relates closely in subject and technique to other works from that period, such as *After Dinner at Ornans* (Musée des Beaux-Arts, Lille). Another question concerns whether or not this is a self-portrait. Charles Léger in 1929 was the first to identify it as such, but this suggestion has been rejected by most later authors and scholars.[3] Photographs of Courbet in profile reveal a refinement of features that is not present in this portrait. On the other hand, they show the same jagged line in the cheek that is seen here. Courbet was a master at creating such ambiguities.   MDS

Oil on canvas
70 × 60 (27½ × 23½)
Signed at lower right: G Courbet
Foundation E. G. Bührle Collection

Gustave Courbet 1819–1877

18   The Houses of the Château of Ornans, c. 1853

In 1856 the poet Max Buchon, Courbet's childhood friend, described the painter's works as "the natural flowering of his personality, in the midst of his family, in that lovely valley of Ornans."[1] Buchon may have been referring to controversial works such as *A Burial at Ornans,* but his comments are equally true of Courbet's landscapes, such as *The Houses of the Château of Ornans,* in which the identity and history of the region he knew so intimately are mingled with his own.

Courbet was greatly attracted to the ruggedly beautiful land around Ornans, with its spectacular bluffs of white rock. One of these cliffs, above Courbet's village, was known as the "château d'Ornans" because a medieval castle once belonging to the dukes of Burgundy had stood there until the seventeenth century. The castle was torn down by order of Richelieu, who, protecting Louis XIII's sovereignty from the independent-minded nobility in the provinces, wanted no potential strongholds to remain. The local people leveled the ruins and built modest dwellings in place of the château. The significance for Courbet of this remnant from the region's earlier political history—whether he saw in it the endurance and power of the ordinary people or the triumph of the present over the past—cannot be precisely determined.[2] One suspects, however, that the inclusion of the château in the background of Courbet's most democratic of canvases, *A Burial at Ornans,* is more than simply topical description.

Courbet first painted a view of the château around 1850 (The Minneapolis Institute of Arts), placing the cluster of houses, perched on the rocky promontory, within a panoramic setting that encompasses the village of Ornans below and the mountainous terrain beyond. He included a laundress in the foreground to add color, scale, and picturesque effect.

Courbet's approach to the scene in the Bührle oil is more bold and direct. He discards the inherited formulas for landscape, the logical progression of foreground, middle-ground, and background, and the requisite figures to provide scale and orientation for the viewer. And instead of highlighting the picturesque setting of the houses, Courbet focuses on the less spectacular approach to the site, the one accessible to him by foot. He finds beauty in the simplicity of the buildings, the rhythm of their dark, sloping roof lines against the sky, and their flat geometry played against the scrubby foliage. There is something of Corot's compositional clarity here, but Courbet, with the directness of the palette knife, makes this view his own.   MDS

Oil on canvas
96.5 × 122 (38 × 48)
Signed at lower left: G. Courbet.
Private collection

Camille Pissarro   1830–1903

19   *Road from Versailles to Louveciennes, 1870*

19a. Pissarro, study for *Road from Versailles to Louveciennes,* Ashmolean Museum, Oxford.

This picture records the artist's mistress, Julie Vellay, and his eldest daughter, Jeanne Rachel, in the narrow front garden at 22 route de Versailles, Louveciennes, the house into which he and his family had moved by 3 May 1869.[1] They left the house at the end of September 1870, some four months after this painting was executed, just before the advance of the Prussians on Paris following the disastrous defeat of the French imperial armies at the Battle of Sedan. Pissarro's family first took refuge in Montfoucault, at the home of Ludovic Piette, then moved to London in early December.

The apparent simplicity of this painting belies its importance in the œuvre of Pissarro. At least one preliminary drawing indicates a concern to balance the compositional elements with a degree of formality not commonly seen as intrinsic to impressionist procedures (see fig. 19a). The plunge into depth of the sunlit road is even more dramatically uncompromising than in *Road from Versailles to Louveciennes (effect of rain)* (Sterling and Francine Clark Institute of Art, Williamstown, Mass.) and *Road from Versailles to Louveciennes (effect of snow)* (The Maryland Institute, Baltimore, on loan to the Walters Art Gallery).[2] With the division of the composition by a tree in the center, which separates the sunlit road from the shadowed garden, this recession points to the influence of Japanese prints. Pissarro, like his fellow impressionists, was already enthusiastic about Japanese art in the 1860s, but his interest was greatly encouraged by Théodore Duret on the latter's return from the Far East in January 1873.

Pissarro's handling of paint here, in its definition of objects, represents a maturity in his technique that emerged by the end of the 1860s, shaped as much by his contact with the work of Courbet and Corot after his arrival in France in 1855 as by his friendships with the impressionists at the Café Guerbois and at the Atelier Suisse from 1859. The blocky, architectonic brushstrokes and the use of carefully chosen dabs of bright color reflect especially the work of Monet and Bazille in the second half of the 1860s. Similarly, however, Pissarro as yet shows little application of the blue-violet tones in shadows, the latter still being described in black.

On several occasions before his departure to England, Pissarro explored the motif of a straight road bordered by buildings or trees and receding into the depth of the composition.[3] None, however, are as crisp in their handling or as dramatic as this one.

MAS

Oil on canvas
100.5 × 81 (39½ × 31⅞)
Signed and dated lower left: C. Pissarro / 1870
Foundation E. G. Bührle Collection

Camille Pissarro 1830–1903

20   *Road from Osny to Pontoise—Hoar Frost, 1873*

Pissarro moved in August 1872 from Louveciennes to Pontoise, where he would be joined by Armand Guillaumin and Paul Cézanne, the latter working beside him to achieve an interchange of motif and technique that would be mutually beneficial over the next five years.

As at Louveciennes (see cat. 19), Pissarro undertook an almost obsessive record of the landscapes around his home.[1] This view of the road from Osny to Pontoise is the second of two compositions that depict the site. The first, showing the landscape in high summer, was almost certainly executed shortly after Pissarro moved to the area.[2] The second, while retaining the same road, with figures on the left and agricultural buildings on the right, explores the changes wrought upon the landscape by a hard winter frost.

The apparently randomly selected view, the thin paint texture, and the application of blue to the shadow area on the left declare a general allegiance to the principles of impressionism. Yet by using the road to establish recession into the depth of the landscape, Pissarro seems to display little interest in challenging the conventions that had governed the construction of traditional landscape, which he blatantly undermined in other works executed during this period, notably *Plowed Fields near Osny* (Collection Durand-Ruel, Paris) and *Old Road from Ennery to Pontoise—Hoar Frost* (Musée d'Orsay, Paris).[3] In this respect the painting has much in common with Sisley's procedures of landscape composition (see cats. 36 and 37).

MAS

Oil on canvas
50.5 × 65 (19⅞ × 25⅝)
Signed and dated lower left: C. Pissarro. 1873
Foundation E. G. Bührle Collection

Edouard Manet   1832–1883

21   Oloron-Sainte-Marie, 1871

Manet served in Paris during the Franco-Prussian War as a lieutenant in an artillery regiment commanded by the painter Ernest Meissonier. On 9 February, nine days after the armistice was signed, he wrote a short letter to Emile Zola to say how sad he was to have just learned that impressionist painter Frédéric Bazille had been killed in the war and that the ground floor of Zola's house had been occupied by a refugee family. He informed Zola that he was going to meet his family in Oloron-Sainte-Marie in the Pyrenees, where they had gone to escape the war: "I'm leaving in a few days to join my wife and mother who are at Oloron in the Basses-Pyrenees. I can't wait to see them. I'll be going by way of Bordeaux. Perhaps I'll pay you a visit. Then I'll speak of things that one cannot write."[1] According to Tabarant, Manet left Paris on 12 February and remained in Oloron until 21 February when he left for Bordeaux (see cat. 22).[2]

Manet began to paint again while in Oloron, having done little during the war. Tabarant maintains that the artist did four paintings before leaving for Bordeaux: the present work, which he calls "Sur une galérie à colonnes, à Oloron," and three others that he describes as sketches.[3] The scene depicted is the second-floor balcony of the house in Oloron rented by Manet's family. The artist's brother-in-law, Dutch painter Leon Koëlla-Leenhoff, is shown leaning on the balcony railing, with a view of the nearby faubourg Sainte-Croix in the background.[4]

The treatment of the cat, the boldly diagonal composition, and the emphasis on architectural features suggest the influence of Japanese prints, which Manet admired.[5] At first the painting seems to be only the record of a passing moment during the artist's short stay in Oloron, but it is Manet's first signed and dated painting after having suffered through the siege of Paris. As such, it is an image that celebrates his delight in the ordinary—a town at peace, a sunny day, the rhythms of nearby rooftops, and a cat at a friend's feet.   CSM

Oil on canvas
42.5 × 62 (16¾ × 24½)
Signed at lower right: Manet / 71
Foundation E. G. Bührle Collection

Edouard Manet   1832–1883

22   *The Port of Bordeaux, 1871*

22a. Manet, *The Port of Bordeaux,* private collection, through the Foundation Wildenstein, Paris.

22b. Manet, *Moonlight over the Boulogne Harbor,* 1869, Musée d'Orsay, Paris.

On 12 February 1871, a few days after the end of the Franco-Prussian War, Manet left Paris for Oloron-Sainte-Marie where his family had gone to escape the conflict. After several days in Oloron (see cat. 21) they left for Bordeaux and remained there for about a week.[1] Manet must have devoted most of his time to painting this view of the harbor of Bordeaux, his first major work since the summer of 1870.

Manet first made a watercolor (see fig. 22a),[2] then this oil painting of the view from the window of a café on the quai des Chartons.[3] Reminiscent of his *Moonlight over the Boulogne Harbor* of 1869 (fig. 22b), *The Port of Bordeaux* depicts a quai where workers load barrels of wine onto a small merchant vessel, the harbor filled with boats and a tangle of tilting masts, and in the distance the Cathedral of Saint-André. Less than a month after the war the harbor must have been bustling with activity, excitement, and a sense of renewal, as the city and the country returned to a normal state of affairs.

During his stay in Bordeaux, Manet probably visited the novelist and critic Emile Zola, then employed as secretary to a member of the government who was in Bordeaux attending a session of the newly elected National Assembly. Manet had written Zola on 9 February to tell him that he might pass through Bordeaux soon and hoped to see him there.[4]

By the early 1870s Zola was no longer the lone champion of Manet and the modern movement. Théodore Duret, in a review published in *L'Electeur Libre* in the spring of 1870, came to the artist's defense and contributed substantially to establishing a fresh critical context in which Manet's work could be understood and appreciated. A passage intended as a general analysis of Manet's work is particularly well suited to the effects that the artist achieved less than a year later in *The Port of Bordeaux*: "No one has the feeling for values and for accent in coloring objects more than he. Everything is resolved in his eyes into variations of color. Every shade or distinct tint becomes a well-marked tone, a special note of the palette."[5] Despite Duret's eloquence, most critics failed to see the strength of Manet's work.   CSM

Oil on canvas
66 × 99.5 (26 × 39⅛)
Signed at lower right: Manet
Inscribed at lower left: Bordeaux
Private collection

23   *La Sultane, 1871*

Beginning with Théodore Duret in 1902, scholars have dated *La Sultane* variously between 1870 and 1876,[1] but as Etienne Moreau-Nélaton pointed out in 1926, the painting is listed in a notebook that Manet used in 1871.[2] Moreover, all of the paintings included in the list were done between 1861 and 1871. In 1932 Paul Colin, without documentation, indicated that this was the first important work Manet painted after returning to Paris in 1871 following the Franco-Prussian War and the Commune.[3] A date of 1871 seems reasonable on stylistic grounds as well.

The model for *La Sultane* is unidentified, but the subject belongs to a category that includes such well-known images of mistresses and prostitutes in Manet's work as *Olympia* of 1863 (Musée d'Orsay, Paris) and *Nana* of 1877 (Kunsthalle, Hamburg). Indeed, in the 1870s the word *sultane* was one of many colloquialisms for a mistress or courtesan.[4]

La Sultane may at first seem to reflect the vogue in nineteenth-century French painting for Middle Eastern subjects, but the prurient aspect is unmistakable. The frontal view of a young woman in a diaphanous shift, handled even more revealingly than the nude *Olympia,* is neither an updated version of Ingres' *The Turkish Bath* of 1862 (Musée du Louvre, Paris) nor an odalisque, but a seductress who lacks both the defiant pride of Olympia and the cultivated banality of Nana. The costumed prostitute stands in a setting decorated to look like a harem or a Middle Eastern brothel. She has lowered her eyes, and her countenance and quiet stance seem to express resignation and fatigue.

In this connection, it is noteworthy that T. J. Clark observes in his essay on Manet's *Olympia* that "Relations between prostitute and client involved, among other things, matters of social class; they often meant a transgression of normal class divisions—a curious exposure of the self to someone inferior, someone lamentable. That doubtless lent spice to the transaction, but only if it were made part of a set of sexual theatricals which became more cumbersome as the years went by. . . . the prostitute was obliged to make herself desirable. . . . It was a game in which the woman most often collaborated and to an extent was trapped."[5]   CSM

Oil on canvas
95.5 × 74.5 (37⅜ × 29⅜)
Signed at lower left: Manet
Foundation E. G. Bührle Collection

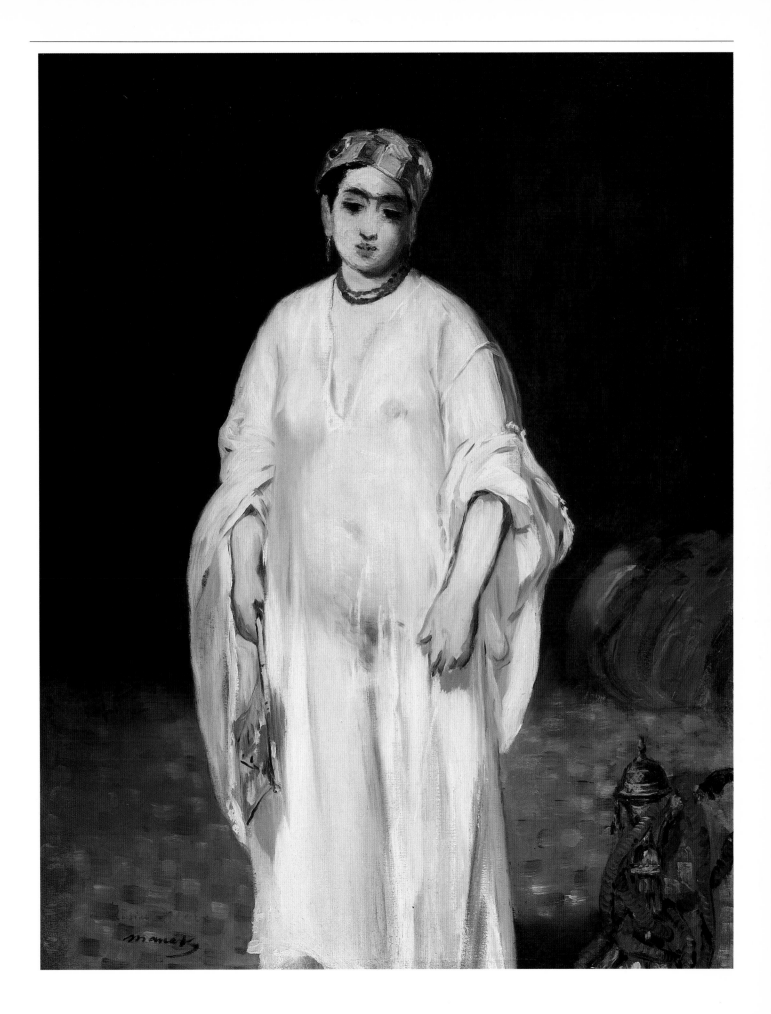

Edouard Manet   1832–1883

24   *The Swallows, 1873*

Manet spent July and August of 1873 in Etaples near Berck-sur-Mer, where he painted *The Swallows* and at least fourteen other works.[1] The figures in the foreground of this painting are the artist's mother, on the left, and his wife.

The plein-air subject and light palette reflect Manet's interest in the technique and subjects of his younger colleagues, especially Monet and Renoir. Nevertheless, the artist apparently found the painting sufficiently conservative to submit it to the jury for the Salon of 1874. He had refused an invitation to participate in the first impressionist group show, which took place at approximately the same time. But of the four works Manet submitted to the Salon, the jury accepted only one painting, *The Railroad* of 1873 (National Gallery of Art, Washington), and one watercolor, *La Polichinelle* of 1873 (private collection, Paris), refusing *The Swallows* and *Masked Ball at the Opera,* 1873 (National Gallery of Art, Washington). It was the first time since 1866 that works by Manet had been rejected for the official exhibition.

The refusal of the two paintings prompted a long article by Stéphane Mallarmé, virtually unknown as either a critic or a poet at the time. He attacked the shortcomings of the jury and deplored the continuing failure to understand Manet's work. With regard to *The Swallows,* he granted "the most superficial critics a single objection in order to refute it later on. . . . it is that, if you wish, his paintings in the colloquial sense are not 'finished' enough. It seems to me that for some the existence of this joke has been called in question by those who first uttered it. What is an 'unfinished work', if all its elements are in accord, and if it possesses a charm which could easily be broken by an additional touch? . . . one never sees the judges deal severely with a canvas which is both insignificant and frighteningly detailed."[2]

The rejection of *The Swallows* and *Masked Ball at the Opera* was also decried by the distinguished critic Philippe Burty, who described the Salon as a "boutique whose doors open only to fabricators with diplomas, to products guaranteed pure and free of 'all foreign substances.'"[3] But another influential critic, Jules Clarétie, derided Manet for precisely those qualities that Mallarmé and Burty had admired: "Manet is one of those who pretend that in painting one can and must be contented with *impression.* We have seen, from these *impressionists,* an exhibition a short time ago on the Boulevard des Capucines, at the studio of Nadar. It was unreservedly disconcerting."[4] In short, Manet's paintings challenged, provoked, and inspired impassioned ideas about the nature of art. Although easily accepted and widely admired today, *The Swallows* contributed meaningfully little more than a century ago to a new understanding of what a painting could be.   CSM

Oil on canvas
65 × 81 (25⅝ × 31⅞)
Signed at lower right: Manet
Foundation E. G. Bührle Collection

25   *The Rue Mosnier with Flags, 1878*

25a. Manet, *The Rue Mosnier with Pavers,* 1878, private collection, on loan to the Kunsthaus, Zurich.

25b. Manet, *The Rue Mosnier with Flags,* Collection of Mr. and Mrs. Paul Mellon, Upperville, Virginia.

To celebrate the success of the Exposition Universelle of 1878, the French government declared 30 June 1878 a national holiday, the Fête de la Paix. But as Theodore Reff summarizes, the day was rife with political significance: "The Fête de la Paix on June 30th was thus, like the fair itself, an affirmation of the country's complete recovery, international acceptance, and material and cultural progress, and was conceived on a larger scale than any during the previous regime, like a continual *fête impériale.* The newspapers and illustrated weeklies were ecstatic that June in describing 'the joy on every face, exuberant and sincere,' and the festive decoration of every street, which in some quarters caused 'the houses to disappear completely behind the bundles of flags.'"[1]

On 30 June 1878 Manet was in his studio on the second floor of 4 rue Saint-Petersbourg (now rue de Leningrad), which he would have to vacate the following week when the lease expired.[2] The studio looked down on the rue Mosnier (renamed the rue de Berne in 1884). He had painted the view once before in the spring (fig. 25a), and apparently he painted it again twice on 30 June. The looseness and speed of execution, the comparative lack of finish, and the absence of a signature and date suggest that the present work was done first. In addition, the longer, fuller shadows in the signed and dated version in the Collection of Mr. and Mrs. Paul Mellon (fig. 25b) suggest a later time of day.[3] But the order and date of execution are supposition. Reff cautions that one of Manet's several drawings and studies of motifs on the rue Mosnier "corresponds closely enough to the [horse and cab in the] first of the paintings of June 30th to suggest that, for all of its exuberant freedom, the latter was prepared by means of such drawings."[4]

Both versions of *The Rue Mosnier with Flags* hint at political significances. The man on crutches on the left side of the Mellon version is most likely a war veteran.[5] He is described by T. J. Clark as "a one-legged man *en blouse*—a veteran of 1870, say, or even worse, of 1871 [the violent civil upheaval in Paris known as the Commune, which followed the Franco-Prussian War]."[6] In the Bührle version the left side of the street is obscured by a swath of red from the tricolor flying from the window of Manet's studio. The artist also seems to have given added emphasis to the red sections of the flags flying from the building across the street; the blue and white sections are considerably less prominent. In this connection, Reff notes "a reminder of the red banners [Manet] had seen during the Commune."[7] Thus in ways that the casual observer may not realize at first, Manet was the quintessential painter of modern life, including the subtle but painful realities of recent French history.   CSM

Oil on canvas
65 × 81 (25⅝ × 31⅞)
Inscribed at lower right:
Certifié d'Ed Manet / Vve Manet
Private collection

26   *The Great Horned Owl, 1881*

26a. Melchior de Hondecoeter, *Dead Rooster,* Musée des Beaux-Arts, Brussels.

This painting is one of six works listed as "panneaux décoratifs" in the 18 June 1883 inventory of Manet's property made in connection with his estate.[1] Four of the panels, including *The Great Horned Owl,* were painted in the summer of 1881 at a house Manet rented at 20 avenue de Villeneuve-l'Etang in Versailles.[2] The sizes of the six canvases are different, however, and the relationship of the panels to each other is tenuous; *The Great Horned Owl* seems to be a wholly independent work of art. Thus it is possible that the paintings were grouped together as a matter of convenience when the inventory was made.

The composition may be indebted to one of Jean-Baptiste Oudry's many still lifes of dead game, several of which include dead birds hanging against a wood-paneled background. Leopold Reidemeister points out that the most compelling possible source in visual terms is Melchior de Hondecoeter's (1636–1695) *Dead Rooster* (fig. 26a),[3] but how and when Manet might have seen it is not known.

Although *The Great Horned Owl* may be indebted to seventeenth- or eighteenth-century prototypes, the modernity of the image is undeniable. The tangle of feathers, the looseness of execution, the upside-down configuration of the owl, and Manet's exceedingly painterly interpretation of the subject, traditionally treated in a trompe-l'œil manner, combine to create deliberate ambiguity. The artist has created a conflict between the image as an illusion and the painting as brushwork, pigment, and tonal harmonies. Of course, Manet delighted in such pictorial tensions throughout his career, evidence of which is the following passage from the essay on Manet that Zola published in 1867: "We are not accustomed to seeing such simple and direct translation of reality. . . . there is such a surprisingly elegant awkwardness. The eye at first perceives color applied in large areas. Soon the objects take shape and fall into place. After a few seconds the whole vigorous effect appears, and it is a truly charming experience to contemplate this luminous and serious painting which interprets nature with a gentle brutality, if I may express myself so."[4]

In paintings such as *The Great Horned Owl* Manet continued to explore and redefine the limits of painting, but ironically, even Zola, his earliest advocate, could not grasp the visual complexities of much of the artist's late work. In 1879 Zola wrote a review of the Salon for the Russian publication *Viestnik Europi (Messenger of Europe)* that includes a passage that could easily have been inspired two years later by the deliberate ambiguities of *The Great Horned Owl:* "He has not been able to forge himself a technique; he has remained the enthusiastic novice who always sees exactly what is going on in nature but who is not confident of being able to translate his impressions in a thorough and definitive fashion."[5]   CSM

Oil on canvas
96.5 × 63.5 (38 × 25)
Signed at lower right: Manet
Foundation E. G. Bührle Collection

27   *The Suicide, 1881*

In 1881 Manet donated this painting to an auction organized by the painter Franc Lamy for the benefit of François Cabaner (1833–1881), also known as Jean de Cabanes or Cabaner, who was dying of tuberculosis in an institution in Amélie-les-Bains. Described by Tabarant as "an eccentric bohemian, a fantastic musician [with a] spirited sense of paradox,"[1] Cabaner was an accomplished composer and lyricist who was a member of the circle of avant-garde artists that gathered first at the Café Guerbois and later at the Café de la Nouvelle Athènes.[2]

Thirty-eight items were donated for the auction by artists such as Renoir, Monet, Pissarro, Cézanne, and Degas,[3] but prices at the sale were generally low. *The Suicide* brought only 65 francs, probably for two reasons. First, the subject must have disconcerted many potential buyers, and it may not be altogether fictional. Second, the style of the work is not what most collectors of paintings by Manet would have wanted. Indeed, Tabarant describes it as "merely an incident of the palette,"[4] and the loose, rapid manner of execution has led to uncertainty about the date. Some scholars assign a date of 1877, while others prefer 1881.

The exact subject and date of the painting are not known, but Zola's preface to the catalogue of the 1881 auction may shed light on both. He suggests that Cabaner's life and work in Paris contributed substantially to his death—in other words, that Cabaner unintentionally committed suicide: "the truth is that [Cabaner] died for his art. ... Twenty years in our inferno in Paris, twenty years of damp living quarters, poor food, feverish nights, and commotions and privations of all sorts, have put him where he is."[5] If one may make inferences based on Zola's remarks, it seems very possible that *The Suicide* refers in a general way, at least as a metaphor, to Cabaner's situation, and that Manet painted it specifically for the auction. Manet, who in 1881 was beginning to show the signs of his own illness, would have known as well as anyone that in certain ways life in Paris could be as lethal as a revolver held in one's own hand.   CSM

Oil on canvas
38 × 46 (15 × 18⅛)
Signed at lower right: Manet
Foundation E. G. Bührle Collection

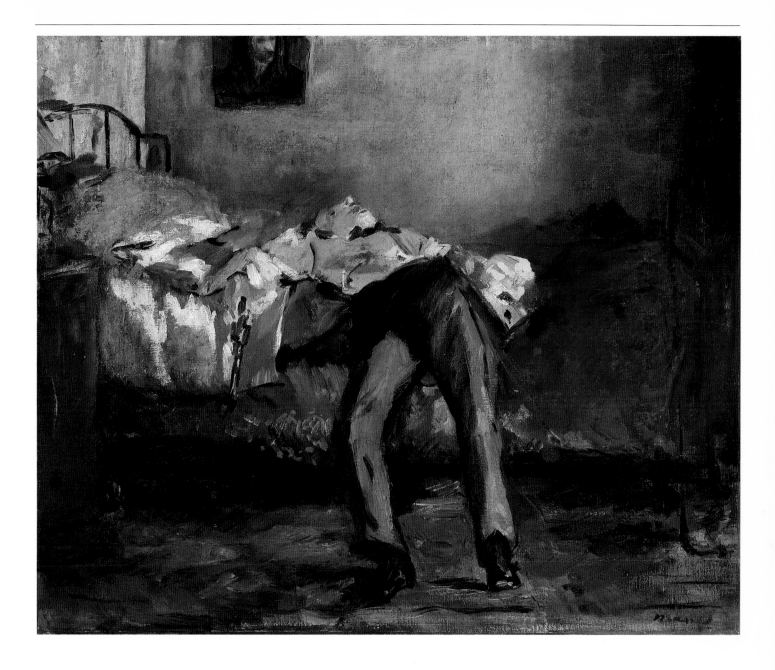

28   *Roses and Tulips in a Vase, 1883*

Tabarant claims that it is difficult to distinguish between the still lifes Manet painted in 1882 at 77 rue d'Amsterdam and others he did the following year in his apartment at 39 rue Saint-Petersbourg during the final decline in his health.[1] More recently, in an essay on the sixteen flower paintings the artist produced from 1881 to 1883, Andrew Forge has cautioned, "no one knows the order in which they were painted. . . . Sufficient information from the past is lacking."[2]

It is likely, however, that *Roses and Tulips in a Vase* is one of Manet's last works, probably painted in February or March 1883. The same crystal vase with an etched dragon appears in *White Lilacs in a Glass* (private collection, France), the work described in the catalogue of the memorial exhibition of Manet's work in 1884 as the artist's "l'avant dernier" painting, executed 28 February 1883.[3] In addition, the marble tabletop, dark backgrounds, and signatures are very similar, further suggesting that the paintings were done at about the same time. The crystal vase with the etched dragon also appears in Manet's last painting, *Roses in a Glass* (private collection), reportedly painted 1 March 1883.[4]

It is likely that the flowers depicted in the present work were given to Manet by one of his close friends, perhaps the elegant courtesan and sometime actress Méry Laurent, who lived closeby.[5] According to Tabarant, "There were always lots of flowers in Manet's studios, but never so many as there were in the rue d'Amsterdam in the early spring of 1883. Lady and gentleman friends had them dropped off with the concierge Aristide when they themselves could not deliver the flowers. Méry Laurent sent them with her housemaid Elisa. With what joy the patient welcomed these messengers of a springtime that he awaited with so much trust! He wanted to paint all of them; at least he would paint some of them."[6] Flowers were an expecially appropriate subject for an artist who was a master of orchestrating touches of color. The blossoms, petals, and stems, as well as the sinuous shape of the dragon etched into the crystal, are analogues of the strokes of color and deliberate rhythms that fascinated Manet from his beginnings as a painter. Clearly the flowers gave him pleasure and inspired him to paint during his final months.   CSM

Oil on canvas
56 × 36 (22 × 14⅛)
Signed at lower left: Manet
Private collection

Edgar Degas 1834–1917

29 *Madame Camus at the Piano, 1869*

29a. Degas, *Madame Camus,* 1869–1870, National Gallery of Art, Washington, Chester Dale Collection.

Mme Camus was the wife of a doctor who treated Degas' eyes. A gifted pianist, she was part of the social circle with which Degas was associated in the late 1860s and early 1870s in which music played a major part. Since most of Degas' portraits were of intimate family and friends, it is not surprising that this musical coterie should have prompted him to paint portraits of a number of musician friends, both amateur and professional. Such portraits include the guitarist Lorenzo Pagans playing for Degas' father, 1871–1872 (Musée d'Orsay, Paris), the bassoonist Désiré Dihau performing in the orchestra at the Opera, c. 1870–1871 (Musée d'Orsay, Paris), or Manet listening to his wife play the piano, c. 1868–1869 (Kitakyushu Municipal Museum of Art).

In all of these portraits Degas places his subjects in everyday settings, surrounded by objects that help define their professions and personalities. Thus Mme Camus is shown in a comfortable bourgeois sitting room, seated at her piano on which is found a precisely rendered score by Beethoven that bespeaks the high standard of her musical accomplishment.[1] The rococo-style mirror, the porcelain figurines atop the piano, and the elaborately wrought wall candelabra evoke a certain feminine fragility that complements her personal grace and delicacy.

In addition to his sitter's surroundings, Degas attached the greatest importance to the expressive potential of pose. Here he seems to have captured the moment when Mme Camus has just swung around on her piano seat to greet the painter/viewer who has interrupted her playing. Although something indefinable in her expression suggests a complex nature, her pose reveals an alert and energetic woman whose forceful character we know Degas admired.[2]

Despite the apparent spontaneity of this portrait, Degas made a number of preparatory studies, as was his frequent practice at this date (see cat. 30 and 31). He submitted this carefully prepared and accomplished portrait to the Salon of 1869, but for reasons that are now impossible to fathom, it was rejected. He was, however, successful at the Salon the following year with a very different portrait of Mme Camus, the beautiful painting in the National Gallery of Art, Washington (fig. 29a), in which he sacrificed the portrayal of character to the more formal concerns of depicting his subject silhouetted against the red glow of artificial light.   AD

Oil on canvas
139 × 94 (54¾ × 37)
Signed (estate stamp) at lower right: Degas
Foundation E. G. Bührle Collection

Edgar Degas   1834–1917

30   *Study for "Madame Camus at the Piano" (Left Hand), 1869*

This is one of seven known preparatory studies for Degas' portrait of *Madame Camus at the Piano* (cat. 29). Degas' academic training, with its emphasis on draftmanship, remained important to him throughout his career, and he prepared carefully for a painting by making drawings from the model, of both the whole figure and individual parts. The various studies for the portrait of Mme Camus therefore provide revealing insights into the way Degas worked.

In addition to this drawing and another drawing in the Bührle collection of the right arm (cat. 31), we know of five other preparatory studies: a squared charcoal drawing of the whole composition, a pastel study of the full-length figure, a detailed pastel study of the face and upper body, a charcoal and pastel study of the room without the figure, and a charcoal and pastel study of the right side of the torso and right arm.[1]

On this beautiful sheet Degas has established the pose of the figure, paying particular attention to the left arm and hand, of which there are two studies. On the same sheet he has made a highly finished drawing of the right arm and hand, which in the painting are extended over the keys of the piano. The outline of the head is summarily but sensitively drawn with a simple charcoal line. The face is all but blank, though the head is somehow eloquent. The bodice of the dress is loosely and lightly sketched in soft chalk, revealing the grainy texture of the paper.

In marked contrast to this sketchy treatment of the head and body is the exceptionally finished rendering of the sleeves and hands. The hands are described here with much greater clarity than in the painting, where they are curiously undefined. But the chief task Degas has set himself here is to depict the velvety black fabric of the sleeves, which he does brilliantly with a dense yet fine black chalk, showing the creases as they catch the light with the most delicate white pastel highlights. These exquisitely drawn sleeves bring to mind the beautiful drapery studies he made for *Semiramis Building Babylon* of c. 1860–1862 (Musée d'Orsay, Paris). They also remind us of Degas' assiduous study and copy of Renaissance masters.   AD

Black chalk and pastel on brown paper
43.5 × 32.5 (17⅛ × 12¾)
Signed (atelier stamp) at lower left: Degas
Foundation E. G. Bührle Collection

Edgar Degas   1834–1917

31   *Study for "Madame Camus at the Piano" (Right Hand), 1869*

Degas has focused his attention in this drawing on the position of Mme Camus' right arm and hand stretched over the piano keyboard, a gesture that contributes so much to her striking pose in the final portrait (cat. 29). The torso and skirt are faintly adumbrated, and the piano and musical score roughly sketched. The right sleeve and hand are much less finished here, however, than in *Study for "Madame Camus at the Piano" (Left Hand)* (cat. 30), where they are meticulously drawn. Yet the sleeve with its transparent black lace cuff and, in particular, the sketchy hand are almost exactly as they appear in the final portrait.

It is curious, given the detailed description of other objects in the painting, that Degas should have left the hands in such an unfinished state. But as this fascinating preparatory drawing reveals, it was clearly his intention to suppress the realistic rendering of the hand. Although it is impossible to determine with any certainty the order in which Degas made these drawings, it seems likely that this sketch is later in the preparatory sequence than the other.   AD

Black chalk and pastel on brown paper
32 × 43.5 (12⅜ × 17⅛)
Signed (signature stamp) at lower right: Degas
Atelier stamp on verso
Foundation E. B. Bührle Collection

32   *Count Lepic and His Daughters, c. 1871*

The subjects of this portrait are Degas' friend Count Ludovic Napoléon Lepic and his two daughters, Eylau and Janine. Lepic, an ardent Bonapartiste, who no doubt named his elder daughter after the Napoleonic battle of 1807, epitomized the suave, worldly upper-class Parisian of the late nineteenth century. He was a man of wide-ranging interests whose study of the theory of evolution and French prehistory led him by 1875 to make models of prehistoric man and animals for the newly founded ethnographic Musée de Saint-Germain. He was also a painter, who participated in the impressionist group exhibitions of 1874 and 1876, as well as a sculptor and a printmaker. Like Degas, Lepic experimented with printmaking techniques, and he was noted for inventing a method known as *eau-forte-mobile* by which he could achieve different effects with individual prints by re-inking the plate with each pulling. He is said to have introduced Degas to the monotype process around 1874 or 1875.

This family portrait is striking for its seemingly unstudied immediacy, which, as so often with Degas, produces the effect of a candid snapshot. Relatively unusually, Degas has placed the figures out-of-doors. The leafy, sunlit setting, heightened by the vived green shutters, adds to the overall impression of freshness and informality, as does the rapid, bravura brushwork. The shifting focus that Degas employs so effectively to convey the changing pattern of light and shade outside also serves to define the three sitters. Whereas the somewhat reserved presence of the count and the amorphous white bundle of his infant daughter recede into the shadowy foliage, Eylau, who dominates the portrait, is in sharp focus and cast in strong light.

Degas, who was a surprisingly perceptive portrayer of children, captures the precocious poise of this little girl who, nevertheless, betrays a hint of self-consciousness in the telling gesture of clutching her skirt. No less astute is the way Degas has caught the nonchalant ease of his friend, Lepic—debonair in his monacle—as well as his slightly detached paternal affection. A few years later Degas would again emphasize these qualities in another portrait of Lepic and his daughters, the *Place de la Concorde,* c. 1875 (formerly Collection Gerstenberg, Berlin; destroyed). Degas painted Lepic again with the printmaker Marcellin Desboutin in about 1876 (Musée des Beaux-Arts, Nice) and on a later occasion with one of his dogs (Lemoisne 1946, no. 950).   AD

Oil on canvas
65.5 × 81 (25¾ × 31⅞)
Foundation E. B. Bührle Collection

Edgar Degas   1834–1917

33   Ballet Class, c. 1880

Degas is known above all as the painter of the ballet, but he was intrigued by the behind-the-scenes world of dance classes or rehearsal rooms more than by performances. He began exploring the theme of the dance class in the early 1870s, and by the end of the decade the equilibrium of these small, precise paintings had given way to a more dramatic, asymmetrical type of composition, exemplified by the Bührle painting. The high viewpoint, seemingly arbitrary cropping, and juxtaposition of empty space with a dense cluster of figures reflects Degas' *japonisme* and his desire to replicate the haphazard nature of perception.

The repetition of compositions, motifs, and poses was fundamental to the way Degas worked. And this particular composition, in which a large, static foreground figure counterbalances a complex group of dancers in motion in the background, clearly preoccupied him, for he repeated it in a number of different formats: *The Dance Class* of 1881 (Philadelphia Museum of Art) and *Ballet Dancers* of c. 1880 (National Gallery, London),[1] a sketchier version of the same composition. The two dancers with raised arms appear in drawings that date from much earlier, and the dancer adjusting her slipper is also found in other paintings, pastels, and drawings.

Inspired toward the end of his career by the pose of the foreground dancer, Degas made a sculpture of a figure looking at the sole of her right foot, which he repeated many times. Indeed, by giving such prominence in this painting to the dancer putting on her shoe, Degas invests the gesture with the weight and resonance of antique sculpture. In many of his dance class scenes, Degas delighted in contrasting such mundane activity with the highly contrived movements of the classical ballet, thereby revealing the artifice behind its seemingly effortless grace.

In Degas' many dance class themes, as with so much of his work, it was the private dimension he explored. Here, what he presents is not a brilliant performance, but an enclosed world where the dancers seem completely unaware of any observer. Like Degas' bathers lost in the private ritual of bathing, these dancers are absorbed in the routines of the dance. The muted tones and pale light that floods in through the windows, catching the matte white and powdery blues of the tutus, contribute to this detached, almost dreamlike mood, which is broken only by the insistent note of the shiny pink ballet slippers on the bench in the foreground.   AD

Oil on canvas
62 × 50.5 (24 ⅜ × 19 ⅞)
Signed (atelier stamp) at lower right: Degas
Private collection

34   *Self-Portrait, 1861*

One of Fantin's principal subjects from 1853 to 1861 was himself. He drew and painted around thirty self-portraits in that time, later explaining that he did so many of them in his youth because the model was readily available and duly submissive.[1] Despite this glib explanation, we sense in the self-portraits the young Fantin's attempts to define himself as an artist.

This self-portrait, painted when Fantin was twenty-five, is one of the most revealing of the group, giving insight into how he viewed himself and wanted to be viewed by others. Many of the self-portraits were no more than sketches given to friends, but this one was intended for public appraisal. It was exhibited at the Salon of 1861, Fantin's first, along with two other portraits. Calling it simply "Etude d'après nature"[2] instead of the traditional "portrait," Fantin underscored his belief that the natural world around him should be the artist's sole subject.[3]

Shown seated in this self-portrait, presumably before an easel, and firmly holding his palette and brushes, Fantin declares art to be his vocation. His direct gaze conveys the seriousness of a young man who stated at nineteen that painting was his only pleasure and only goal in life.[4] Fantin filters his own image through one inherited from the Romantics. The dramatic spotlighting of his head and the hint of arrogance in his posture owe much to the concept of the artist as an intense, highly individualistic, and exceptional human being. Yet contradicting this youthful display of self-confidence, almost arrogance, he depicts himself drawing back into the shadows, revealing a reticence that was characteristic of both Fantin and his art.

If the Bührle painting declares Fantin's intentions and ambitions as an artist, it also looks back to his formation as one. Fantin learned to paint primarily by studying and copying Old Masters in the Louvre. Rembrandt's series of self-portraits, in particular that of 1660,[5] and his expressive use of *chiaroscuro* are obvious influences here.

MDS

Oil on canvas
81.5 × 66 (32⅛ × 26)
Foundation E. G. Bührle Collection

35   *Climbing Roses and Peaches, 1873*

After the early self-portraits, Fantin rarely returned to the subject. Instead he concentrated on painting still lifes, imaginative subjects, and portraits of others. The still lifes—of flowers, for the most part—number in the hundreds and make up almost half of his painting œuvre. The reason for this is simple: Fantin made his living from them.

Fantin regarded his still lifes as more than just his "bread and butter," however. He saw them as a way of sharpening his powers of observation and at the same time concentrating on the pure act of painting. He believed that the subject was less important than what the artist did with it. But others were not convinced. For many, still life retained the stigma of being the genre at the bottom of the academic subject hierarchy. This outmoded, but entrenched view persisted in the Salons where Fantin sought approval; and discouraged, he refused to exhibit his still lifes there after 1876.[1]

There are no traces of conflict in the paintings themselves, where all is tranquility and harmony. Fantin was a studio artist, who remained indoors while the young impressionists ventured out to paint nature on its own terms. Nevertheless, within these self-imposed confines, Fantin was able to bathe his flowers in light and air. And he made his surfaces breathe by scraping the paint down to the canvas in certain places to create "interstices"—as artist and critic Jacques-Emile Blanche called them—between areas where the paint was thickly applied.[2]

Climbing Roses and Peaches is also testimony to Fantin's exquisite sense of compositional and tonal unity, which is reconciled with a faithful rendering of the objects. Against his usual neutral background Fantin places the objects to form a perfectly balanced triangle. The rose lying between the saucer and basket of peaches is a key element. With the four peaches, it counters the larger basket, and linked as it is in color and shape with the roses above, it prevents the canvas from appearing to split horizontally.

The cut rose on the table, dying without water to sustain it, introduces an elegiac element into the painting. It recalls the many examples of seventeenth-century still-life painting in which the rose was the symbol of the transience of life. It is unlikely that Fantin, who in the 1870s became more and more attached to the painting of the past, was not aware of this tradition.   MDS

Oil on canvas
54.5 × 55.5 (21½ × 21½)
Signed and dated at upper right: Fantin 73
Private collection

Alfred Sisley   1839–1899

36   The Road to Saint-Germain at Marly, 1874–1875

The area of the Seine basin defined by Louveciennes, Marly-le-Roi, and Bougival was strictly speaking Sisley's territory during the "heroic" years of impressionism. Sisley had been preceded by Pissarro in Louveciennes in May 1869, and by Monet in Bougival in June the same year. Renoir was also a regular visitor to both places throughout the summer and autumn of that year. It was Sisley, however, who was most loyal to this small area. He had moved there in the autumn of 1870, following the outbreak of the Franco-Prussian War, which brought with it the collapse of his father's business. Settling first in Louveciennes, then in Marly-le-Roi in 1875, he was lured by the cheaper rents of suburban properties, the range of rural motifs, and the ease of access to his market and art suppliers in Paris.

Marly-le-Roi was noted for its proximity to Louis XIV's Château de Marly. The château had been destroyed during the Revolution, but the grounds had remained, with their alleys of formal trees, boundary walls, and a semicircular basin that had come to serve both as a watering spot for animals and as a lavoir for the women of Marly-le-Roi and Louveciennes. The basin lay at the point where the routes from Marly-le-Roi and Louveciennes merged on their progress northward to Saint-Germain-en-Laye. This view appears to be looking north down the hill from Marly-le-Roi, with the basin suggested behind the trees on the right. In keeping with some twenty-two paintings by Sisley of Marly-le-Roi, the Bührle painting neither celebrates the grandeur of its architectural remains nor conveys nostalgia for its more glorious past. Rather, as in the similar *Watering Hole at Marly in Winter* (Collection Jacques Guerlain, Paris),[1] this work depicts the road in normal use, plied by horses and carts and lined by domestic architecture. The only hint of its nobler past lies in the regular procession of trees that mark the route's descent.

Sisley was more ready than his fellow impressionists to retain a traditional approach to the composition of landscapes. In the Bührle painting the viewpoint was selected so that the natural elements of road and trees would establish recession into depth. Furthermore, the composition was framed by a repoussoir tree on the right. In contrast, the tonal range and handling of paint reflect the practices of impressionism in the mid-1870s. Unlike his snow scenes of earlier in the decade, such as *First Snow at Louveciennes* of c. 1870 (Museum of Fine Arts, Boston),[2] where shadow was still defined in terms of black, the palette in this work was expanded to suggest a pale yellow reflection of the sun on snow in the left foreground and the blue chill of shadow on the right.   MAS

Oil on canvas
45.5 × 55 (17⅞ × 21⅝)
Signed at lower right: Sisley
Foundation E. G. Bührle Collection

37 *Summer at Bougival, 1876*

The reputation of Bougival, well established by the mid-nineteenth century, attracted the boating confraternity as well as writers and artists, who flocked there in hordes in the 1860s.[1] Most of the impressionists worked in this area during the latter half of the decade. From 1872 Sisley painted regularly at Bougival, where he found that its riverscapes, along with those at Port Marly just to the north, provided variants of the landscapes he had recorded around Marly-le-Roi and Louveciennes, where he had settled in 1870 (see cat. 36).[2]

The Bührle collection's painting reveals a bend in the Seine River as it flows toward the escarpment upon which lies Saint-Germain-en-Laye. It is related to at least two other views of the same motif: *Banks of the Seine at Bougival* (Collection Lord Radcliffe, London) and *Bouvigal* (private collection), both of 1876.[3] All three paintings give prominence to the path leading toward a group of cottages in the background, although *Bougival* shows the house in the distance at somewhat closer range, while *Banks of the Seine* employs a viewpoint slightly further around to the left.

Emphasis on the path confirms Sisley's selection of a naturally composed viewpoint, which when taken in conjunction with the Bührle painting's inclusion of framing trees on the left, suggests that the artist was following traditional landscape procedures to create a picturesque view. This hypothesis can be taken a step further by considering the purpose of the solitary figure walking along the path. His unhurried movement through a balanced composition may reflect the artist's desire to establish a bucolic, indeed idyllic, mood in the rural scene.

The right side of the painting undermines the classical interpretation, however. Here, as in *Banks of the Seine,* the dominant features are a steamer, its black smoke cutting across the blue sky, and a bridge, forming a defiant horizontal line that immediately establishes the presence of a road from Bougival to Chatou and thence to the city of Paris. By juxtaposing the emblems of city and countryside, Sisley seems to be representing in this landscape the particular function that the Seine basin fulfilled for Paris during the nineteenth century. In guide books and in novels such as Flaubert's *L'Education sentimentale* and Henry James' *The Ambassadors,* escape from the crowded urban experience of Paris was accomplished by retreating to a villa, a riverside inn, or a walk through a countryside, which, relative to Paris, appeared to approximate the unsullied landscape of nature in its perfect state.   MAS

Oil on canvas
47 × 62 (18½ × 24⅜)
Signed and dated at lower right: Sisley. 76
Foundation E. G. Bührle Collection

38   *The Thaw in L'Estaque* or *The Red Roofs, c. 1870*

Cézanne spent the winter of the Franco-Prussian War, 1870–1871, in the village of L'Estaque, just to the west of Marseilles. He went there with Hortense Fiquet, with whom he had been living since 1869 (see cat. 39), and stayed in a small house that his mother owned. Although it seems that Cézanne was sought in Aix for conscription into the army, he was not discovered in L'Estaque. He remained there throughout the war as well as the period of civil upheaval that followed in Paris known as the Commune. He returned to Aix in March 1871.[1]

In the catalogue of the recent exhibition devoted to Cézanne's early work, Sir Lawrence Gowing notes: "His typical work [at L'Estaque]... was *Melting Snow at Estaque,* the fearful image of a world dissolved, sliding downhill in a sickeningly precipitous diagonal between the curling pines which are themselves almost threateningly unstable and Baroque, painted with a wholly appropriate slipping wetness and a soiled non-colour unique in his work. Such a picture reveals by contrast the value of the solidity and stability to which the rest of Cézanne's life was devoted."[2] It must be added that only four works from Cézanne's months in L'Estaque are known and that all are dark and foreboding. In *The Thaw in L'Estaque* it seems that the war and perhaps the Commune had affected his mood. The sky threatens, the twisted trees cling precariously to the slope, the road seems to go nowhere, and the houses seem toylike and unsubstantial.

When the dealer Ambroise Vollard later asked Cézanne what he had done during the Franco-Prussian War, the artist replied laconically, "Listen, Monsieur Vollard, I worked a lot out-of-doors *[sur le motif]* at Estaque. Except for that there was no other event of importance in my life during the years 1870–1871. I divided my time between the field and the studio."[3] It was significant, however, that during this time Cézanne turned his attention to working "sur le motif," a key tenet of impressionism, and became preoccupied by landscape painting. He had come to the end of the dark, brooding, expressive work of his youth and was about to turn to the brighter palette and constructive brushstroke that mark the beginning of his mature work. Cézanne also acknowledged to Vollard that the period was difficult for him, and he concluded with the comment: "But know, Monsieur Vollard, that at that moment I was working on a landscape that was not going well. Also I remained in Aix for a while afterward in order to work from nature."[4]   CSM

Oil on canvas
72.5 × 92 (28½ × 36¼)
Private collection

Paul Cézanne   1839–1906

39   *The Artist's Wife in an Armchair, c. 1878; 1886–1888*

39a. Photograph of Cézanne's *The Artist's Wife in an Armchair,* in Leo and Gertrude Stein's apartment in Paris, 1906, The Cone Archives, The Baltimore Museum of Art.

Cézanne probably met Hortense Fiquet, a professional artists' model, in Paris early in 1869, when she was nineteen and he was thirty. Soon they were living together, and in 1872 she gave birth to their only child, a son named Paul. Cézanne did not inform his family of the liaison at first, but in 1886 he and Fiquet were married with the artist's parents as witnesses. Cézanne's relationship with his wife seems never to have been ideal, but apparently because of the artist's devotion to his son the marriage did not fail completely.[1]

The Artist's Wife in an Armchair is one of about twenty-five portraits that Cézanne painted of his wife. It was most likely done in an apartment in Paris at 32 rue de l'Ouest, where Cézanne lived for various periods between 1879 and October 1882.[2] Venturi dates the portrait to 1879–1882, but van Buren, noting that the style of Mme Cézanne's dress was popular between 1878 and 1882, suggests a date of 1879.[3] Rewald, however, observes that on stylistic grounds the painting is probably the result of two separate periods of activity: "The discreet wallpaper of bluish floral sprays in the background of [the] portrait can be identified with lodgings Cézanne occupied in 1879–80 *[sic]* . . . but the much less volumetric head of the sitter appears to have been painted several years later." Rewald suggests that the portrait was painted c. 1878 and reworked in 1886–1888.[4]

Cézanne communicates very little emotion in most of his portraits. The facial expressions of his subjects are usually equivocal or neutral, and this portrait is no exception. There is hardly a hint of the relationship between the artist and the sitter. Indeed, the viewer is engaged principally with the formal rather than the personal aspects of the image: the curve of Mme Cézanne's chest is echoed in the shape of the chair above her left shoulder; the shape of her right arm is repeated in the arm of the chair; and the color and brushwork used for her dress are variations on the color and pattern of the wallpaper. The sitter's dark, almond-shaped eyes stare out from her bourgeois surroundings, but the artist neither imparts nor implies much about her as a person. As Rewald notes, "Hortense's only contribution to her husband's life as an artist was in posing for him repeatedly without moving or talking."[5]

The Artist's Wife in an Armchair was once owned by Leo and Gertrude Stein and hung in Miss Stein's apartment at 22 rue de Fleurus in Paris. Picasso saw it there, and Fernande Olivier, his mistress at the time, later described it as "that beautiful likeness of the painter's wife in a blue dress, sitting in a garnet-colored armchair."[6] Whether it actually influenced Picasso's famous portrait of Miss Stein we will probably never know (fig. 39a).[7]   CSM

Oil on canvas
92.5 × 73.5 (36⅜ × 28⅞)
Foundation E. G. Bührle Collection

40   *Still Life with Petunias, c. 1885*

Still Life with Petunias is one of at least thirty-four still lifes of flowers that Cézanne painted during the course of his career. It was probably painted in Aix-en-Provence in the conservatory of the Cézanne family house, the Jas de Bouffan, purchased by the artist's father in 1859. Although Venturi and others place this work in the years 1875–1876,[1] a date in the mid-1880s is more likely. The painting was probably done at about the same time as a group of watercolors of pots of geraniums that Rewald assigns to c. 1885.[2] In addition, the rhythms and the massing of leaves and foliage are not unlike effects depicted in three watercolors of a slightly later date, about 1885–1888.[3]

The composition of the Bührle painting is nearly musical in its subtle and often complex orchestration of harmonies, shapes, colors, contours, and groups of brush-strokes. Although there is great variety in the visual interrelationships, the artist avoids repeating elements that are exactly the same. None of the terracotta flower pots is depicted as a whole, independent form; and each is distinguishable accord-ing to slight differences of shape, color, and detail, such as the chipped rim. Pots overlap pots, flowers cover parts of pots and interrupt contours, and the pots are in different planes. Furthermore, lines that ought to be parallel or follow the form of a predictable curve are allowed to bend. The edge of the tabletop bows upward as it moves from left to right, and the curved contours of the bottom of flower pots are slightly flattened. Similarly, leaves and flowers echo one another rhythmically but never according to a predictable, formulaic pattern. Each shape, contour, and brushstroke responds to the exigencies of the composition as a whole.

Addressing Cézanne's still lifes generally, Schapiro observes: "Stable, but of endlessing shifting, intense color, while offering on the small rounded forms an infi-nite nuancing of tones, his still life is a model world that he has carefully set up on the isolating supporting table, like the table of the strategist who meditates imaginary battles between the toy forces he has arranged on his variable terrain. Or the still life of Cézanne may be likened to a solitary pictorial chess, the artist seeking always the strongest position for each of his freely selected pieces."[4] Schapiro's comments underscore the quality of such works as *Still Life with Petunias* as among the most intellectually challenging still lifes executed during the nineteenth century. Indeed, the present work is ample evidence that Cézanne infused his still lifes with a degree of seriousness and complexity unrivaled by any of his contemporaries.   CSM

Oil on canvas
46 × 55.5 (18⅛ × 21⅞)
Private collection

41   *The Boy in the Red Vest, 1888–1890*

41 a. Cézanne, *Boy in a Red Vest*, 1888–1890, Collection of Mr. and Mrs. Paul Mellon, Upperville, Virginia.

When this painting appeared on view for the first time in a one-man exhibition at the Galerie Vollard in 1895, the influential critic Gustave Geffroy praised it as a work that could "withstand comparison with the most beautiful figures in painting."[1] It has since become one of Cézanne's most famous images and a work that appears in virtually every significant essay on the artist's development.

Venturi states that the sitter is an Italian youth, traditionally identified as Michelangelo di Rosa, who worked as a professional model and is here dressed as a peasant from the Roman Campagna. He appears in four other paintings by Cézanne and two watercolors done between 1888 and 1890 (fig. 41a).[2] Evidently Cézanne employed this model when living at 15 quai d'Anjou in Paris, for decorative elements associated with that apartment are visible in works that depict young di Rosa. Rewald notes that the apartment had "a wainscot or molding, accompanied by a narrow wine-red band. . . . there was also, near the fireplace, a small curtained door or opening."[3] The wainscot can be seen in the background behind the sitter's head, and a curtain appears at the upper left.

Many of Cézanne's figures of the 1890s are seated and rest their heads on one hand. The pose is well known in the history of art from such iconic images as Dürer's *Melancolia I,* Michelangelo's depiction of the damned in the Sistine ceiling, and Carpeaux's *Ugolino and His Sons.* Cézanne's use of the pose can be traced to canvases of the 1860s, but it does not appear in his work during the 1870s and most of the 1880s. According to Reff, the pose "carried for Cézanne from the beginning a burden of romantic pathos and private guilt that represents an essential side of his artistic personality, one that resurfaces, after the Impressionist and constructive periods of the seventies and eighties, in such deeply melancholy images as the *Young Italian Girl* and the *Boy with a Skull.*"[4]

Throughout the painting lines and planes inexplicably bend, merge, break, and curve. The arc that describes the outer contour of the boy's body flows in a continuum from his collar to his thigh. The brushwork, horizontality, and palette seen in his left thigh continue the rhythms of the overhanging tablecloth. At the lower left the junction of the boy's pants and chaps coincides with the edge of the seat, identifying different planes with a single point in space. And as many critics note, the figure's right arm is much too long. Thus the composition is a carefully woven fabric of exaggerations, distortions, apparently arbitrary touches of color, and ambiguities that seem to contradict the illusionistic goals of the painting. As Schapiro observes, "Cézanne's art . . . lies between the old kind of picture, faithful to a striking or beautiful object, and the modern 'abstract' kind of painting, a moving harmony of colored touches representing nothing."[5]

CSM

Oil on canvas
80 × 64.5 (31½ × 25⅜)
Foundation E. G. Bührle Collection

42   *Vase of Flowers and Apples, c. 1890*

42a. Cézanne, *Tulips in a Vase,*
1890–1892, Norton Simon Art
Foundation.

42b. Cézanne, *A Vase and Column,* c. 1890, private collection,
Amsterdam.

Cézanne uses the same olive jar as a vase here that he uses in other paintings and works on paper, with slight variations in shape and glaze.[1] It appears in his *Tulips in a Vase* (fig. 42a) and *Tulips and Apples* (The Art Institute of Chicago), both of 1890–1892. Although these still lifes are similar in subject to the Bührle picture, they lack its resonant and complex background.

A watercolor in a private collection in Amsterdam, *A Vase and Column* of c. 1890 (fig. 42b),[2] may be directly related to the Bührle painting. It depicts the olive jar with foliage and what appears to be the same topmost flower, as well as a vertical shape in the background that is probably not a column but a section of decorative and architectural detailing, as in the Bührle *Vase of Flowers and Apples.* Another watercolor, *Foliage in a Jar* of 1890–1892 (private collection, Paris), may be a preliminary study of the lower half of the pot.[3]

The rectilinear shapes of the table top and the divisions of the background provide a rhythmic and compositional foil for the curvilinear forms of fruit, the vase, and the flowers. As Schapiro has written of the *Tulips and Apples* in Chicago, "It is a harmony of opposed elements, a strange balance of contrary qualities, united through hidden analogies and a most sensitive play of color."[4]

The two pieces of fruit in the foreground—probably oranges but usually described as apples—are particularly important to the success of the composition. They offset the compositional weight of the vase and flowers, and they anchor the implicit diagonal thrust of the leaning flower stems at the right, the shadow of the vase, and the line in the lower right background defining what seems to be the junction of the floor and the wall. The vase seems to extend slightly to the left in response to the visual weight and position of the oranges.

Vase of Flowers and Apples, one of only seven still lifes in which Cézanne combined fruit and flowers,[5] is also noteworthy for the richness and variety of the brushwork. Certain passages are like transparent washes of watercolor, others are painterly and cursive, while others are directional and rhythmic. In his essay on meaning in Cézanne's still lifes, Schapiro offers an observation that is particularly apt here: "What appears most ordered in the still-life picture issues from the painter's visible brush-strokes and alludes hardly at all to the purposes that give neatness and charm to the table in ordinary life. He endows these strokes with a subtle cohesion and a harmony of colors that transfigure the whole as a work of art while intensifying in the objects the appearance of the existence and familiar."[6]

CSM

Oil on canvas
56 × 46.5 (22 × 18¼)
Private collection

43   *Self-Portrait with Palette, c. 1890*

43a. Cézanne, *Self-Portrait*, drawing in a sketchbook, private collection, New York.

This is the largest of Cézanne's many self-portraits and the only example that includes elements other than the artist's own head and upper torso. Moreover, it is the only self-portrait in which he identifies himself specifically as an artist.

Cézanne presents himself as a painter who is partly obscured by his own art. The interrupted rectangles of his palette and the stretcher, skillfully played off against the rectangle of the image as a whole, both yield information about the artist and shield him. By aligning the left edge of the palette with the outer contour of his arm and terminating his cluster of brushes at the contour that delineates the outside edge of his jacket, he draws attention to the critically important aspect of his work that Schapiro describes as "parallel lines, connectives, contacts, and breaks which help to unite in a common pattern elements that represent things lying on the different planes in depth."[1] Indeed, upon close examination we find a rich pattern of rhythms, harmonies, analogous shapes, brushstrokes, and touches of color that come together in the creation of the overall composition.

Cézanne thus reveals significant information about his technique and his intellect but little about himself. Schapiro calls it "one of the most impersonal self-portraits we know."[2] It is carefully calculated, guarded image by the man who later wrote to his friend, the provençale poet Joachim Gasquet: "All my life I've worked in order to be able to earn my living, but I thought I could paint good things without drawing attention to one's private life. Of course an artist attempts to elevate himself intellectually as much as he can, but the man must stay in the background. The pleasure must stay in the work."[3]

The date of *Self-Portrait with Palette* is a matter of continuing debate. Venturi and others place it in the years 1885–1887, but Reidemeister dates it to 1884, and Rewald ascribes it to c. 1890.[4] Reidemeister notes the similarity of the head to a sketchbook drawing previously assigned to 1877–1882 (see fig. 43a), which Chappuis has dated both 1880–1882 and 1884, and which Andersen places in 1883–1884.[5] Despite the putative connection with the drawing, Rewald's date is the most convincing on stylistic grounds. The lack of emphasis on clearly defined parallel brushstrokes; the relatively large, softly modulated areas of translucent color; and an overall tendency toward simplification and abstraction argue strongly for a date closer to 1890 than to 1884.   CSM

Oil on canvas
92 × 73 (28¾ × 36¼)
Foundation E. G. Bührle Collection

Paul Cézanne   1839–1906

44   Mont Sainte-Victoire, 1904–1906

In 1902, at the age of sixty-three, Cézanne had a new studio built on the side of a hill known as Les Lauves just north of Aix-en-Provence. The studio was finished in September, and it must have been at about that time that the artist discovered a site nearby from which to depict Mont Sainte-Victoire, a motif that had interested him for more than thirty years. "Climbing the fairly steep road beyond the studio to the crest of Les Lauves," writes John Rewald, "he found a new exhilarating panorama stretching away to his right. From here Sainte-Victoire, remote but imposing, no longer appeared as the chopped-off cone that he had contemplated from Château Noir or Bibémus, but as an irregular triangle, its long back gently rising to the abrupt, clifflike front that tapered off to the horizontal extension of the Mont du Cengle."[1]

Most scholars assign the Bührle view of Mont Sainte-Victoire to the years 1904–1906,[2] but its exact date has remained impossible to determine. Gowing suggests that there may be at least an indirect connection with a passage in a letter that Cézanne wrote to Emile Bernard on 15 April 1904: "Lines parallel to the horizon give breadth, whether it is a section of nature or, if you prefer, of the spectacle which the Pater Omnipotens Aeterne Deus spreads out before our eyes. The lines perpendicular to this horizon give depth, but nature for us men is more depth than surface, whence the need to introduce into our vibrations of light, represented by the reds and yellows, a sufficient amount of blueness to give the feeling of air."[3]

While the play of vertical and horizontal elements is unquestionably an important aspect of the picture, Cézanne's reference to an omnipotent, eternal being, albeit in the context of very general remarks to Bernard, is also noteworthy. It suggests that in the late work there is meaning and significance that most critics and scholars have ignored in the effort to define the artist's role in the rise of modernism and the origins of cubism. Moreover, if we accept Cézanne's comments about the implicit meaning of horizontals and verticals, then *Mont Sainte-Victoire* is more than a carefully studied fabric of brushstrokes and color. In discussing the views of Mont Sainte-Victoire painted from Les Lauves, Reff summarizes: "Eight times or more [between 1902 and 1906] the same simple image recurs, stripped of the compositional complexities of the previous decades, reduced to the elemental earth, mountain, and sky. And as the variants succeed each other, they become more passionate in execution and more spiritual in content, the peak seeming to embody that striving upward from the darkness of the valley toward the luminous sky in which Cézanne's own religious aspiration can be felt, yet at the same time dissolving in the torrent of energetic brushstrokes, fusing with the air filled with similar strokes all around it."[4]

CSM

Oil on canvas
66 × 81.5 (26 × 32⅛)
Private collection

Claude Monet   1840–1926

45   *Camille Monet with Dog, 1866*

The subject of this painting is Camille Doncieux, whom Monet married in 1870. He painted this portrait of her when she was nineteen, shortly after she had become his model and companion. Camille was a stylish young woman who brought a new dimension of grace and elegance into Monet's life. Her sophisticated clothes were clearly an important part of her appeal to Monet, and in his many portraits of her he seems to delight in her ever-changing wardrobe. She posed for at least two of the elegant women in his large *Women in a Garden* of 1866–1868 (Musée d'Orsay, Paris) and was again the fashionable model for *Woman in a Green Dress* (Kunsthalle, Bremen), which was a sensational success at the Salon of 1866.

The style and technique of this portrait are typical of Monet's work in the mid-1860s. The strong light/dark contrasts and bold colors applied with broad strokes of the brush, the palpable texture of paint, especially noticeable in the dog's fluffy coat, the striped fabric of the dress, and the creamy impasto of Camille's skin clearly owe a debt to Manet and Courbet, both of whom Monet knew well at this date. By depicting his subject so close to the picture plane, Monet conveys a sense of physical immediacy that is particularly evocative of the portraits of women Courbet painted the year before in 1865 at Trouville, where Monet had worked with him briefly.

In his later portraits of Camille, Monet rarely achieved such a direct and powerful characterization as he did here. Once he had adopted his impressionist style, he nearly always portrayed Camille out-of-doors, where her individuality was sacrificed to his exploration of the play of light and atmosphere. In this portrait, however, Monet gives a clear idea of her character as well as her appearance. Her strong features and thoughtful expression suggest an intelligent and forceful woman. Neither her fashionable dress nor the presence of the dog, a device that often established a frivolous erotic note in the rococo tradition, detract in any way from the sitter's air of dignified poise. Although one often senses a certain aloofness in Monet's many portraits of Camille, it seems that this unusually intimate portrayal had a special meaning for him, for he kept it in his studio until his death in 1926.   AD

Oil on canvas
73 × 53.5 (28¾ × 21)
Signed at upperright: Claude Monet / 1866.
Private collection

Claude Monet   1840–1926

46   *The Dinner, 1868–1869*

46a. Monet, *Interior, after Dinner,* 1868–1869,
National Gallery of Art, Washington, Collection of Mr. and
Mrs. Paul Mellon.

This small study of a family dinner was probably painted during the winter of 1868–1869 when Monet rented a house at Etretat on the Normandy coast. Although it has traditionally been identified as the Sisley family, there is no basis for this identification. The figures portrayed are most likely Monet's mistress Camille, with her back to the viewer, and their infant son Jean, then aged about a year, with two unidentified friends and a maid who enters at the rear.

The sense of warmth and domestic comfort that the painting exudes reflects Monet's pleasure in family life and his newly found financial security. Owing to the support of his first patron, a M. Gaudebert from Le Havre, who commissioned a portrait of his wife, Monet was able to enjoy a relatively long respite from the extreme financial hardship he had endured in the previous few years. In this relaxed mood he painted a series of landscapes, seascapes, and interior views of the house.

Two other works are related to the Bührle painting in subject and setting. One small sketch-like painting, *Interior, after Dinner,* of 1868–1869 (fig. 46a), is a very similar view of the same gathering but shows the scene after the meal, when the table has been cleared, the child and the maid have retired, the women sit sewing by the fire, and the man leans against the fireplace. A much larger, more ambitious, and more fully resolved painting of a family meal that takes place in a different part of the same room in daylight is *The Luncheon* of 1868 (Frankfurt, Städelsches Kunstinstitut). In this work Monet lavishes much greater attention on the objects on the table and the individual poses and facial expressions of the figures.

In *The Dinner* such details are sacrificed to the study of light and shadow. The figures are caught in the dazzling pool of light cast by the hanging lamp or engulfed in the shadowy depths of the room beyond. This interest in the effects of nocturnal light may owe something to contemporary prints by Courbet, Legros, and especially Whistler in which the graphic medium lent itself so effectively to strong chiaroscuro.[1] It represented only a brief and atypical moment in Monet's career, however. Only a few months after painting *The Dinner,* he turned his attention to the effects of outdoor light, which from then on became his principal subject.   AD

Oil on canvas
50.5 × 65.5 (19⅞ × 25¾)
Signed at lower left: Claude Monet
Foundation E. G. Bührle Collection

Claude Monet   1840–1926

47   *Camille Monet, Son, and Nurse in Garden, 1873*

In the summer of 1873 Monet was living with his wife Camille and their young son Jean at Argenteuil, then a new suburban community on the Seine not far from Paris. Argenteuil became a popular meeting place for impressionist painters in the early 1870s and a center of the rapidly evolving plein-air style. Both Manet and Renoir visited Monet there and painted his garden.

The paintings Monet made of his gardens at Argenteuil are redolent with a sense of well-being. His work was selling well at the time through his dealer Durand-Ruel, and this afforded him temporary relief from the grueling poverty that had dogged him for much of the previous decade. The modern suburban villa visible in the background of this painting, the substantial garden, Mme Monet's chic Parisian clothes, and the well-dressed child tended by a maid are all evidence of the leisure, bourgeois lifestyle that this prosperity allowed.

This is one of fifteen views that Monet painted of his garden at the first of two houses he rented in Argenteuil. He was a passionate gardener and even in his rented houses devoted considerable time to growing flowers, creating a private domain of beauty that also served as a principal subject for his art. The motif of the garden would culminate in his numerous paintings of Giverny. But in these late garden paintings he depicted almost abstract forms of plants in an elemental context of sky and water, whereas in the small domestic views of the 1870s he presented an orderly suburban paradise occupied by formally dressed people and well-groomed flowerbeds.

Much of the visual drama of this garden scene springs from the contrasting zones of bright sunlight and cool, violet-gray shadow. The figure of Camille dominates the foreground and controls the composition, seeming to absorb the vibrant mass of flowers and foliage into her contained, shadowed presence. Her face is blurred, lost in the shade of the black parasol that counterbalances the vivid red and green of the flowerbed. The seemingly casual arrangement of figures is characteristic of the impressionists' aim to replicate the way we actually perceive things. Several critics have interpreted the separation of the figures as a sign of estrangement within the family. Whether or not this was the case, the lack of interaction introduces an unexpected malaise into this otherwise pleasurable scene.   AD

Oil on canvas
60.5 × 81 (23⅞ × 31⅞)
Signed at lower left: 73 Claude Monet
Private collection

Claude Monet 1840–1926

48 *Poppies near Vétheuil, 1879*

In January 1878 Monet moved to Vétheuil, a village forty miles down the Seine from Paris, where he remained until the winter of 1881. This was a time of great personal hardship for him. He was practically destitute, and in September 1879 his wife Camille died after a long illness. Yet he nevertheless threw himself into an intensely productive period of work. His move to Vétheuil signifies a definitive withdrawal from urban life, for he never again painted Paris or its suburbs but devoted himself almost exclusively to landscape and later to views of his garden at Giverny. The serene countryside along the banks of the Seine around Vétheuil inspired numerous paintings that capture different conditions of light and weather. This is one of a number of views of Vétheuil looking across from Lavacourt on the opposite bank of the Seine.

Although the landscapes Monet painted during the harsh winter of 1878–1879 convey a sense of sadness, not a hint of his private troubles is allowed to diminish this radiant view of a field of poppies in high summer. The cultivated environment of his own gardens is so often the subject of Monet's painting, but it is clear that the riotous abundance of this untamed field of flowers was equally compelling to him. Images of women and children in summery meadows, the emblems of fecund growth around them, are a common subject in impressionist painting. Here the tiny figures of the woman and children gathering poppies, who are all but submerged in the splendid vitality of nature, become almost literally flowers of the field.

In this work we see Monet at the height of his impressionist style. He no doubt set up his easel on the spot and employed a rapid, spontaneous brushstroke to convey the light and atmosphere of the outdoors. His fine-tuned response to the nuances of tone and texture in the scene before him is apparent in his minute and constant shifts of color and touch. A soft palette of browns, grays, greens, creams, and blues applied with a modulated touch records the peaceful panorama of the Seine valley landscape beneath a shifting sky of fleecy clouds, while the majestic field that dominates the foreground is rendered with staccato dabs of vibrant red that sing out against the surrounding grasses of green and yellow, perfectly encapsulating the shimmering heat of a summery's day. AD

Oil on canvas
71.5 × 90.5 (28⅛ × 35⅝)
Signed at lower right: Claude Monet
Foundation E. G. Bührle Collection

Auguste Renoir   1841–1919

49   *Portrait of the Painter Alfred Sisley, 1864*

49a. Renoir, *Portrait of William Sisley*, 1864, Musée d'Orsay, Paris.

Traditionally scholars have ascribed Renoir's portrait of Alfred Sisley to 1868, but in 1985 Anne Distel asserted on stylistic grounds that it must have been painted earlier. It seems to have been done at about the same time as Renoir's portrait of Sisley's father William, a painting that is signed and dated 1864 (fig. 49a).[1] The palette, the rendering of form, and the treatment of the background are very similar, and the canvases are virtually identical in size.

Renoir and Sisley probably met in 1862 when both entered the Ecole des Beaux-Arts and studied in the atelier of Charles Gleyre, where Claude Monet and Frédéric Bazille were also students. In 1864 when Gleyre closed his studio and stopped teaching, the four young painters suddenly found themselves without a formal affiliation. Bazille and Sisley were supported by their relatively wealthy families, but Renoir and Monet were not so fortunate. The portraits of Sisley and his father may have been commissioned as a way for Sisley to provide financial assistance for his gifted but impecunious friend. According to Distel, little is known about Sisley's father, "but legend has it that he was a man of some means who allowed his son Alfred to devote himself to painting."[2]

Renoir's portrait of Sisley has its origins in a long tradition of nineteenth-century images of the *haute bourgeoisie*.[3] But the sitter's attitude and demeanor reflect the realism characteristic of avant-garde painters of the mid-1860s, including Henri Fantin-Latour, whom Renoir met in 1862 and with whom he often visited the Louvre.[4] Sisley's relatively informal pose, with one hand in a pocket, anticipates the intention expressed by Edgar Degas about five years later when he wrote in one of his notebooks: "Make portraits of people in familiar and typical positions."[5]

By the time the portrait was painted, Renoir must have known Sisley well. They had been together in Gleyre's studio for more than a year and had worked together in April 1863 with Monet and Bazille in the village of Chailly in the Fontainbleau Forest. By the spring of 1865 Renoir was living in Sisley's apartment at 31 avenue de Neuilly, near the Porte Maillot, and that year they worked together in Marlotte. Between 1866 and 1876 Sisley served as Renoir's model for figures in such important works as *Cabaret de la Mère Anthony* of 1866 (Nationalmuseum, Stockholm), *The Engaged Couple* of 1868 (Wallraf-Richartz Museum, Cologne), *Garden on the rue Cortot, Montmartre* of 1876 (The Museum of Art, Carnegie Institute, Pittsburgh), and *The Bower* of 1876 (Pushkin Museum, Moscow). In addition, Renoir painted Sisley's portrait again in 1874 (The Art Institute of Chicago).   CSM

Oil on canvas
82 × 66 (32¼ × 26)
Foundation E. G. Bührle Collection

50   *Harvesters, 1873*

Renoir focuses here on the pictorial aspects of a traditional nineteenth-century French subject seldom depicted by the impressionists. He celebrates light and color, the fullness of the harvest, and the harmony of laborers and the land. But the bravura brushwork, orchestration of color, and brilliant rendering of light seem to have interested him more than the subject itself. The scene reflects neither the truths about peasant life extolled in works by Jean François Millet nor the mechanization that was rapidly changing agricultural production in the second half of the century. As Richard Brettell observes, "The Impressionists pictorialized agriculture in its pre-modern, or traditional forms, and it seems from their paintings, drawings, and prints that they ignored, or were utterly ignorant of, the considerable advances in the area evident in the popular press and official statistics of their time."[1]

Although Renoir's approach to the subject avoids social and historical issues, the patently modern manner of execution infuriated certain contemporary critics in 1874 when the painting was included in the first impressionist group show. Louis Leroy attacked it in his famous review in *Le Charivari,* often cited as the source of the term "impressionists." Leroy's review, written as a dialogue with the academic landscape painter Joseph Vincent as they visited the exhibitions, contains the following sarcastic passage:

"*... stupid people who are finicky about the drawing of a hand don't understand a thing about impressionism, and great Manet would chase them out of his republic.*" [Vincent]

"*Then Monsieur Renoir is following the proper path; there is nothing superfluous in his* Harvesters. *I might almost say that his figures . . .*"

"*... are even too finished.*"

"*Oh, Monsieur Vincent! But do look at those three strips of color, which are supposed to represent a man in the midst of the wheat!*"

"*There are too many; one would be enough.*"

I glanced at [Vincent]; his countenance was turning a deep red.[2]

The influential critic Ernest Chesneau dismissed the painting as one of "two that are only experiments without result," but he admired two other works among the six Renoir exhibited.[3] *Harvesters* was not disliked by everyone, however. Marc de Montifaud described one work in the show, *L'Avant-Scene,* as a "painting of great quality" and a "success" corroborated by two of the other works exhibited, one of which was *Harvesters.*[4] Clearly the painting was an important point of discussion in the 1874 group show, and as such played a significant role in the rise of the impressionist movement.   CSM

Oil on canvas
60 × 74 (23⅝ × 29⅛)
Signed at lower left: Renoir. 73.
Private collection

51   *Young Woman in a Feathered Hat, 1880*

51 a. Renoir, *La Place Clichy,* 1880, Fitzwilliam Museum, University of Cambridge.

51 b. Renoir, *La Place Pigalle,* 1880, private collection, London.

Young Woman with a Feathered Hat is directly related to Renoir's *La Place Clichy* (fig. 51a) and *Place Pigalle* (fig. 51b), both of 1880. At first it seems to be a study for *La Place Clichy,* but at least two authorities believe that the Bührle canvas followed the Fitzwilliam picture.[1] Denys Sutton has observed that the Bührle picture is most likely an image extracted from the more ambitious composition in Cambridge and worked up as an independent image with an integrity of its own. He notes that *Young Woman in a Feathered Hat* "is more finished in appearance than either of the other two works."[2] In addition, close examination reveals thin touches of blue, pink, and green in the background that may refer to passages in the background of the Fitzwilliam picture, further reinforcing Sutton's argument.

The remarkable immediacy of the young woman, the vantage point, and the abrupt cropping of the figure suggest the influence of photography.[3] The image could have been caught by a camera as the woman moved across the viewer's field of vision. Analogous compositions do not exist in photographs of the late 1870s and early 1880s, however, because the necessary combination of lens and film did not yet exist. Although the partially glimpsed individual who catches one's attention randomly and momentarily on the street was to become an integral aspect of the visual vocabulary of modern urban life, such subjects were relatively new in the 1870s and 1880s and interested only certain avant-garde painters.

Young Woman in a Feathered Hat could be used to illustrate passages from Edmond Duranty's landmark essay of 1876, "The New Painting," the first attempt to define the principal stylistic innovations and attitudes toward subject matter characteristic of the emerging modern movement: "What we need are the special characteristics of the modern individual—in his clothing, in social situations, at home, or on the street. . . . Attitude will tell us whether a person is going to a business meeting or returning from a tryst. . . . The very first idea was to eliminate the partition separating the artist's studio from everday life, and to introduce the reality of the street. . . . Our lives take place in rooms and in streets, and rooms and streets have their own special laws of light and visual language."[4] In short, Renoir was among the leading practitioners of the changes in style, subject, and approach that established the modern movement and led to a new understanding of art.   CSM

Oil on canvas
55 × 38 (21⅝ × 15)
Signed at upper right: renoir.
Private collection

52   *Portrait of Mademoiselle Irène Cahen d'Anvers, 1880*

52a. Renoir, *Portrait of Alice and Elisabeth Cahen d'Anvers*, 1881, Museo de Arte de São Paulo, Brazil.

In a letter of 4 July 1880 Paul Cézanne reported to Emile Zola, "I hear Renoir has some good commissions for portraits."[1] Indeed, since the enormous success in the Salon of 1878 of Renoir's portrait of the wife and children of the publisher Georges Charpentier (The Metropolitan Museum of Art, New York), he had received several portrait commissions from wealthy Parisians. During the summer of 1880 Cézanne may have heard that Renoir was at work on a portrait of the eight-year-old daughter of the successful banker Louis Cahen d'Anvers. Renoir met the Cahen d'Anvers family through the critic and editor Théodore Duret and the collector Cernuschi,[2] and Mme Cahen d'Anvers commissioned the portrait of Irène in 1880. According to Daulte, Renoir painted it in two sittings at the Cahen d'Anvers home on the rue Basanno.[3] The following year he did a double portrait of Irène's two sisters, Alice and Elisabeth (fig. 52a), and her father's younger brother Albert (formerly Galerie Beyeler, Basel).

The style of the portrait of Irène is a combination of the loose, feathery brushwork characteristic of Renoir's classic impressionist manner of the mid-1870s and the more conservative approach that he often adopted for commissioned portraits.[4] In order to satisfy the requirements of formal portraiture and the need to render a suitable likeness, such works are often tighter and more linear, anticipating his "dry" style of the early 1880s.

In 1883 the portrait of Irène was included in Renoir's first one-man show, one of a series of exhibitions devoted to the work of individual contemporary artists that the Galerie Durand-Ruel organized that year in its new premises on the boulevard de la Madeleine. Twenty-five of the seventy works in the show were portraits, an indication of how imortant portraiture had become to the artist's livelihood. The preface to the catalogue was written by Duret, who emphasized the qualities that continue to make Renoir one of the most admired late nineteenth-century French painters: "[In Renoir] we recognize at first sight the ability to paint woman in all her grace and delicacy, which has led him to excel particularly in portraits. The artist has fully displayed this gift of charm from the beginning, and it is in his ability as a painter and colorist that we must observe his progress and development."[5]   CSM

Oil on canvas
65 × 54 (25⅝ × 21¼)
Signed and dated at upper right: Renoir. 80.
Foundation E. G. Bührle Collection

Paul Gauguin   1848–1903

53   *Mette Gauguin, 1878*

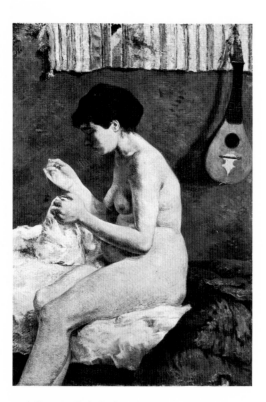

53a. Gauguin, *Nude Study* or *Suzanne Sewing*, 1880, Ny Carlsberg Glyptotek, Copenhagen.

The date and identity of the sitter for this portrait have been based on the inscription at the lower right signed by Pola Gauguin, the artist's fourth child: "I the undersigned certify that this painting was painted by my father Paul Gauguin in the year 1878 and that it represents the portrait of my mother. Oslo, July 1929, Pola Gauguin." Although Pola's authority regarding his father's paintings has at times been questioned, the style is consonant with Gauguin's incipient impressionism of the late 1870s, and the figure undoubtedly represents Mette, here at age twenty-eight.[1] Gauguin had already carved her likeness in marble the previous year and would place the sculpture in the fifth impressionist exhibition of 1880.[2]

A handsome, independent Danish woman who married Gauguin in 1873, Mette Gad had born two of her five children by the time she sat for this portrait. In 1878 the future looked bright for the young couple. They resided in Paris at 74 rue des Fourneaux, and Paul, who was still engaged in a lucrative business career, was an ambitious collector of contemporary art. He had been able to exhibit one of his own paintings at the Salon of 1876, the first and only time he took part in this official, state-sponsored exhibition. Beginning in 1879, he would paint regularly in the company of Camille Pissarro, whose influence is evident in this work, and he would be asked to take part in the independent exhibitions of the impressionists.

In the manner of Berthe Morisot's domestic portraits of women, Gauguin painted his wife in the conventional act of sewing.[3] Mette's shoulder-length hair is pulled back, and a heavy sweater covers her high-collared dress. Light from an unseen window illuminates the figure "contre-jour," leaving her profile in shadow. She is enclosed by the array of patterns and textures that vaguely describe the features of the room. The striped cloth at the right seems to be a fragment of a rug that Gauguin used as a prop in several other early paintings.[4]

Considering its genre subject, *Mette Gauguin* is of an unusually ambitious size. It was probably the departure point for a very dissimilar portrait, *Nude Study* or *Suzanne Sewing* from 1880 (fig. 53a), which is of nearly the same dimensions.[5] The scimitar that floats inexplicably beneath the mirror introduces a bizarre note, although it may simply be a decorative curio acquired during the artist's travels in the merchant marines. Given that Gauguin would abandon his family in 1885, it is tempting to read the object as an ominous portent of the couple's future strife.   MP

Oil on canvas
115 × 80.5 (45¼ × 31⅝)
Foundation E. G. Bührle Collection

Paul Gauguin   1848–1903

54   *Pape moe, 1893*

54a. Gauguin, *Pape moe,* 1893–1894, The Art Institute of Chicago, Gift of Mrs. Emily Crane Chadbourne.

In "Noa Noa," Gauguin's fanciful narrative about his first Tahitian voyage, the artist recounts that during a grueling hike in the forest he came upon a naked woman drinking at a waterfall: "Then—though I had made no sound—as a frightened antelope instinctively senses a stranger, she cocked her head, scrutinizing the thicket where I was hidden. . . . Violently she dived, crying out the word *'tachae'* (fierce). . . . I rushed to look down into the water: no one, nothing but an enormous eel winding between the small stones of the bottom."[1]

Although Gauguin identified this experience as the subject of *Pape moe,*[2] the anecdote probably records more of an apocryphal afterthought than an actual event. As one of the final paintings from Gauguin's first Tahitian trip, *Pape moe* in fact preceded the written account and was closely based on a documentary photograph by Charles Spitz, a businessman and photographer who lived in Papeete, the Tahitian capital. Gauguin seems to have been particularly fond of Spitz's image, for he generated from it not only the Bührle picture but two watercolors (see fig. 54a), one monotype, and a polychromed wood relief.[3] Only in the oil version did the artist so effectively transform the lush tropical foliage of the photograph into dense tapestried color.

Gauguin included elements in his picture that were omitted from the chapter in "Noa Noa." Ostensibly female, but effectively androgynous, the figure in the painting who leans to drink from the golden stream gazes directly at a strange fishlike head that floats above an enchanted, rainbow-colored pool. This apparition has been likened to other supernatural creatures who appeared to Gauguin's Tahitian women,[4] women who by virtue of their communion with nature were endowed with special intuitive powers. *Pape moe*'s essential spiritual message is revealed by its many formal and iconographical affinities with *Hina tefatou* (Museum of Modern Art, New York).[5] In that mythological painting from 1893, the Tahitian moon goddess Hina implores her son Fatu to grant eternal life to mankind. But Fatu, whose head looms ominously above the pool of a grotto, is implacable. According to Tahitian legend, however, the regenerative powers of the magic water give Hina the power to be reborn each month.[6]   MP

Oil on canvas
99 × 75 (39 × 29⅝)
Signed and dated at lower right:
P. Gauguin 93 / PAPE MOE
Private collection

Paul Gauguin   1848–1903

55   *Still Life with Sunflowers on an Armchair, 1901*

55a. Odilon Redon, *Les Origines*, pl. 2, *Il y eut peut-être une vision première essayée dans la fleur*, 1883, National Gallery of Art, Washington, Rosenwald Collection.

In a letter to Gauguin in late 1899 the Parisian dealer Ambroise Vollard promised to buy the artist's entire artistic output but urged him specifically to do flower paintings. Suspicious as always of Vollard's motives, Gauguin warned him, "I do not copy nature. . . . With me everything happens in my exuberant imagination and when I tire of painting figures (which I like best) I begin a still life and finish it without any model. Besides this is not really a land of flowers."[1]

Gauguin was too ill to paint the following year, but in 1901 he produced a spectacular series of still lifes, two of which are in the Bührle collection. Completed before the artist left Tahiti for the Marquesas Islands in September, *Still Life with Sunflowers* is one of four canvases from 1901 that depict sunflowers.[2] Gauguin harvested these blossoms from the garden he had planted with seeds imported from Europe. The flowers are casually arranged in a homely basket propped on a chair, as if just gathered from the garden. They seem bedraggled by Tahiti's stifling heat and humidity.

Like many paintings from Gauguin's second trip to Tahiti, this still life draws in part on an earlier composition.[3] In *Pour faire un bouquet* of 1880 (private collection), a basket of flowers sits atop a chair with a white cloth draped over its back, and an open door provides a view to the garden beyond. This unorthodox use of chairs as surrogate tables anticipated the device as employed by van Gogh in two famous Arles canvases from 1888.[4] In turn, Gauguin's sunflower series constitutes a poignant reminiscence of the Dutch painter.[5]

The Bührle collection's *Still Life with Sunflowers* most closely resembles a slightly larger sunflower still life in the State Hermitage Museum, Leningrad, in which a native woman is framed by the window's embrasure to the right of the chair. In the Bührle picture Gauguin supplanted this spatially ambiguous "picture-within-a-picture" with a seascape in which two Tahitians bathe in the sea near a pirogue. The book and inkwell on the windowsill reinforce its function as a sill rather than a picture frame. As if to mitigate the illusion, however, Gauguin depicted in the shadows behind the chair a surrealistic blossom with an eye as its center. This botanical oddity is a direct descendent of the ocular blossoms invented by the symbolist painter Odilon Redon (see fig. 55a).   MP

Oil on canvas
66 × 75.5 (26 × 29¾)
Signed and dated at lower right: P. Gauguin 1901
Foundation E. G. Bührle Collection

Paul Gauguin   1848–1903

56   Idyll in Tahiti, 1901

Idyll in Tahiti is one of the last images Gauguin painted of Tahiti. In September of 1901 he sailed to Hivaoa in the Marquesas, where he died less than two years later. Gauguin produced only a handful of landscapes in 1901, preoccupied as he was by an important series of still lifes. Despite ever worsening health, entanglements with the authorities, and constant fretting about money, Gauguin enjoyed a period of relative well-being during his final months on Tahiti, to which the placid mood of *Idyll in Tahiti* attests.

The stretch of coastal land depicted here is probably near Punaauia on Tahiti's western shore, where Gauguin had settled upon his return to the islands in 1895. He purchased two parcels of land in Punaauia in 1897, but rather than the traditional bamboo huts seen in the background of the painting, he built a large wooden house to which he attached a studio.

It has been noted recently that Gauguin copied the large sailing vessel at the upper left from a painting by Johan Barthold Jongkind from 1861.[1] Jongkind's painting had belonged to the collector Gustave Arosa, once Gauguin's legal guardian, and Gauguin must have carried a photograph of the painting with him to Tahiti. The same ship appeared in a similar composition by Gauguin from 1899, *Te tiai na oe ite rata* (private collection),[2] where it probably represented the eagerly awaited mailboat, Gauguin's only link to the European world he never completely abandoned. In translation, that title reads "Are you waiting for a letter?" As Bengt Danielsson has pointed out, the words must echo a question repeatedly put to the artist by his island neighbors.[3]

The painting of 1899 depicts entwined coconut palms, whose arching silhouettes appear in many of Gauguin's Tahitian landscapes, including *Idyll in Tahiti*. Typically, the artist reshaped the landscape to suit his needs in subsequent works, and in the Bührle painting two Tahitians carry provisions along a sloping path that opens up in the foreground. Gauguin saturated the area with an intense orange-red hue, suggesting the incendiary effect of a tropical sunset and dramatically setting off the complementary color of the surrounding grasses.   MP

Oil on canvas
74.5 × 94.5 (29 ⅜ × 37 ¼)
Signed and dated at lower right: P. Gauguin 1901
Foundation E. G. Bührle Collection

57   *Still Life with Fruit, Basket, and Knife, 1901*

57a. Gauguin, *Still Life with Grapefruits,* 1901, private collection, Lausanne.

Still Life with Fruit, Basket, and Knife is the most classical of Gauguin's still-life compositions from his second Tahitian voyage. Judiciously constructed, it exhibits stylistic kinship with another canvas of the same dimensions, *Still Life with Grape-fruits* (fig. 57a), which has been recently dated to 1901.[1] In both works the still-life elements are arranged along a cloth depicted in cool pastel hues and placed on a large brown trunk (presumably the one in which Gauguin packed his belongings for Polynesia). In the Bührle picture, however, Gauguin forsook the decoratively patterned wallpaper of *Still Life with Grapefruits* in favor of a generalized background of softly brushed, warm tonalities. The backdrop and the face of the trunk are perfectly aligned with the picture plane, which throws into relief the solid volumes of the fruits and vegetables.

Gauguin turned to Cézanne for inspiration when he produced the present still life, just as he returned to van Gogh when painting sunflowers the same year. It is well known that the prize of Gauguin's own art collection was Cézanne's renowned *Still Life with Compotier* from 1879–1880 (private collection), with which he reluctantly parted in 1897.[2] Gauguin frequently mimicked the constructive parallel strokes of Cézanne's brush, and here he includes a knife to the left in direct homage to Cézanne's picture. As late as 1901, in a kind of ongoing artistic dialogue with his European contemporaries, Gauguin continued to measure his own accomplishments in still life against the standard of Cézanne.

Gauguin gathered produce for this still life from the garden he had first planted in 1899, in which he had raised vegetables from seeds sent by his closest friend in Paris, Daniel de Monfreid.[3] The European vegetables in this painting, such as the eggplant at the right, sit alongside a basket filled with mangoes, the quintessential Tahitian delicacy. To judge from the painting, the garden was a success, and in June of 1901 Gauguin requested seeds, specifying gourds, for the garden he planned to sow in the Marquesas.[4]

MP

Oil on canvas
66.5 × 76.5 (26⅛ × 30⅛)
Signed and dated at lower left:
Paul Gauguin 1901
Private collection

Vincent van Gogh 1853–1890

58 *The Bridge at Asnières, 1887*

58a. Emile Bernard, *The Bridge at Asnières,* 1887, Collection, The Museum of Modern Art, New York, Grace Rainey Rogers Fund.

The Bridge at Asnières was painted during the summer of 1887. Its personalized combination of impressionist and neo-impressionist technique reflects the wide variety of sources and influences to which van Gogh had been constantly exposed since arriving in Paris in March 1886. Indeed, the summer of that year he reported to the English painter H. M. Levens: "There is much to be seen here – for instance Delacroix, to mention only one master. In Antwerp I did not even know what the impressionists were, now I have seen them and though *not* being one of the club yet I have much admired certain impressionists' pictures – *Degas* nude figure – *Claude Monet* landscape."[1]

Van Gogh also described to Levens "a series of color studies in painting [still lifes of flowers]" made for the purpose of "trying to render intense color and not a gray harmony." More than a year later, in a letter to his sister Wilhelmina, he was still preoccupied with ideas about color and again referred to the color studies: "what is required in art nowadays is something very much alive, very strong in color, very much intensified . . . Last year I painted hardly anything but flowers in order to get accustomed to using a scale of colors other than gray."[2]

When van Gogh painted *The Bridge at Asnières,* he had absorbed impressionist and neo-impressionist ideas about color and brushwork but had not adopted a particular system or come under the influence of a specific painter or theory.[3] The use of parallel brushstrokes and broken color suggests the influence of Signac and Seurat, whose work he admired, but the subject is more likely indebted to Monet's bridge pictures of the 1870s.[4] The rather complex composition may reflect the artist's strong interest in Japanese prints, which he collected and admired.[5] In short, from the dozens of influences and ideas he had experienced during the previous eighteen months, van Gogh fashioned a technique and an approach to the subject that is unmistakably his.

The scene depicted is the railroad bridge at Asnières, with the Pont de Lavallois in the background, not far from the island of the Grande Jatte. Most likely van Gogh was introduced to the area by Emile Bernard, whose parents had a house there.[6] A photograph taken in 1887 shows van Gogh and Bernard seated together at a table on the quai in Asnières.[7] Bernard, too, painted a view along the quai, but later in the autumn (fig. 58a). Whereas van Gogh's painting is an accomplished work by a young artist still experimenting with the latest ideas about technique, Bernard's treatment shows an artist more comfortable with exaggeration and simplification. CSM

Oil on canvas
53.5 × 67 (21⅛ × 26⅜)
Foundation E. G. Bührle Collection

59   *Apricot Trees in Blossom, 1888*

Between 24 March and 20 April 1888, not long after arriving in Arles, van Gogh devoted much of his energy to paintings and drawings of flowering orchards. Nine of the paintings were meant to form three triptychs, the first contributions toward a "scheme of decoration" the artist planned to continue in the spring of 1889: "You see, we may consider this year's nine canvases as the first design for a final scheme of decoration a great deal bigger... which would be carried out along just the same lines next season."[1]

Ronald Pickvance suggests that *Apricot Trees in Blossom* was intended as a wing of one of the triptychs.[2] Jan Hulsker places it among a group of six paintings of orchards that occupied the artist during late March.[3] But the editors of the most recent edition of de la Faille's catalogue raisonné of van Gogh's œuvre identify the painting with a work that the artist mentioned in a letter written 9 April: "I have another orchard, as good as the pink peach trees, apricot trees of a very pale pink."[4] It is also possible, however, that the present work is the first orchard picture van Gogh painted in Arles, cited in a letter written 24 March: "I have just finished a group of apricot trees in bloom in a little orchard of fresh green."[5]

In the broad context of the artist's life and work, the orchard scenes reflect both his increasingly pantheistic view of nature and his own renewal after two years of decadence and difficulty in Paris. In addition, van Gogh's images of flowering orchards are directly related to his emphasis on subjects that reflect the natural continuum of birth (blossoms), death (harvest), and regeneration (sowing). Twice van Gogh used paintings of flowering trees to commemorate or celebrate birth. In the spring of 1888 he painted *Orchard in Blossom* (private collection, Switzerland) on the occasion of his brother's birthday.[6] Two years later he painted *Blossoming Almond Tree* (Rijksmuseum Vincent van Gogh, Amsterdam) in honor of the birth of his nephew.[7] In dedicating one of the orchard paintings to the memory of the contemporary Dutch artist Anton Mauve, he specifically identified Mauve with a continuum that transcends death.[8]

Most of the images of flowering orchards painted in Arles in the spring of 1888 were intended as sections of triptychs, a pictorial mode closely associated with altarpieces and religious paintings. It seems clear, therefore, that the artist meant the orchard paintings to have an implicit spiritual dimension in addition to their role in his projected "scheme of decoration."   CSM

Oil of canvas
54.5 × 65.5 (21½ × 25¾)
Signed at lower right: Vincent
Private collection

60 *The Sower, 1888*

60a. Van Gogh, *The Sower,* 1888, Rijksmuseum Vincent van Gogh, Amsterdam.

This is one of two closely related images of a sower van Gogh painted in the fall of 1888. In a letter to his brother Theo at the end of November he included a sketch "of the latest canvas I am working on, another Sower. An immense citron yellow disk for the sun. A green-yellow sky with pink clouds. The field violet, the sower and tree Prussian blue. Size 30 canvas."[1] The Bührle painting is unquestionably this canvas. Pickvance argues that the smaller version in the Rijksmuseum Vincent van Gogh (fig. 60a) is a highly developed sketch that closely approximates the finished composition, but others believe it is "a small replica" of the Zurich painting.[2]

Sowers were the subject of several important paintings and drawings van Gogh executed in June and October 1888,[3] but the theme interested him throughout his career. In 1880 he informed Theo that he owned a print of Millet's *The Sower* and had made five drawings after it;[4] in September 1881 he did several drawings of sowers in Etten;[5] in 1882 he drew a pair of sowers at work to illustrate that "there is more drudgery than rest in life";[6] in 1889 and 1890 he executed several drawings of sowers as well as two paintings after Millet's *The Sower.*[7] Van Gogh's interest in the theme can be traced at least as far back as 12 June 1877, almost three years before he became an artist, when he wrote to Theo about a sermon he had heard on the parable of the sower, noting that it "made a deep impression of me."[8]

In the Bührle and Amsterdam paintings the sun becomes a halo for the sower, and the sower a sainted husbandman in van Gogh's canon of pantheism. The result is a secularized Christian image. In effect, the painting is an apotheosis of a sower, a deification of a field hand. It also reflects van Gogh's ongoing preoccupation with the cycle of birth, death, and regeneration, a theme that underlies much of the work he produced between 1888 and 1890.

It has been noted that *The Sower* seems to reflect van Gogh's admiration of Japanese prints[9] and that the composition may have been influenced by Gauguin's *The Vision after the Sermon,* summer of 1888 (The National Galleries of Scotland, Edinburgh).[10] In fact, Gauguin included a drawing of the composition in a letter he sent van Gogh in late September 1888.[11] He also stayed with van Gogh in Arles from October to December 1888, and the two engaged in ongoing discussions, sometimes disagreeing, about the role of simplications and exaggerations in their work. *The Sower* seems to be of special significance in this context, because it is the only work van Gogh signed during the two months Gauguin was in Arles.[12]   CSM

Oil on burlap, mounted on canvas
73 × 92.5 (28¾ × 36⅜)
Signed on tree trunk at lower right: Vincent
Foundation E. G. Bührle Collection

61 *Olive Orchard, 1889*

Between June and December 1889 van Gogh produced at least fifteen paintings of olive orchards.[1] He found the subject especially difficult but always fascinating, and on 28 September he wrote his brother Theo: "I am struggling to catch [the olive trees]. They are old silver, sometimes with more blue in them, sometimes greenish, bronzed, fading white above a soil which is yellow, pink, violet-tinted orange, to dull red ocher. Very difficult though, very difficult."[2]

Ronald Pickvance and Jan Hulsker have suggested that this may be the painting van Gogh identified as the "small copy" he made for his mother or sister in September 1889.[3] But the work is not particularly small nor is it a copy or replica after the *Olive Orchard* in the Rijksmuseum Kröller-Müller (F 585). It is possible that van Gogh painted the Bührle picture in late November, when he wrote to Emile Bernard that he was "working at present among the olive trees, seeking after the various effects of a gray sky against a yellow soil."[4] There is not a trace of early or late fall vegetation on the ground around the trees, which increases the likelihood that the painting was done in late November or early December.

The significance of olive trees in the context of van Gogh's work is pronounced but elusive. He explained to his brother in a letter written in Arles in late April that "the rustle of an olive grove has something very secret in it, and immensely old. It is too beautiful for us to dare to paint it or to be able to imagine it."[5] In another letter, written about a year later, he refers to the "symbolic language" of the olive trees.[6] In addition, van Gogh cited his paintings of the olive orchards as evidence of the marked differences between his own work and that of Gauguin and Bernard: "What I have done is a rather hard and coarse reality beside their abstractions, but it will have a rustic quality and will smell of the earth."[7]

In olive trees, as in wheat fields, cypresses, and sunflowers, van Gogh found an innate expressiveness that was evidence to him of a higher order of meaning, a spiritual force in nature. As such, the subject was particularly well suited to the pantheistic vision that informs much of his imagery between 1888 and 1890 and his stylistic development in the second half of 1889. He found the motif worthy of Delacroix, an artist whom he venerated throughout his career, and of Puvis de Chavannes,[8] but ironically he could not see that his olive orchard paintings pointed not to the past but the future.   CSM

Oil on canvas
53.5 × 64.5 (21⅛ × 25⅜)
Private collection

62 *Wheat Field with Cypresses, June 1889*

62a. Van Gogh, *Wheat Field with Cypresses,* 1889,
Rijksmuseum Vincent van Gogh, Amsterdam.

On 8 May 1888 van Gogh committed himself to the asylum of Saint-Paul-de-Mausole in Saint-Rémy-de-Provence. His doctor, Théophile Peyron, confined him to the grounds for about a month, but early in June he permitted the artist to work in the surrounding landscape. *Wheat Field with Cypresses* was among the group of extraordinary paintings van Gogh produced in the weeks that followed.[1] Among other works painted during this period of intense activity were *The Starry Night* (The Museum of Modern Art, New York; F 612), both versions of *Cypresses* (The Metropolitan Museum of Art, New York, and Rijksmuseum Kröller-Müller, Otterlo; F 613 and F 620), and the earliest of the olive orchard paintings that he did before the end of the year.[2]

Pickvance points out that van Gogh's "discovery of the cypress was the cardinal event of June 1889," that the motif was "audaciously thrust into prominence" in *The Starry Night* in mid-June, and that "by the end of the month, the series of cypress canvases was fully launched, with [*Cypresses,* F 613], its large upright pendant now in Otterlo [F 620], and the horizontally contrasting *Wheat Field with Cypresses.*"[3] The artist clearly regarded *Wheat Field with Cypresses* as a work of special significance, for on 2 July he sent a drawing after the completed painting to his brother (see fig. 62a), and in September he made painted variants for his sister and mother.[4]

Van Gogh was fascinated by the cypresses as the natural equivalents of architectural forms, "as beautiful in lines and proportions as an Egyptian obelisk."[5] He admired their inherently expressive character and compared their color to a musical note.[6] He later wrote of their spiritual significance and said the cypresses were "the contrast and yet the equivalent" of his images of sunflowers, which he associated with gratitude.[7]

Like the cypresses, wheat fields are among van Gogh's most important metaphors. Wheat, for the artist, was "the germinating force" in the cycle of life and the creative process.[8] Indeed, just after finishing *Wheat Field with Cypresses,* he wrote to his sister: "The history of [wheat] is like our own; for aren't we, who live on bread, to a considerable extent like wheat, at least aren't we forced to submit to growing like a plant without the power to move, by which I mean in whatever way our imagination impels us, and to being reaped when we are ripe, like the same wheat?"[9] He later expanded the metaphor, writing to Theo that even if he failed as an artist he knew that this work had value as part of a broader process: "I feel so strongly that it is the same with people as it is with wheat, if you are not sown in the earth to germinate there, what does it matter? — in the end you are ground between the millstones to become bread."[10]   CSM

Oil on canvas
73 × 93.5 (28¾ × 36¾)
Private collection

63   *Blossoming Chestnut Branches, 1890*

63a. Van Gogh, *Blossoming Almond Branch,* 1890,
Rijksmuseum Vincent van Gogh, Amsterdam.

Van Gogh associated blossoming branches with birth, renewal, and the beginning of the cycle of life, and he painted two small still lifes of a blossoming almond branch soon after arriving in Arles in late February 1888, which express a new sense of hope after two difficult years in Paris.[1] In addition, the many paintings of flowering fruit trees he painted that spring seem closely related to the renewed purpose he felt in his own life and work. He began work on another painting of a blossoming almond branch (fig. 63a) following the birth of his nephew on 2 February 1890.[2]

He sent that *Blossoming Almond Branch* to Paris on 29 April and saw it when he visited his brother, sister-in-law, and nearly four-month-old nephew in Paris in May.[3] Having been discharged from the asylum in Saint-Rémy on 16 May, he was on his way to live twenty miles from Paris in the village of Auvers-sur-Oise.[4] Theo had arranged to place him in the care of Dr. Paul Gachet, who had been recommended by Camille Pissarro.

Not long after van Gogh arrived in Auvers, he returned to his interest in blossoming foliage.[5] He may have been inspired to paint the flowering chestnut branches in Auvers after seeing *Blossoming Almond Branch* in his brother's apartment. He was also very conscious of his own new beginning. The late spring and early summer vegetation in Auvers must have filled him with a sense of renewal. But his letters also indicate an underlying anxiety as a result of his changing circumstances. And although Theo wrote on 30 June, "you have found your way, old fellow, your carriage is steady on its wheels and strong,"[6] Vincent ended his own life before the end of July.

The packed composition and agitated brushwork of *Blossoming Chestnut Branches* seem related in spirit to the similarly energetic *Wild Vegetation in the Hills,* a drawing done in Saint-Rémy in the summer of 1889 (Rijksmuseum Vincent van Gogh; F 1542). But the palette—especially the blues, reds, and greens—the relatively dry handling of the paint, and the rhythmic brushstrokes are closely related to the palette and technique of the two portraits van Gogh painted of Dr. Gachet in June 1890. The doctor and amateur artist, who formed a significant collection largely as a result of his friendships with several contemporary artists, owned several of the paintings that van Gogh painted during his brief seventy days in Auvers, including *Blossoming Chestnut Branches.*   CSM

Oil on canvas
72.5 × 91 (28 ½ × 35 ⅞)
Foundation E. G. Bührle Collection

Georges Seurat   1859–1891

64   *Study for "Sunday Afternoon on the Island of La Grande Jatte,"*
     1884–1885

64a. Seurat, *Sunday Afternoon on the Island of
La Grande Jatte,* 1884–1885, The Art Institute of Chicago,
Helen Birch Bartlett Memorial Collection.

Seurat exhibited his first monumental figure painting, *Bathing at Asnières* (National Gallery, London),[1] at the Salon des Indépendents in May 1884. According to Signac, Seurat then went daily over the next six months to the little island of Grande Jatte in the River Seine, between Clichy and Courbevoie, to prepare studies for his second major exhibition work, *Sunday Afternoon on the Island of La Grande Jatte* (fig. 64a).[2] Although doubt remains as to how quickly Seurat produced the finished painting, it was certainly completed in time for the second Salon des Indépendents, planned for March 1885. When this Salon was postponed, Seurat reworked the canvas and exhibited it at the eighth and final impressionist exhibition the following year.

Bathing at Asnières and the even more ambitious *Grande Jatte* were probably intended as statements on modern history painting.[3] Seurat proceeded according to a method derived from his academic training:[4] preliminary compositional studies were developed in drawings of specific details and in oil sketches that determined the overall distribution of color and relationship between colors. Before painting *Grande Jatte* itself, Seurat produced at least three subsidiary canvases, twenty-six drawings, and thirty-two compositional studies in oil on panel, of which the Bührle painting is one.

Seurat seems to have begun *Grande Jatte* by defining the form of the landscape, disposition of figures, and distribution of color. Such studies were undertaken on the spot. A subsequent stage involved more precise plotting of individual sections of the composition. The left and center sections are the focus in the Bührle panel. In both stages Seurat used *balayé* or crisscross brushstrokes, which he had employed initially in 1881 to translate the hatching of his conte crayon drawings into color. Unlike the finished painting, however, or later figure studies such as that in the Fitzwilliam Museum, Cambridge,[5] or larger compositional sketches such as that in The Metropolitan Museum of Art, New York,[6] Seurat's small oil studies did not seek to analyze the precise relationship between light and the primary and complementary colors juxtaposed on the canvas as dots or brushstrokes.

The Bührle collection's sparsely populated study is related to several drawings, notably two studies of the dog in the center.[7] It contains other figures that also appear in the final painting, such as the man with an umbrella standing in profile and the woman seated at the river's edge. The man in the top hat at the right was moved toward the left and given a walking stick in the finished work, replacing a figure in a similar pose who sports a bowler in the Metropolitan Museum sketch. The trees act as screening devices in both the sketch and the finished painting, and the tree on the riverbank and the dominant central motif of a forked tree are also established.   MAS

Oil on panel
15.5 × 24.7 (6⅛ × 9¾)
Foundation E. G. Bührle Collection

65 *Study for "Invitation to the Sideshow," 1887–1888*

65 a. Seurat, *Invitation to the Sideshow (La Parade),* 1887–1888, The Metropolitan Museum of Art, Bequest of Stephen C. Clark, 1960.

This small work is preliminary for Seurat's *Invitation to the Sideshow* (fig. 65a), exhibited at the Salon des Indépendents in 1888 along with *The Models* (Barnes Foundation, Merion, Pa.).[1] The latter work was still in progress in late 1887 when Seurat embarked on the equally ambitious *Sideshow,* whose urban, nighttime setting is in contrast to the semirural, daytime settings of earlier large figure subjects such as *Bathing at Asnières* and *Sunday Afternoon on the Island of La Grande Jatte* (see cat. 64) and his series of landscapes from the preceding three years.

Seurat had been interested in the subject of saltimbanques and traveling players since 1881, and here he portrays a "parade," or group of entertainers, performing outside a circus tent to entice passers-by to enter. The scene is from the Cirque Colvi, a large, well-organized circus that had performed for the Foire aux Pains d'Epices at the Place de la Nation in eastern Paris in April and May 1887.[2]

The Bührle painting appears to have been completed in a very short time, possibly as a relief from the slow production of *The Models.*[3] The oil sketch on panel, lightly squared in chalk, seems to have served three purposes: planning the configuration of the composition, which differs from the finished painting only in that it does not include the tree on the left; defining the main distribution of color; and in accordance with academic procedure, providing the basis for the transfer of the composition and related studies to the larger scale of the final painting. This comprehensive approach may have been essential because of the nocturnal, transient nature of the subject.[4] For the large figure paintings of 1884 and 1885–1886, Seurat could return to the scene for further study and revision. Cirque Colvi offered no such opportunity.

In nineteenth-century French painting and popular imagery, the subject of the sideshow became either a platform for political satire or an analogue of the artist/performer as social outcast.[5] The latter may have been intended in Seurat's *Sideshow.* The performers bid for the approval of an audience representative of contemporary French society—the lower classes on the left, the bourgeoisie on the right—just as the artist has to seek the support of his public. The painting also demonstrates a careful application of Charles Henry's theories of the emotional implications of color and the psychological implications of the direction of line. *Sideshow* should perhaps be seen more as an exercise in non-naturalism than in the application of a scientific analysis of the optical relationship between light in nature and color on the canvas.[6]   MAS

Oil on panel
16.5 × 26 (6½ × 10¼)
Foundation E. G. Bührle Collection

66   *The Redheaded Girl, c. 1886*

The sitter for this study is almost certainly Carmen Gaudin, a model whom Lautrec discovered in 1885 in the street outside a Paris restaurant where he was dining with a fellow student, Henri Rachou.[1] The same model appears in profile in *The Laundress* of 1886–1887 (private collection),[2] identified by the shape of her nose and mouth and the arrangement of her hair with its longish fringe left uncaught by the bun at the nape of her neck. She also appears in *The Redhead at Montrouge-Rosa* of 1886–1887 (Barnes Foundation, Merion, Pa.) and in four studies, dated by Dortu to 1885, where she wears the same black, low-collared dress as that worn by the model in this work.[3]

Given the similarity of the Bührle painting to the other four studies, it would seem that this work should also be dated to c. 1885–1886 rather than to 1889 as suggested by Dortu. The earlier date is supported by the handling of paint and the tonality of the palette. Unlike the painting of the same model dated by Dortu to 1889, *Redheaded Woman in the Garden of M. Forest* (private collection), with its dominant tones of green and violet, this work has the subdued tonal values of *Portrait of Jeanne Wenz* of c. 1886 (The Art Institute of Chicago).[4] Furthermore, the work shows no evidence of Lautrec's experiments with the short, crisscross brushstrokes he adopted in 1887 or the linear, graphic handling of paint found in his pictures of two years later.

The model's position in an outdoor setting is also significant. As early as 1881 Lautrec had written to a childhood friend: "I have tried to draw something real, not ideal."[5] This ambition was immediately evident in such pictures as *Head of a Man—M. Etienne Devisme* (Musée d'Albi) and paintings of figures in landscapes or gardens executed at Celeyran in 1882.[6] Lautrec was certainly aware of Bastien-Lepage's large-scale paintings of peasants in landscape settings, which had been shown to great critical acclaim at the Salon since 1876. He must have also looked at similar treatments by Monet and Renoir of single figures in confined outdoor spaces.

The existence of four related studies of the same sitter may indicate that Lautrec's decision to pose his model in profile had no more significance than his need to study her from different viewpoints. The profile pose occurs in Lautrec's work from 1881 onward, however, and it had the potential to reduce the degree of naturalism in a painting since it deprived the model of any individual facial expression.[7] By eliminating inessential details and concentrating on the main physical characteristics of his models, Lautrec appears to have drawn on the examples of both Japanese prints and Italian quattrocentro portraiture.[8] The result is the creation of a hieratic image of his subjects that removes them from the territory of naturalistic representation.   MAS

Oil on canvas
55 × 50 (21⅝ × 19⅝)
Signed with monogram at bottom left: T-L
Private collection

67 *The Two Friends, 1895*

Lautrec first mentions frequenting the twilight world of Montmartre in a letter to his mother dated 15 August 1884.[1] Although he refers only to cafés in this letter, he is known to have become a habitué of the rich and varied brothel life that abounded in the streets around the Butte. He called on his experiences of this world for a number of paintings, culminating in the moving series of lithographs entitled *Elles,* published in 1896.

Lautrec had initially explored lesbian themes in 1892,[2] possibly inspired by the commission to decorate the walls of a brothel on the rue d'Amboise. It is uncertain whether Lautrec actually lived in brothels for extended periods of time,[3] but his depictions of life in these establishments were certainly the product of long hours of study inside their walls. As with his more general views, this record of a more intimate scene in the daily existence of prostitutes passes no moral judgment. Rather, it celebrates a nobility of emotion and expresses the artist's profound understanding of the sadness that pervades the life of his two models.

Lautrec explored the subject of two lesbian prostitutes in two other paintings of the same period, both equally classic and monumental in their treatment of the theme: *Abandon* or *The Two Friends* (Collection Peter Nathan), and *The Sofa* (The Metropolitan Museum of Art, New York).[4] All three paintings show the women expressing tenderness, lying on a couch half-dressed. The paintings are executed in *huile d'essence* on cardboard, which reflects the delicate fragility of the subject and also reveals the fluid drawing line. This latter is a reminder both of Lautrec's academic training and of his skillful manipulation of lithographic ink and chalk in the creation of the prints that complemented his paintings from 1891 onward.

The representation of lesbian subjects was not common in nineteenth-century art, although a notable precedent for Lautrec would have been Courbet's *Sleeping Women* of 1865 (Musée du Petit Palais, Paris). Another important source would have been Japanese Shunga prints of the eighteenth and nineteenth centuries, examples of which Lautrec was known to own, in which any differentiation between the male and female reclining lovers would not have been immediately evident to the Western eye.   MAS

Huile d'essence on cardboard
64.5 × 84 (25⅜ × 33⅛)
Signed with monogram at lower right: T-L
Foundation E. G. Bührle Collection

68   Messaline, 1900

This painting is one of a group of works created by Lautrec during his sojourn in Bordeaux over the winter of 1900–1901. It represents a scene from Isidore de Lara's operetta *Messaline,* which, with Offenbach's *La Belle Hélène,* formed part of the winter season at Bordeaux's Grand Théâtre. The operetta, based on Théophile Gautier's adaptation of Juvenal's Sixth and Tenth Satires, recounted the tragedy of Emperor Claudius' nymphomaniac wife. This subject had been treated by at least two of Lautrec's contemporaries: Aubrey Beardsley created illustrations in 1895 that were published in 1899, and Alfred Jarry reworked the subject as a novel that was published in 1901.

After a physical and mental collapse had forced Lautrec to be hospitalized in spring 1899, his health remained precarious. He was in Bordeaux and Arcachon the summer of 1900, and rather than returning to Paris in the autumn, he decided to stay in Bordeaux near his mother, who was staying at the family's Château de Malromé. He took an apartment on the rue of Cauderan and a studio on the rue Porte-Digeaux, and he gained privileged access to the backstage and wings of the Grand Théâtre itself.

It is from the wings that Lautrec appears to have recorded the subjects of his paintings and lithographs of both *La Belle Hélène* and *Messaline.* He had long been fascinated by the theater, and he sought to depict the performers not only from the conventional view across the footlights, as did many of the impressionists, notably Degas, but also from eccentric angles such as from the wings or a high box, where he could capture the fleeting moment when the performer was illuminated by the footlights.

In this painting the exaggerated lighting dramatically picks out the faces and arms of two performers, yet the tonality of the painting is somber, typical of the shift in Lautrec's palette in the late 1890s.[1] It is tempting to interpret the darker palette as a reflection of the artist's physical and psychological degeneration, but the same change can be seen in the work of his contemporaries, notably that of Cézanne.

Lautrec made at least three studies from the wings of the Grand Théâtre, probably preparatory to three more finished studies and three finished paintings.[2] At least one lithograph is also based on this theme.[3] Although the studies suggest Lautrec's reliance on direct observation for his finished compositions, certain remarks in his correspondence cast doubt on this supposition. Twice in December 1900 Lautrec wrote to Joyant, first asking for "any photographs, good or bad, of Lara's *Messaline?* I am working on the production and the more documentation I have the better," and later requesting "the programmes and the texte of *L'Assommoir* and *Messaline.*"[4] This implies a continuing search for a balance between the directly observed and the imaginatively conceived in his work, by which he sought to distill the essence of his subjects.   MAS

Oil on canvas
92 × 68 (36¼ × 26¾)
Signed with monogram in red at lower right: T-L
Foundation E. G. Bührle Collection

69   *The Blue Rider, 1903*

The figure of the horseman was of great significance in Kandinsky's world of ideas and in his work. It emerges as the hero of Russian legends and fairy tales, takes the shape of Saint George, and becomes the emblem, in many variations, for the almanac *Der Blaue Reiter,* which had been in the planning stages since 1910 and was first published in 1912. The horseman must have represented energy, motion, and strength to the young artist, so eager for achievement.

Kandinsky at this time lived in Munich with Gabriele Münter, taught his painting class at the Phalanx school in Kallmünz near Regensburg in the summer of 1903, and was primarily occupied with landscape painting. In his memoirs he says: "During this time of disappointments in studio work and outdoor painting I produced an especially large number of landscapes, which, however, did not give me much satisfaction, so that I used only very few of them in later paintings. . . . I spent little time thinking about houses and trees, but covered the canvas with colored stripes and blotches and let them sing as loudly as I could. Within me chimed the sunset hour in Moscow. Before my eyes was the powerful spectrum of the sky of Munich, bursting with color, tolling in its shadows. Afterward, especially at home: always deep disappointment. My colors seemed too weak, flat, the study a failed effort to catch the power of nature."[1]

Kandinsky had admired Monet's haystacks in Russia in 1896 at an exhibition of French art. He must have seen works by van Gogh at the Secession exhibitions in Berlin and Munich and would have recognized the dearth of objects in the landscape compositions, large fields of color attenuated in the foreground, and the high horizon line near the top of the painting.

In the Bührle landscape Kandinsky created a unique mood. Sonorous colors project the glow of the evening light, with long, dark shadows. The scene takes on the character of a dream, a kind of mythic reality, underscored by the presence of the rider. The horseman in the landscape heralds Kandinsky's efforts to find a plain, painterly, rhythmic means of expression, which subsequently opened the way to abstraction.   MH

Oil on canvas
52.5 × 55 (20⅝ × 21⅝)
Signed at lower right: KANDINSKY.
Private collection

70   *Races at Longchamp, c. 1897*

70a. Bonnard, *The Cab Horse,* c. 1895, National Gallery of Art, Washington, Ailsa Mellon Bruce Collection.

Horse races have been held at Longchamp in the Bois de Bologne near Paris since 1857. Bonnard, however, seems less interested than Manet and Degas in the racehorses and their breakneck speed. Instead he depicts incidental or peripheral scenes observed within the ranks of the spectators. The horse-drawn carriage is a familiar theme in Paris street scenes, as in Bonnard's *Cab Horse* of c. 1895 (fig. 70 a), where passers-by are defined in outline only, crowding boulevards and plazas. The Bührle painting focuses on one insignificant moment behind the viewing stands, far away from the racecourse barriers, yet we are captivated by the unusual viewpoint and the imaginative palette.

Bonnard had learned from Japanese prints that when objects are truncated at an angle and placed in the foreground, they seem to move the motif closer to the viewer and also partly block out the background. By providing glimpses beyond the man, horse, and carriage that dominate the foreground plane here, Bonnard restores the picture's dynamic spatial depth. Despite the primary figures' proximity to the viewer, the light hues seem to diminish the weight of their bodies and the physical weight of the paint, and this guides the viewer's eye to the background and the fashionable hats of the ladies, the small strolling figures, and the trio of trees that establish contrast in color and rhythm to the bright outlines of the women in the forward carriage.

The humor of Bonnard's pictorial world always lies in his choice of unusual views, the hint of caricature in his forms, and the play of color accents independent of weather and atmosphere. This distinguishes him from the impressionists and establishes his ties with Degas and Toulouse-Lautrec. Bonnard seems to have found the greatest freedom for new artistic interpretation in ordinary, unspectacular motifs.

Maurice Denis has written: "A painting—before it becomes a warhorse, a nude, or some anecdote—is essentially a formal arrangement of color on a flat surface."[1] This famous quote was interpreted visually by the Nabis, following in the footsteps of Gauguin, Bernard, and Serusier. But Bonnard quickly divorced himself from rigorous theories and trusted his intrinsic power of vision. He also discovered the camera, which afforded him not only many images to support his memory but new inspirations from quick shots of subjects that were partly blocked in the foreground. The Bührle painting is closely related to the triptych *The Races at Longchamp* dated 1897 (present location unknown).[2]

MH

Oil on cardboard on wood
30.5 × 42 (12 × 16½)
Signed at lower left corner: Bonnard / 1899
Private collection

Pierre Bonnard 1867–1947

71   *The Luncheon, 1899*

In the 1890s and around the turn of the century Bonnard repeatedly returned to his family home, Grand-Lemps in the Dauphiné, to paint everyday family scenes like this one, with women and children gathered at the table. He observes a fleeting moment, with the children's secret plea to grandmother Mertzdorff and his sister Andrée Terrasse daydreaming.

The young artist had received his first public recognition with posters and humorous illustrations. Among artist friends he was known as "le Nabis japonard." In these spontaneous family scenes he now seems more intensely engaged in the issues of painting, light, and color. The human figure is dematerialized, loses physical presence, in deference to purely formal and painterly qualities.

Bonnard evidently searched for new ways to turn a table into the key element in a picture. The bright surface and oval shape of the table here, seen from above, together with all the colorful components of a meal, determine the formal canon of the painting and define the rhythmic order of the figures grouped around the table. The horizontal and vertical lines of the room, depicted as a flat area, posit a further formal division. The eye-catching red of the fruit stands out as the central point, as though this color were the origin of the entire pictorial idea. It is rivaled by deep blacks, luminous white, and the vivid, painterly pattern of the wallpaper, so that it seems as though the room is vibrating with color, urging our eyes to wander over the entire surface.

The image radiates a curious sensual and dynamic force, and the pictorial elements seem to have taken on an independent value and function. This masterful early work reveals Bonnard's great talent for painting and touches on the themes —figures in interiors— that would occupy him all his life and would lead to ingenious, surprising works of art.   MH

Oil on cardboard
54.5 × 70.5 (21½ × 27¾)
Signed at upper left corner: Bonnard / 1899
Foundation E. G. Bührle Collection

Edouard Vuillard 1868–1940

72 *At the Theater, c. 1898*

Music, literature, and theater belonged to the world of the young generation of painters in the 1890s who called themselves the Nabis (prophets) and pursued their destiny outside the official art schools, succeeding the group of Pont-Aven, the impressionists, and the symbolists. Poster designs, programs, or theater set designs gave them their first opportunities for income and recognition. Work was executed rapidly and sketchily, usually in large format, with glue-based colors that dried quickly. Forms were simplified and stylized, situations heightened through caricature, colors elevated symbolically. One recalls Gauguin's words, proclaimed by Maurice Denis: "That every work of art contain a transposition, a caricature, the passionate equivalent of a received sensation."[1]

The theater was doubly a facilitator of such impressions. The glaring stage lights sharpened outlines and intensified the visual impression of color. When the shy, taciturn Vuillard said of himself: "I was never anything but a spectator,"[2] he directed the viewer's focus over the rows of seats and the heads of the audience to the stage and his work, meaning to evoke the collective atmosphere of the theater, which unites stage and auditorium in one realm of experience. Such scenes of the theater, with both near and far views, had already been realized by Seurat and Degas.

Vuillard, however, departs from the high contrast of the stage lights and transforms the scene into color. The red gowns of the artists and of the decorative sets, which may even be by his own hand, seem the very source of light and flood the room with warm, sensual hues. All activity takes place on the same pictorial plane, and the viewer's eye must move around to grasp it. Form, color, and theme lead to new decorative as well as expressive painting and attain independent pictorial values.

We know that Vuillard as well as Bonnard often worked for the Théâtre Libre, the Théâtre d'Art, or L'Œuvre, but here the location is unidentifiable, which contributes to the anonymity of the scene. The lively, warm colors, the loose, nervous brushstroke, the diffusion of paint over the picture surface all indicate a date in the late 1890s.   MH

Oil on cardboard
49 × 39 (19 ⅜ × 15 ⅝)
Signed at lower right corner: E Vuillard
Foundation E. G. Bührle Collection

Edouard Vuillard   1868–1940

73   *The Visitor, c. 1903*

73a. Vuillard, *The Model in the Studio*, c. 1903–1906, Kimbell Art Museum, Fort Worth.

After 1900 the Nabis began to work more and more independently. Bonnard and Vuillard continued their experiments in painting but looked for subjects more frequently in their intimate circle of family and friends and worked from the model. Their relationship to painting and the object remained spontaneous and based less on theories or symbolic images than was that of Maurice Denis or Paul Serusier. They relied entirely on keen visual and creative abilities. Nothing was too banal to be transformed in a painting.

Vuillard maintained his bachelor existence, renting an apartment in Paris with his mother in March 1988 at 28 rue Truffaut, which he vacated again in October 1904. Often a surviving lease is the only sure way to date works by this artist. The Bührle painting shows Vuillard's studio, where he worked from the model and also occasionally received visitors. The same studio appears in his *Model in the Studio* of c. 1903 (fig. 73a). It also appears in a work by Bonnard of 1899, *Grandmother* (present location unknown), for which Vuillard's mother and her granddaughter served as models.

Vuillard here arrived at a more realistic interpretation of the room as compared with earlier works, where layers of flat, patterned planes defined the space. Here he employs perspective and light falling at an angle to model the objects, which project from the background as sculptural forms. As in *At the Theater* (cat. 72), the impulse for the painting seems to derive from one color, the intense black of the dress, the fireplace, and the bag on the mantelpiece. Black establishes the rich contrasts in the painting and the interlocking structure of the composition. Hard edges contrast with the soft flow of the dress.

Despite the realistic rendering of this scene, abstract values create their own pictorial hierarchy. In addition, the meaning of the picture cannot be interpreted with certainty. The woman's identity is not known, although the man's overcoat and the contemplative, waiting posture of the woman suggest an artist-model relationship. Vuillard has masterfully combined here a brief moment in the model's pose, the solid spatial structure, and the dynamic quality of light to give the painting both stability and movement.   MH

Distemper on paper on canvas
60 × 51 (23⅜ × 20⅛)
Signed at upper right corner: E Vuillard
Foundation E. G. Bührle Collection

74   *The Pont Saint-Michel, Paris, c. 1900*

74a. Matisse, *Pont Saint-Michel,* private collection.

Cityscapes seen from an elevated viewpoint were a specialty of the Nabis and also bring to mind the aged Pissarro, who captured in his paintings of the 1890s the pulsating rhythm of boulevards and quais as seen from the garrets of the city. Around the turn of the century Matisse kept his distance from the bustle of the *Revue Blanche,* then the voice of the avant-garde. As head of a family, he not only had to contend with financial concerns but also strove for artistic independence and was plagued by serious doubts about his own direction.

Matisse and his young wife lived at 19 quai Saint-Michel, and from his studio, he painted the sights of the Seine River—upstream as in *Notre Dame* (The Museum of Modern Art, New York) and downstream as in *The Pont Saint-Michel.* The Bührle painting is probably one of his earliest versions, showing the quai, the bridge, the Palais de Justice with the tip of the Sainte-Chapelle, and from afar, the roofs of the Louvre.

Upon Matisse's return from Toulouse in 1899, he encountered the gray light of Paris, which, in strong contrast to the resplendent colors of the south, must have inspired the silvery harmony in this painting. What catches the eye, however, is not the suffusive haze but the pattern of the bridge, quai, streets, and ships. Through the weight of the clouds, smoke, and roofs, they determine the formal configuration of the painting. The foreground is indicated by one thin, vertical strip at the left, the edge of a house, which is of little consequence to the composition.

Matisse directs the field of vision toward a unified picture plane without obstructions. Although he portrays specific daylight and atmospheric conditions, his focus is already the cityscape itself. Later variations indicate his fascination with the geometric, linear pattern seen through his window (fig. 74a).[1] The focus here is not on the window, with its juxtaposition of interior and exterior, not ephemeral moments, but on the view itself, its inner structure. As he later explained in *Notes d'un peintre*: "A quick impression of a landscape only provides a moment of its existence. I prefer, while insisting on its character, to risk the loss of charm and obtain more stability."[2]

MH

Oil on canvas
60 × 73 (23⅝ × 28¾)
Signed at lower left corner: H. M.
Foundation E. G. Bührle Collection

75   *Guy de Charentonay (recto of no. 76), 1906–1909*

When Gustave Moreau died in 1898 without a successor to his liberal views and stature as a teacher at the Ecole des Beaux-Arts, Rouault and his friends Henri Matisse and Albert Marquet suffered a profound existential crisis. Rouault was left on his own, burdened with great financial worries, and overcome with deep spiritual distress. As he struggled to find new pictorial content and definition, his encounters with characters from the impoverished quarters of Paris pervaded his imagery, replacing the historical topics that academic training had impressed on him. The artistic embodiment of this existential quest is seen in his depictions of the gloomy, stirring creatures who subsist at the edge of society.

The portrait of young Guy de Charentonay is an exception in this series. Three versions exist, of which this is the largest. It is a gripping portrait of enormous internal tension. Distrust, even fear, is expressed in the boy's features, as he looks out of the corner of his eye. The composition of the work, with the protruding wall and the view into more distant areas, is identical to many of Rouault's bordello and circus scenes.

The strikingly modeled head and master draftmanship recall Rouault's academic schooling and his strong commitment to great epochs of the past. Cézanne-like blues dominate. The white collar of the boy in his black clothes seems to illuminate his entire face. Rouault's signature is the same as in his circus scenes, and this portrait evokes the same feeling as his night figures. He is able to portray the child with brief, sketchy brushstrokes. "Drawing is a burst from the awakening mind,"[1] he says. The inner fervor and sympathy of the artist for his subject seem directly imparted through his brush, making him a fauvist as well as an expressionist painter.

The artist's heirs do not know whether or not the work was commissioned. Rouault was acquainted with the family but did not maintain friendly relations.   MH

Graphite, pastel, and gouache on paper
70 × 56 (27⅝ × 22)
Signed at upper right corner:
vague traces of the initials G R painted over
Private collection

76 *Clown with a Big Drum (verso of no. 75), 1906–1909*

76a. Rouault, *Parade,* 1907, Kunstmuseum, Basel.

Circus girls, prostitutes, acrobats, and clowns appear in Rouault's work from 1902–1903 on (fig. 76a). They are creatures of the night, on display under the artificial spotlights of the theater, or patiently waiting in the wings. The artist catches their faces in larger-than-life portraits, though they are more stereotypes than individuals, set on peculiar, ambiguous ground. He renders them anonymously, as confessional representatives of a corrupt world of hopelessness and sorrow. As silent witnesses to Rouault's compassion, they convey both his sympathetic and his accusatory stance. They personify the lineage of Daumier's mordant figures or Toulouse-Lautrec's demi-mondaines.

Rouault's ardent engagement is particularly evident in his clown paintings, culminating in his self-portraits as a clown. Yet Rouault is not so much questioning his artistic existence as trying to establish it within an existential context, rooted in religion, of illusion and reality. In a letter of 1905 he noted: "I clearly saw that the clown was me, it was us. . . . It's life that gives us this rich and spangled costume, we are all more or less clowns, we all wear a spangled costume, but if we are surprised as I surprised the old clown oh! then who will dare say that he is not seized to the very core of his being by an immeasurable pity. To extract one's art from the expression of an old nag of a saltimbanque (man or horse) is crazy pride or perfect humility if one is made for that."[1]

Both this work and the image on the recto (cat. 75) seem rapidly executed, laid down in rudimentary, summary lines and forms expressive of character. The impenetrable strength of these figures and the extraordinary freedom in execution reflect the existential struggle of the artist for his art: "until now my artist's conscience has remained pure . . . but the struggle seems so arduous and so difficult for me that I ask no one to follow me."[2]   MH

Graphite, pastel, and gouache on paper
70 × 56 (27⅝ × 22)
Private collection

77   *Banks of the Seine at Chatou, 1906*

Vlaminck's friendship with André Derain had introduced him to painting and to the circle of the fauves. In April 1906 all of his work was purchased by the art dealer Ambroise Vollard, who had already done the same for Matisse and Derain. This made it possible for Vlaminck to immerse himself completely in the adventure of painting.

While his painter friends left to paint in coastal towns during the summer months— Matisse to Collioure, Marquet and Dufy to Normandy, Derain to England and Estaque—Vlaminck remained faithful to the Seine area, working in Chatou, Bougival, Argenteuil, and Le Pecq. This individualistic, self-taught man, trusting his instinct and his abilities, endeavored to find an autonomous, emotive idiom of painting apart from any existing rules. "I try to paint with body and soul and not pay attention to any style," he told his friends.[1] Vlaminck later even claimed the invention of fauvism as his own. His pictures from 1904/1905, however, show impastoed hues much heightened with white, and only later, under the influence of works by Matisse and Derain in Collioure from the summer of 1905, do purer and thinner applications of paint and more audacious interpretations become apparent in his own work. In 1905 Vlaminck again fell under the spell of van Gogh, whose paintings he had studied at the Salon des Indépendants during a retrospective.

In 1906 a certain calming occurs in the composition and brushwork of Vlaminck, although some inner tension is still evident. He began to employ complementary colors. The trees in the present painting are blue, then red, the fences yellow. Walls and quai are ablaze with the same glowing colors. The hills, bridge, and boat appear in saturated blue, and the leaves of the tree by the river banks turn magically to gold. The topography is still recognizable as the quai of Chatou, though the landscape takes on an extravagant quality, as if drawn from a fantasy. "Alone, the series of colors on the canvas, with all their strength and resonance, could, in orchestrating themselves, translate the colored emotion of this landscape," the artist later recounted.[2]

Almost all paintings by Vlaminck from this period have the same seductive strength. They are the result of an especially happy, unconstricted phase of painting, which clearly attest to the wild, Nordic temperament of the artist in the tradition of van Gogh and at the same time consolidate his mission as a fauve. "Painting, I wanted it to be alive, emotional, tender, fierce, natural like life."[3]   MH

Oil on canvas
54 × 65 (21¼ × 25⅝)
Signed at the verso: Vlaminck
Private collection

Maurice de Vlaminck   1876–1958

78   Still Life with Oranges, 1906/1907

The years 1905–1907 were among the most turbulent and experimental for painters of Vlaminck's generation. Although in 1906 Vlaminck was still very much under
the influence of van Gogh, his style of painting changed toward the end of the year.
His colors remained luminous but turned toward cooler, deeper shades, and his
brushstroke became broader.

Saturated red and blue dominate the present composition, overwhelming the
pallid color of the fruit. Vlaminck here seems to emulate Gauguin in his choice of
color as well as in his flat application of paint. One is reminded of Gauguin's words to
his friend Schuffenecker: "A great feeling can be translated immediately. Meditate
on it, and find in it the simplest form."[1] In the fall of 1906 the Paris Salon presented a
memorial exhibition for Gauguin, which offered a fresh opportunity to examine his
paintings. Their simple, imposing language of form and high-keyed color fields evidently gave Vlaminck's painting new direction. He seems to have recognized a
kindred creative spirit in Gauguin's works: "Between Gauguin and his painting, I
find a frenzied desire for invention, a will to create, at any price, an original style.
Brushes in hand, he searches for what he fails to find in himself."[2]

Vlaminck was also familiar with Cézanne's still lifes and was in the habit of
stopping by Ambroise Vollard's small gallery in the rue Laffitte. The fall Salon of
1907 mounted an homage to Cézanne, who had died recently in Aix-en-Provence.
Impressions merged. Vlaminck probably observed there the close-up focus and the
simple, rhythmic construction of Cézanne's still lifes of everyday household objects.
The various pots in Vlaminck's Bührle still life are still accentuated with highlights
for increased luminosity, and zones of shadows are used to achieve three-dimen-
sionality. But the artist here works out new spatial and pictorial formulas. Compared with his *Still Life with Oranges* of 1906 (formerly Collection Leigh Block,
Chicago), a very similar version, this painting should be dated somewhat later, in
the winter of 1906/1907 at the earliest.   MH

Oil on canvas
45.5 × 55 (18 × 21¾)
Signed at lower left corner: Vlaminck
Foundation E. G. Bührle Collection

Franz Marc 1880–1916

79 *The Dog in Front of the World, 1912*

According to J. A. Schardt, Marc received the inspiration for this painting when he went for a walk in Sindelsdorf. "He and his wife rested on an incline, and next to them sat the dog Russi, who stared quietly and steadily into the scenery so that Marc said: 'I'd like to know for once what goes on inside that dog when he sits there and contemplates the landscape!'"[1]

The collected energy of the seated pose and the sculptural rendering of the dog is continued in the dynamic properties of the countryside. Trees, rocks, and hills seize the vitality of nature in sequences of undulating arcs and flowing lines, which evoke a cosmic configuration. Impelled by Kandinsky's spiritual imagination, Schönberg's music, and the new spatial dynamic in the work of the futurists and orphists, Marc departed from the single vantage point perspective. He looked for internal laws of already highly abstract character to express the substance of the picture. Even though the impression of the hill is preserved—that is, depth is conveyed in the layering of arcs that makes up the hill—Marc describes a moving, streaming force field instead of realistic space. Visual experience seems poeticized, associated with a range of otherworldly color.

Marc made the acquaintance of Robert Delaunay in Paris in the fall of 1912, immersed himself in orphist sensibilities, and further investigated abstract solutions. The Bührle painting should be dated before September 1912, during a phase of intensely intellectual examination of pictorial form, as Marc explained in the magazine *Pan:* "Nature is everywhere, within us and outside us; there is only one thing that is not completely nature, but more its extension and elucidation, and whose power comes from a source unknown to us, and that is art. Art was and is in its essence at all times the boldest departure from nature and naturalness, the bridge into the spiritual realm, the necromancer of humanity. Incomprehension and fear of its new guise we understand, but not criticism."[2] Those words today seem almost uncannily prophetic.   MH

Oil on canvas
111 × 83 (43¾ × 32⅝)
Signed at lower right corner: Marc
Private collection

80 *Mare with Foals, November 1912*

80a. Marc, *Blue Horse II,* 1911, Kunstmuseum, Bern.

In 1912 Marc worked closely with Kandinsky on the publication of the almanac *Der Blaue Reiter.* As Kandinsky remembers it, "we both loved blue, Marc horses, I riders. The name came about all by itself!"[1] In images of animals Marc saw new possibilities to place the organic and rhythmic arrangements found in nature into an existential context based on form and color.

Marc had already observed the new cubist and futurist movements and had seen works by Gauguin and van Gogh in Paris and in exhibitions of the Sonderbund and the Secession. He regularly visited Cassirer in Berlin and Thannhauser in Munich and was familiar with fauve tenets and neo-impressionist color theories. They encouraged the young artist to look beyond mere retinal perception to a more mystical content in his paintings. He wrote to the publisher Reinhard Piper: "I see no happier medium to 'animalize' art, as I would like to call it, than the image of the animal. Therefore I reach for it. . . . My sculpture is a cautious attempt in the same direction. Through multiple parallels and oscillating lines I suggest the circulation of blood in the heads of the two horses. The observer should sense the inner trembling of the animal spirit and not wonder about the breed of the horse. I intentionally eradicated from the horse any trace of a particular breed."[2]

What Marc had learned from working on the small bronzes of 1908/1909, he translated into painting in 1911/1912, placing blue or yellow horses in anonymous landscapes with colorful striations for hills, as in *Blue Horse II* of 1911 (see fig. 80a). The luminosity of the colors and the decorative rendering of animal and landscape are strongly reminiscent of Gauguin's *The White Horse* of 1898 (Musée d'Orsay, Paris). In comparison to Gauguin, however, Marc aimed from the beginning for expressive, forceful lines, exaggerated volume, and strong rhythms. In the Bührle painting he also segmented the pictorial space. His examination of cubism and orphism—he had seen Delaunay in Paris in the fall of 1912—is especially evident in these crystalline forms. The space of the landscape is abandoned in favor of a new geometric order, as revealed in the paintings of late 1912. MH

Oil on canvas
76 × 90 (29⅞ × 35⅜)
Signed at upper right corner: M.
Private collection

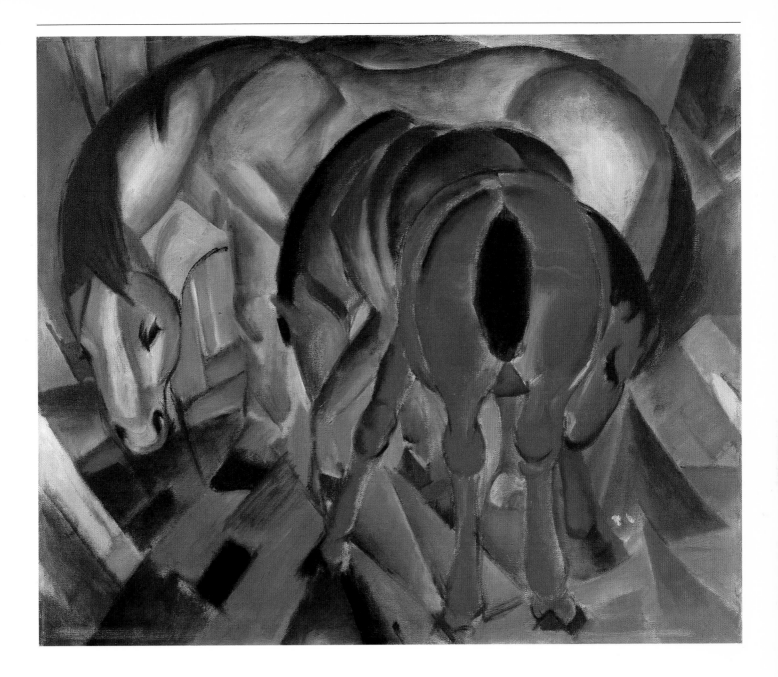

André Derain   1880–1954

81   *The Table, 1904/1905*

This large interior by Derain from the fauve period (1903–1905) has hardly any parallel in his œuvre and is not easily datable. During this time Derain, like his friend Vlaminck, lived in Chatou, a suburb of Paris. In September 1904, after almost three years of military service, he resumed his study of painting. He had followed the Paris art scene with great interest, attending exhibitions at the Salon, and had seen a group of Cézanne's works in 1904. That same year Matisse had his first exhibition at the gallery of art dealer Ambroise Vollard.

The present interior demonstrates an astoundingly unrestrained manner of painting. Colors are applied in a thick impasto and possess a corresponding radiance. The dazzling red seems brushed in heavy strokes over already existing layers of paint. White and ocher are effectively heightened, and dark areas and contours define discrete forms. The style seems infused with violence, as if the artist had attempted to destroy any artistic conventions in a burst of rage.

Derain had seen the van Gogh exhibition at the Bernheim-Jeune Gallery in 1901, and probably the special exhibition of his work in 1905 at the Salon des Indépendants. These paintings were pivotal for the younger generation. Derain's brushstrokes now become bold and uninhibited, his colors rush over the surface of the canvas in vibrating dabs and broken lines. The space is viewed from above, seen as broad chromatic fields of equal value so that planes and volumes correspond to each other without any indication of depth.

This spatial conception, with its fragmented objects and seemingly arbitrary selection of partial views, also recalls the works of the older Nabis and exemplifies how the young Derain had assimilated all the new pictorial definitions and fervently tried to interpret them on his own, as Guillaume Apollinaire attested later: "Derain passionately studied the masters. The copies he made of their work prove the care that he took to know them. At the same time, with unequaled temerity, he passed over all that was most audacious in contemporary art in order to rediscover, with simplicity and freshness, the principles of art and the disciplines that flow from it."[1]

Color and form in the Bührle painting seem unleashed in a state of battle, dating the painting to the winter of 1904/1905, before Derain's collaboration with Matisse at Collioure. There his palette brightened, and he increasingly employed complementary colors and more systematically explored neo-impressionist theories. MH

Oil on canvas
94 × 85 (37 × 33½)
Signed at lower left corner: Derain
Foundation E. G. Bührle Collection

Pablo Picasso   1881–1973

82   *The Italian Girl, 1917*

82a. Picasso, *Harlequin,* 1915, Collection, The Museum of Modern Art, New York, acquired through the Lillie P. Bliss Bequest.

On 17 February 1917 Picasso traveled to Rome with Jean Cocteau for eight weeks, to join Sergey Diaghilev and the troupe of the Ballets Russes and to prepare for a commission he had received for the set design for *Parade.* He rented a studio in the via Margutta with a view of the Villa Medici. The city gave him an opportunity to reacquaint himself with antiquity and classical form.

The artist's creations during World War I reflect a development bordering on figurative abstraction. Stimulated by his work in collage and sculpture, his paintings of that time show striations and layers of flat arrangements of form. One example is his *Harlequin* of late 1915 (see fig. 82a). In these works Picasso retained the structure of the objects despite radical dissection of the form, but he did not take the final step toward complete abstraction, as Kandinsky had done. In Rome he even reapproached realism and made numerous drawings. He is said to have visited many museums and points of interest, usually accompanied by Stravinsky. Cocteau noted: "Antiquity comes alive like new in this Arab Montmartre."[1]

Two large paintings came from Picasso's studio in Rome: *Harlequin* and *Woman with a Necklace* (Musée national d'art moderne, Centre Georges Pompidou, Paris) and *The Italian Girl* in the Bührle Collection. While both works stand out for their strict cubist construction, *The Italian Girl* astonishes with its lively southern colors, used in conjunction with a penetrating black. Baroque formal elements such as a curving marble banister serve as icons, unfolding a highly decorative and at the same time monumental display before our eyes. Roman sculptural architecture is mixed with ornament and exuberant coloring.

Did Picasso find his model for this painting in the streets of Rome, as some sketches suggest? New impressions always conjured up images from the past for Picasso. During his affair with Olga Koklowa the paintings of Ingres resurfaced in his memory. Did the women in Rome remind him of Corot's likenesses? The design commission from Diaghilev introduced a new romanticism and classical opulence to Picasso's work first seen in *The Italian Girl.*   MH

Oil on canvas
149.5 × 101.5 (58⅞ × 40)
Signed at the upper left corner: Picasso / ROME 1917
Foundation E. G. Bührle Collection

83 *The Port of L'Estaque, 1906*

Braque joined the fauves as their last and youngest collaborator and exhibited in the
Salon des Indépendants with his colleagues from 1906 on. His real breakthrough in
the fauve style, however, did not occur until the end of the year when he spent time
in L'Estaque during the winter months. In the summer of 1906 he had worked with
Othon Friesz in Antwerp and Le Havre, where his palette became more luminous.
His composition of the landscape, though, was still based on a well-defined linear
configuration, as in *Ship at Le Havre* of 1905 (Foundation E. G. Bührle Collection).

In 1906 Braque had eagerly absorbed all the impressions of the lively Salon exhibitions in Paris and had probably also seen the Matisse exhibition at Druet. Under
the flood of southern light in L'Estaque near Marseilles, he began painting in a personalized neo-impressionist style. These pictures are comparable to attempts by
Matisse and Derain in the previous year at Collioure. Braque quickly assimilated every new discovery, from Cézanne to Seurat, and all that had been accomplished by
his colleagues. Fauvism at this time had become a recognized, though still debated
style. He later remarked: "Fauve painting had impressed me with what it had that
was new, and that suited me. ... I was twenty-three years old. ... This physical
painting pleased me."[1]

It is difficult to follow the progress in Braque's development, because he later
destroyed many works from this period, but especially in comparison to Derain and
Matisse we can see how liberal his interpretation of divisionist painting theories was
from the beginning. His view of the port at L'Estaque was composed not only by
analyzing light and color and, like Vlaminck, engaging in explosive acts of painting
but also by creating sensuous rhythms of form and color that swirl across the surface in a pattern. It would not be surprising if Braque had painted such works in the
studio. In 1907, under the influence of Gauguin and Cézanne and with his recently
gained expertise in painting, the volume of his color became denser and heavier.
Constructional elements as well as firmer handling of the line subsequently led to his
first pre-cubist paintings.   MH

Oil on canvas
38 × 46 (15 × 18⅛)
Foundation E. G. Bührle Collection

84   *The Violinist, 1911/1912*

84a. Braque, *Woman with a Mandolin,* 1910, Bayerische Staatsgemäldesammlung, Munich.

84b. Braque, *Man with a Guitar,* 1911, Collection, The Museum of Modern Art, New York, acquired through the Lillie P. Bliss Bequest.

In the summer of 1911 Braque worked with Picasso in Céret, a small town in the French Pyrenees. This collaboration is known as one of the happiest and most productive in the history of art. Tirelessly they explored cubist fragmentation and achieved such a closeness that even friends could not always distinguish the work of one from the other. Their pieces show increased faceting in the interpretation of the subject and in the articulation of the painted surface, resulting in linear nets, geometric fields, floating symbols, and incorporeal areas of light and shadow. The sand-colored shades of these paintings mirror the austere rocky vistas of the Pyrenees, sun-drenched in browns and yellows at dusk.

Although these works focus on formal and stylistic concerns, many have personal themes. They are either still lifes or subjects related to music; Braque is said to have been a very talented musician and played many instruments, among them the violin and the accordion. Did Picasso create a monument to Braque in the large *Accordion Player* of 1911 (The Solomon R. Guggenheim Museum, New York)? Is a self-portrait hidden in Braque's *Violinist?* Frequently the dealer D. H. Kahnweiler gave titles to the works of art for the purpose of identification, but the self-contained compositions elude conclusive interpretation.

Musical instruments were often depicted in works by Picasso and Braque. The motif of a woman with a mandolin had appeared in Picasso's œuvre in 1909, inspired by a painting by Corot of this theme. Picasse did an oval variation in 1910,[1] reiterated by Braque as an oval in 1910 (fig. 84a). There, isolated forms and the pose of the woman are still easily readable, whereas in *The Violinist* energetic lines converge at the top, forging a pyramidal construction. Aside from a few remaining cues, the human figure dissolves into the structure of the painting. The face attains a kind of negative value through the concentration of light, while the violin and the structure of the chair retain a certain physical weight. Compared with Braque's *Man with a Guitar* of 1911 (fig. 84b) and *The Portuguese* of 1911 (Kunstmuseum, Basel), his *Violinist* exhibits a previously unseen condensation of form, creating an illusion of depth through clusters of light and the impression of vibrating color, suggesting that Braque made this painting in the winter of 1911/1912.   MH

Oil on canvas
100 × 73 (39⅜ × 28¾)
Signed on the verso: G. Braque
Foundation E. G. Bührle Collection

85   Portrait of Emil G. Bührle, 1951/1952

This portrait, commissioned by the sitter, Emil G. Bührle (1890–1956), shows the industrialist and art collector in the office of his company in Zurich-Oerlikon. Holding a sheaf of papers in his right hand and raising his left, he seems to regard the observer with calm and watchful eyes. The papers allude to Bührle's status as a businessman, and the works of art represent his love of paintings and sculpture.

On the left, in a prominent position, stands a late Egyptian royal portrait bust, once part of a full-length statue. It is carved of black diorite with a classically tied royal (Nemes) headdress and what appears to be an apotropaic sacred asp. On the back wall is a landscape of Lake Geneva by Ferdinand Hodler, painted by the artist in the fall of 1912 from the window of the sickroom of his beloved friend Valentine Godé-Darel.

Kokoschka, a contemporary of Emil Bührle's, began this portrait in early November 1951. Painting every morning in sessions that lasted up to six hours, he had hoped to finish before the end of the month, but the project extended until Christmas: "He [E. Bührle] has high praise for it, but he also notices where it needs improvement."[1] Convinced that he had completed the portrait, Kokoschka returned to London on 26 December, St. Stephen's Day. Yet Bührle was not entirely satisfied with the result, and Kokoschka had to briefly rework the painting in April 1952 before Bührle accepted ownership on 1 May.

Kokoschka, unlike most twentieth-century artists, overwhelmingly preferred portrait painting to landscapes. At the beginning of the 1950s three out of five of his paintings were portraits. Typical of the artist's late portraits is a sketchiness that replaces the exactitude of earlier works. Despite the looseness of its execution, however, the Bührle portrait achieves a solid, stable composition through its emphasis of diagonals. Broad, sweeping brushstrokes define the setting in brilliant colors, with shades of blue and turquoise accentuating Bührle's gray suit and recurring in the Egyptian sculpture. The brushstrokes fuse into a subtly differentiated web of colors in this arresting portrait.   CB

Oil on canvas
125 × 90 (49¼ × 35⅜)
Signed at bottom, left of center: O K
Private collection

Appendix

The six most important exhibitions of the Emil G. Bührle Collection and their abbreviations:

Zurich 1958 = *Sammlung Emil G. Bührle,* Kunsthaus, Zurich, June—September 1958.

Berlin 1958 = *Französische Malerei von Manet bis Matisse,* Schloss Charlottenburg, Berlin, October—November 1958.

Munich 1958–1959 = *Hauptwerke der Sammlung Emil Georg Bührle,* Haus der Kunst, Munich, December 1958—February 1959.

Edinburgh and London 1961 = *Masterpieces of French Painting from the Bührle Collection,* The Royal Scottish Academy, Edinburgh, August—September 1961; The National Gallery, London, September—November 1961.

Lucerne 1963 = *Sammlung Emil Georg Bührle, Französische Meister von Delacroix bis Matisse,* Kunstmuseum, Lucerne, August—October 1963.

Frans Hals
1 Portrait of a Man

PROVENANCE: Earl of Cowper, Panshanger; Lady Cowper, Panshanger; Lord Desborough, Panshanger; N. Katz, Basel; purchased by Bührle in 1946.

EXHIBITIONS: *Exhibition of Dutch Art, 1450–1900*, Royal Academy of Arts, London, 1929, no. 109; *Dutch Old Masters*, Art Gallery, Manchester, 1929, no. 41; *Europäische Kunst 13.–20. Jahrhundert*, Kunsthaus, Zurich, 1950, 21, pl. 6; *Drie Eeuwen Portret in Nederland*, Rijksmuseum, Amsterdam, 1952, no. 53; *Holländer des 17. Jahrhunderts*, Kunsthaus, Zurich, 1953, no. 49; Zurich 1958, no. 68; Munich 1958–1959, no. 85, ill.; *Im Lichte Hollands*, Kunstmuseum, Basel, 1987, no. 38.

LITERATURE: Wilhelm von Bode, *Studien zur Geschichte der holländischen Malerei* (Brunswick, 1883), 92, no. 152; Ernst Wilhelm Moes, *Frans Hals, sa vie et son œuvre* (Brussels, 1909), no. 161; Cornelis Hofstede de Groot, *Beschreibendes und kritisches Verzeichnis der Werke der hervorragendsten holländischen Maler des XVII. Jahrhunderts*, 10 vols. (Esslingen, 1907–1928), 3: no. 283; Wilhelm von Bode and M. J. Binder, *Frans Hals, sein Leben und seine Werke*, 2 vols. (Berlin, 1914), 2: no. 278, ill.; Wilhelm R. Valentiner, *Frans Hals, Klassiker der Kunst* 28 (Stuttgart and Berlin, 1921), no. 276 (2d rev. ed., 1923, no. 292); Numa S. Trivas, *The Paintings of Frans Hals* (London and New York, 1941), no. 106, fig. 138; E. Hüttinger, *Holländische Malerei im XVII. Jahrhundert* (Zurich, 1956), 31–32; Manuel Gasser and Willy Rotzler, *Kunstschätze in der Schweiz: Hundert Meisterwerke der Malerei, der Skulptur und des Kunstgewerbes in öffentlichen, kirchlichen und privaten Sammlungen der Schweiz* (Zurich, 1964), no. 52; Seymour Slive, *Frans Hals*, 3 vols. (London, 1970–1974), 1:208; 2: pls. 336, 339; 3:111, no. 219; Claus Grimm, *Frans Hals* (Berlin, 1972), 120, no. 168; *Foundation Emil G. Bührle Collection* (Zurich and Munich, 1973), no. 153.

Jan van Goyen
2 The Castle Montfoort

NOTES: 1. Both Montfoort and IJsselstein Castles were located along the idyllic Hollandse IJssel river in the province of Utrecht. The Castle Montfoort, founded in the twelfth century, was largely destroyed by the French when Louis XIV invaded the Netherlands in 1672. Only an entrance building and part of the walls with one polygonal tower are still extant. / 2. Beck 1972–1987, 2: nos. 690 and 693.

PROVENANCE: Probably First Lord Manvers; Captain Arthur Campbell, London; sale, Christie's, London, 23 April 1904, no. 18; Dr. E. Hölscher, Mühlheim-Rhine; sale, Berlin (Lepke), 5 December 1916, no. 31; K. W. Bachstitz, The Hague (cat. 1, fig. 89); J. F. H. Menten, Zurich-Lausanne, 1919; purchased by Bührle in 1946.

EXHIBITIONS: *Europäische Kunst 13.–20. Jahrhundert*, Kunsthaus, Zurich, 1950, 21; *Holländer des 17. Jahrhunderts*, Kunsthaus, Zurich, 1953, no. 35; *Alte Meister aus der Sammlung E. G. Bührle*, Schloss Jegenstorf, 1955, no. 6; Zurich 1958, no. 73; Munich 1958–1959, no. 79.

LITERATURE: Cornelis Hofstede de Groot, *Beschreibendes und kritisches Verzeichnis der Werke der hervorragendsten holländischen Maler des XVII. Jahrhunderts*, 10 vols. (Esslingen, 1907–1928), 8: no. 165; Hans-Ulrich Beck, *Jan van Goyen*, 3 vols. (Amsterdam and Doornspijk, 1972–1987), 2: 315, no. 691.

Pieter Jansz. Saenredam
3 Interior of the St. Bavo Church, Haarlem

NOTE: 1. Construction of the St. Bavo Church began in 1328 and continued until 1538, with many later changes and additions.

PROVENANCE: D. Katz, Dieren (1934); J. H. Smidt van Gelder, Arnhem; F. Nathan, Zurich; purchased by Bührle in 1955.

EXHIBITIONS: *Schilderijen en teekeningen Pieter Jansz. Saenredam 1597–1665*, Museum Boymans, Rotterdam, 1937–1938, no. 7, fig. 5; *17e Eeuwse Meesters uit Gelders Bezit*, Gemeentemuseum, Arnhem, 1953, no. 57; Zurich 1958, 69, no. 77, fig. 21; Munich 1958–1959, no. 144; *Pieter Jansz. Saenredam*, Centraal Museum, Utrecht, 1961, no. 46, ill.; *Im Lichte Hollands*, Kunstmuseum, Basel, 1987, no. 88.

LITERATURE: P. T. A. Swillens, *Pieter Janszoon Saenredam, Schilder van Haarlem, 1597–1665* (Amsterdam, 1935), no. 96, fig. 87; Walter A. Liedtke, *Architectural Painting in Delft* (Doornspijk, 1982), 152 n. 152; Saskia Nihom-Nijstad, *Reflèts du siècle d'or*, Institut Néerlandais (Paris, 1983), 121; *Foundation Emil G. Bührle Collection* (Zurich and Munich, 1973), no. 165.

Aelbert Cuyp
4 Thunderstorm over Dordrecht

NOTE: 1. Beckett 1962–1969, 3: 118–119.

PROVENANCE: Collection of the Tollemache family, Ham House, England, since the seventeenth century; Earl of Landerdale, Ham House; Earl of Dysart, Ham House; Sir Lionel Tollemache, Ham House; Marlborough Fine Art, London; purchased by Bührle in 1954.

EXHIBITIONS: *Alte Meister aus der Sammlung E. G. Bührle*, Schloss Jegenstorf, 1955, no. 4; Zurich 1958, no. 76, ill.; Munich 1958–1959, no. 33; *Schok der Herkenning*, Mauritshuis, The Hague, 1970–1971, no. 61; *Shock of Recognition*, The Tate Gallery, London, 1971, no. 54.

LITERATURE: Charles Roundell, *Ham House: Its History and Art Treasures*, 2 vols. (London, 1904), 2:105; Cornelis Hofstede de Groot, *Beschreibendes und kritisches Verzeichnis der Werke der hervorragendsten holländischen Maler des XVII. Jahrhunderts*, 10 vols. (Esslingen, 1907–1928), 2: no. 708; G. F. Hartlaub, "Der Blitz in der Kunst," *Atlantis* 27 (1955): 84; Ronald B. Beckett, *John Constable's Correspondence*, 4 vols. (Ipswich, 1962–1969), 3: 118–119; Stephen Reiss, *Aelbert Cuyp* (London, 1975), 55, no. 27, pl. 4; *Foundation Emil G. Bührle Collection* (Zurich and Munich, 1973), no. 151.

Willem van Aelst
5 Hunting Still Life with Dead Partridge

PROVENANCE: Private collection, Germany; F. Nathan, Zurich; purchased by Bührle in 1955.

EXHIBITIONS: Zurich 1958, no. 83.

Pieter de Hooch
6 The Cardplayers

PROVENANCE: Probably sale, Amsterdam, 24 November 1806, no. 30; sale, Christie's, London, 1819; sale, P. van Cuyck, Hôtel Drouot, Paris, 17 February 1866, no. 47; sale, Auguiot, Hôtel Drouot, Paris, 1 March 1875, no. 12; Isaac Pereire, Paris, 1911; Gustave Pereire, Paris; Alfred Pereire, Paris; Wildenstein and Company, New York, 1933–1941; purchased by Bührle in 1953.

EXHIBITIONS: *Five Centuries of European Painting*, Los Angeles, 1933, no. 16; *Avery Memorial Opening Loan Exhibition*, Wadsworth Atheneum, Hartford, 1934, no. 25; *Vermeer: oorsprong en invloed: Fabritius, De Hooch, De Witte*, Museum Boymans, Rotterdam, 1935, no. 34; *Vermeer Tentoonstelling*, Rijksmuseum, Amsterdam, 1935, no. 152a; *Seventh Anniversary Exhibition of German, Flemish and Dutch Painting*, Nelson Gallery of Art, Kansas City, 1940–1941, no. 28; *Holländer des 17. Jahrhunderts*, Kunsthaus, Zurich, 1953; *Alte Meister aus der Sammlung E. G. Bührle*, Schloss Jegenstorf, 1955, no. 49; Zurich 1958, no. 80; Munich 1958–1959, no. 86.

LITERATURE: John Smith, *A Catalogue Raisonné of the Works of the Most Eminent Dutch, Flemish and French Painters*, 9 vols. (London, 1829–1849), 4: no. 26; William Thoré-Bürger, "Van der Meer de Delft." *Gazette des beaux-arts* 21 (1866): 550, no. 12; Henry Havard, "Pieter de Hooch." *L'Art et les artistes hollandais* 3 (1880): 131; Cornelis Hofstede de Groot, *Beschreibendes und kritisches Verzeichnis der Werke der hervorragendsten holländischen Maler des XVII. Jahrhunderts*, 10 vols. (Esslingen, 1907–1928), 1: no. 264; Clotilde Brière-Misme, "Tableaux inédits ou peu connus de Pieter de Hooch," *Gazette des beaux-arts* 15 (1927): 372–374, ill.; Wilhelm R. Valentiner, *Pieter de Hooch, Klassiker der Kunst* 35 (Berlin and Leipzig, 1929), 269–270, ill.; C. H. Collins Baker, "De Hooch or not De Hooch?" *The Burlington Magazine* 57 (1930): 198; Wilhelm R. Valentiner, "Zum 300. Geburtstag Jan Vermeers, Oktober 1932. Vermeer und die Meister der holländischen Genremalerei," *Pantheon* 10 (1932): 318, fig. 198; Lawrence Gowing, *Vermeer* (London, 1952), 108–109, no. 59, ill.; Roland E. Fleischer, "Ludolf de Jongh and the Early Work of Pieter de Hooch," *Oud-Holland* 92 (1978): 56, fig. 15; Peter C. Sutton, *Pieter De Hooch* (Oxford, 1980), 23, 43, 81, no. 25, pl. 22.

Giovanni Battista Tiepolo
7 Diana Bathing

NOTES: 1. Cf. Hüttinger 1958, 218. / 2. Ovid, *Metamorphoses*, 3:138. / 3. Piovene and Pallucchini 1968, nos. 15 and 19 B. / 4. Hüttinger 1958, 219. / 5. Ovid, *Metamorphoses*, 2:409.

PROVENANCE: Count Francesco Algarotti, Venice; Bonomo Algarotti; Countess Algarotti-Corniani; Maurice de Rothschild, New York; purchased by Bührle in 1956 from Dr. A. Kauffmann, London.

EXHIBITIONS: Zurich 1958, no. 86; Munich 1958–1959, no. 156.

LITERATURE: Eduard Hüttinger, "Bad der Diana," *Arte Veneta* 12 (1958): 218–220, ill.; Guido Piovene and Anna Pallucchini, *L'opera completa di Giambattista Tiepolo* (Milan, 1968), no. 210; Michael Levey, *Giambattista Tiepolo: His Life and Art* (New Haven and London, 1986), 132–133, ill.; *Foundation Emil G. Bührle Collection*, 2d ed. (Zurich and Munich, 1986), no. 148, ill.

Antonio Canal, or Il Canaletto
8 Santa Maria della Salute

NOTES: 1. Constable 1976, no. 171. / 2. Constable 1976, nos. 162, 172, 224, 251 a, 258 a, 341, and 351. / 3. Constable 1976, nos. 251 a and 258 a.

PROVENANCE: Dukes of Buccleuch, Dalkeith Palace near Edinburgh; E. Speelman, London, 1952; purchased by Bührle in 1953 from Marlborough Fine Art Ltd., London.

EXHIBITIONS: *Royal Academy Exhibition in the British Institute*, London, 1840, no. 103(?); 1860, no. 50(?); *Alte Meister aus der Sammlung Bührle, Zürich*, Schloss Jegenstorf, Bern, 1955, no. 31; *Schönheit des 18. Jahrhunderts*, Kunsthaus, Zurich, 1955, no. 59; Zurich 1958, no. 87; Munich 1958–1959, no. 9.

LITERATURE: Eduard Hüttinger, *Venezianische Malerei* (Zurich, 1959), 73, ill. 96; *Schätze aus Museen und Sammlungen in Zürich* (Zurich, 1969), 296; W. G. Constable, *Canaletto: Giovanni Antonio Canal,* 2d ed. (Oxford, 1976), 1:119 n. 1; 2: no. 172; André Corboz, *Canaletto; Una Venezia immaginaria* (Milan, 1985), 1:240, 251; 2: no. P183; *Foundation Emil G. Bührle Collection,* 2d ed. (Zurich and Munich, 1986), no. 141, ill.

Antonio Canal, or Il Canaletto
9 The Grand Canal

NOTES: **1.** Constable 1976, nos. 162, 172, 224, 251 a, 258 a, 341, and 351. / **2.** Constable 1976, no. 223.

PROVENANCE: Dukes of Buccleuch, Dalkeith Palace near Edinburgh, E. Speelman, London, 1952; purchased by Bührle in 1953 from Marlborough Fine Art Ltd., London.

EXHIBITIONS: London 1840, no. 76(?); Bern 1955, no. 30; Zurich 1955, no. 58; Zurich 1958, no. 88; Munich 1958–1959, no. 10.

LITERATURE: Constable 1976, 2: no. 224; Corboz 1985, 2: no. P182; *Foundation Emil G. Bührle Collection,* 1986, no. 142.

Jean-Baptiste Greuze
10 Portrait of the Painter Laurent Pécheux

NOTE: **1.** In Rome Pécheux came under the influence of Anton Raphael Mengs, an early practitioner of the new, international classicism, and Pompeo Batoni, who made a specialty of painting portraits of foreigners on the Grand Tour.

PROVENANCE: Galerie Wildenstein, Paris; purchased by Bührle in 1941.

LITERATURE: Jean Martin and Charles Masson, "Catalogue raisonné de l'œuvre peint et dessiné de J.-B. Greuze," in Camille Mauclair, *Jean-Baptiste Greuze* (Paris, 1906), no. 1,201; Luigi Cesare Bollea, *Lorenzo Pécheux* (Turin, 1936); Edgar Munhall, *Jean-Baptiste Greuze, 1725–1805* [exh. cat., Wadsworth Atheneum] (Hartford, Conn., 1976–1977); Brigitte Zehmisch, in *Foundation Emil G. Bührle Collection,* 2d ed. (Zurich and Munich, 1986), no. 1.

Francisco Goya
11 Procession in Valencia

NOTES: **1.** *Catalogue des tableaux anciens des écoles espagnole, italienne, flamande, et hollandaise, composant la galerie de M. le Marquis de Salamanca* (Paris, 1867). / **2.** Marginal notes in the copy of the catalogue in the Frick Reference Library give the prices as 3,600 French francs for the *Bullfight* and 2,500 for the *Procession.* / **3.** Xavier de Salas, "Sur les tableaux de Goya qui appartinrent à son fils," *Gazette des Beaux-Arts* 63 (1964): 99–110. / **4.** Gassier and Wilson 1971, nos. 253, 967, 1,626. / **5.** Francis George Very, *The Spanish Corpus Christi Procession: A Literary and Folkloric Study* (Valencia, 1962), 107. / **6.** Nigel Glendinning, "El Asno Cargado de Reliquias in los *Desastres de la Guerra* de Goya," *Archivo Español de Arte* 35 (1962): 221–230; George Levitine, "Goya, les emblêmes, et la revanche de l'âne portant des reliques," *Gazette des Beaux-Arts* 93 (April 1978), 173–178. / **7.** Janis Tomlinson, "'Goya y lo Popular' Revisited: On the Iconography of *The Wedding,*" *Pantheon* 42 (1984), 23–29.

PROVENANCE: Collection of Mariano (or Javier?) Goya; sale, Collection of the Marqués de Salamanca, Paris, 3–6 June 1867; Collection of Baron van der Heyden and Hauzeur, London, by 1925; Collection of the Viscountess Kemsley, London; purchased by Bührle in 1955.

EXHIBITIONS: *Spanish Paintings, Ancient and Modern,* London, 1920–1921, no. 129A; *Exposition d'Art ancien espagnol, organisée par la Demeure historique,* Hôtel Jean Charpentier, Paris, 1925, no. 30; Zurich 1958, no. 98.

LITERATURE: Jutta Held, *Farbe und Licht in Goyas Malerei* (Berlin, 1964), 191–192 (questions attribution to Goya); Pierre Gassier and Juliet Wilson, *The Life and Complete Work of Francisco Goya* (New York, 1971), 249, no. 952; *Foundation E. G. Bührle Collection* (Zurich and Munich, 1973), 328–329; Marianne H. Takács, "Scènes de genre de Goya à la vente de la collection Kaunitz en 1820," *Bulletin du Musée Hongrois des Beaux-Arts* 44 (1975), 107–121.

Jean-Auguste-Dominique Ingres
12 Portrait of Monsieur Devillers

NOTES: **1.** Most of the official uniforms worn by imperial civil servants were already in use during the Consulate (1799–1804). Embroidered motifs, such as the ears of wheat, identified the wearer's profession, whereas the amount of embroidery denoted his rank. See Delpierre 1958, 5 and 22 n. 50. / **2.** Naef 1977–1980, 4: no. 77. / **3.** Naef 1977–1980, 4: no. 78.

PROVENANCE: Collection Lang, Galerie Bernheim jeune, Paris (from 1911); with a New York dealer, then a Zurich dealer; purchased by Bührle in 1955.

EXHIBITIONS: Paris, Salon of 1814(?); *Ingres,* Galerie G. Petit, Paris, 1911, no. 17; *Französische Kunst des 19. und 20. Jahrhunderts,* Kunsthaus, Zurich, 1917, no. 116; *Exposition Ingres,* Hôtel de la chambre syndicale de la curiosité et des beaux-arts, Paris, 1921, no. 16; *Udstillingen af fransk Malerkunst fra den første Halvdel af det 19 Aarhundrede,* Ny Carlsberg Glyptotek, Copenhagen, 1928, no. 91; *Cent Ans de portrait français,* Galerie Bernheim jeune, Paris, 1934, no. 46; *Les Artistes français en Italie,* Musée des Arts Décoratifs, Paris, 1934, no. 214; *Quelques Tableaux d'Ingres à Gauguin,* Galerie Bernheim-Jeune, Paris, 1935; *Exposicion de Pintura Francesa,* Montevideo, Uruguay, 1940, no. 42; *The Painting of France since the French Revolution,* M. H. de Young Memorial Museum, San Francisco, 1940–1941, no. 58; Zurich 1958, no. 102; Edinburgh and London 1961, no. 1.

LITERATURE: Henry Lapauze, *Ingres: sa vie et son œuvre* (Paris, 1911), 111–114, 156–157; Georges Wildenstein, *Ingres* (London, 1956), no. 79; Madeleine Delpierre, "Les Costumes de cour et les uniformes civils du premier Empire," *Bulletin du Musée Carnavalet* 11 (November 1958), 2–23; Eduard Hüttinger, *Sammlung Emil G. Bührle* [exh. cat., Kunsthaus] (Zurich, 1958), no. 102; Douglas Cooper, *Masterpieces of French Painting from the Bührle Collection* [exh. cat., The National Gallery] (London, 1961), no. 1; Hans Naef and Charles Lerch, "Ingres et M. Devillers," *Bulletin du Musée Ingres,* no. 15 (September 1964), 5–14; *Ingres* [exh. cat., Petit Palais] (Paris, 1967–1968); Daniel Ternois and Ettore Camesasca, *Tout l'Œuvre peint d'Ingres* (Paris, 1971), no. 66; Hans Naef, *Die Bildniszeichnungen von J.-A.-D. Ingres,* 5 vols. (Bern, 1977–1980), 1:255–261, and 4: nos. 77, 78; Leopold Reidemeister, in *Foundation Emil G. Bührle Collection,* 2d ed. (Zurich and Munich, 1986), no. 5.

Camille Corot
13 A Girl Reading

NOTES: **1.** Bazin 1973, 61. / **2.** Asselineau 1851, 54. This visitor may well have seen *A Girl Reading* in Corot's studio.

PROVENANCE: Sale, Collection Bascle, Paris, 1883; purchased by Bührle in 1948.

EXHIBITIONS: *Maîtres modernes,* Galerie Durand-Ruel, Paris, 1878, no. 115; *Europäische Kunst, 13.–20. Jahrhundert,* Kunsthaus, Zurich, 1950, no. 23; Biennale, Venice, 1952, no. 20; *Europäische Meister 1790–1910,* Kunstmuseum Winterthur, 1955, no. 47; Zurich 1958, no. 119; *Corot,* Kunstmuseum, Bern, 1960, no. 43; Edinburgh and London 1961, no. 2; Lucerne 1963, no. 4.

LITERATURE: Charles Asselineau, "Intérieurs d'Atelier: C. Corot," *L'Artiste* 7 (15 September 1851): 53–55; Alfred Robaut, *L'Œuvre de Corot: Catalogue raisonné,* 4 vols. (Paris, 1905), 2: no. 393; Etienne Moreau-Nélaton, "L'Histoire de Corot et de ses œuvres," in Robaut 1905, 1; Eduard Hüttinger, *Sammlung Emil G. Bührle* [exh. cat., Kunsthaus] (Zurich, 1958), no. 119; Douglas Cooper, *Masterpieces of French Painting from the Bührle Collection* [exh. cat., The National Gallery] (London, 1961), no. 2; *Figures de Corot* [exh. cat., Musée du Louvre] (Paris, 1962); Germain Bazin, *Corot* (Paris, 1973); Antje Zimmermann, "Studien zum Figurenbild bei Corot" (diss., University of Cologne, 1986), 150–152; Jean Selz, *La Vie et l'œuvre de Camille Corot* (Paris, 1988), 134–136.

Eugène Delacroix
14 A Turkish Officer Killed in the Mountains

NOTES: **1.** Johnson 1981–1986, 1: no. 113. / **2.** André Joubin, *Journal de Eugène Delacroix,* 3 vols. (Paris, 1932), 1: 99. / **3.** Escholier 1926, 1: opp. p. 182; Johnson 1981–1986, 1: no. 138; and Delteil 1908, no. 55. / **4.** Lord Byron, "The Giaour," in *Byron,* ed. Jerome McGann (Oxford, 1986), lines 668, 659–660. / **5.** The *palampore* also appeared in Thomas Stothard's 1814 illustration of Hassan's death, which Delacroix may have known. Géricault's print (Delteil 1924, no. 95), made after an oil sketch that is now lost (Eitner 1983, 358 n. 108), was published in October 1824. / **6.** See also the almost contemporary painting *The Execution of Marino Faliero* (1826, Wallace Collection, London).

PROVENANCE: Sale, H. Didier, Paris, 3 May 1849; M. J. Leroy, Paris; sale, Arsène Houssaye, Paris, 29 March 1854; sale; Paris, anonymous, 8 May 1861; sale, Barthélemy, Paris, 14 December 1871; to M. Brun-Rodrigues; sale, Ad. Liebermann, Paris, 8 May 1876; sale, Baron de Beurnonville, 29 April 1880; Baron d'Erlanger, Paris; sale, Leo d'Erlanger and Gerald d'Erlanger, London, 25 March 1946; to Messrs. Tooth; sold by them to Mrs. A. E. Pleydell-Bouverie, London (1949); purchased by Bührle in 1952 from an English dealer.

EXHIBITIONS: Galerie Lebrun, Paris, 1826, no. 47 (as *Un officier turc tué dans les montagnes)?*; *Anthology,* Galerie Tooth & Son, London, 1949, no. 9 (as *Mort de Hassan*); *Landscape in French Art, 1550–1900,* Royal Academy of Arts, London, 1949–1950, no. 190; *Eugène Delacroix,* Wildenstein and Company, London, 1952, no. 10; *Europäische Meister 1790–1910,* Kunstmuseum, Winterthur, 1955, no. 68; Biennale, Venice, 1956, no. 5; Zurich 1958, no. 112; *Centenaire d'Eugène Delacroix,* Musée du Louvre, Paris, 1963, no. 60; *Eugène Delacroix,* Kunsthaus, Zurich, 1987–1988 (as *Un officier turc tué dans les montagnes*).

LITERATURE: Adolphe Moreau, *E. Delacroix et son œuvre* (Paris, 1873), 224; Alfred Robaut, *L'Œuvre complet de Eugène Delacroix* (Paris, 1885), no. 201; Loys Delteil, *Le Peintre-graveur illustré: Ingres et Delacroix* (Paris, 1908), no. 55; Loys Delteil, *Le Peintre-graveur illustré: Théodore Géricault* (Paris, 1924), no. 95; Raymond Escholier, *Delacroix: Peintre, Graveur, Ecrivain,* 3 vols. (Paris, 1926), vol. 1; George Heard Hamilton, "Delacroix, Byron, and the English Illustrators," *Gazette des Beaux-Arts,* 6th ser., 36 (October-December 1949): 261–278; Lee Johnson, "Delacroix at the Biennale," *The Burlington Magazine* 98 (September 1956): 327; Eduard Hüttinger, *Sammlung Emil G. Bührle* [exh. cat., Kunsthaus] (Zurich, 1958), no. 112; Maurice Serullaz, *Mémorial de l'exposition Eugène Delacroix* [exh. cat., Musée du Louvre] (Paris, 1963), no. 74; Lee Johnson, "The Delacroix Centenary in France—II," *The Burlington Magazine* 106 (June 1964): 259–265; Paul Joannides, "Colin, Delacroix, Byron, and the Greek War of Independence," *The Burlington Magazine* 125 (August 1983): 495–500; Lorenz Eitner, *Géricault: His Life and Work* (London, 1983); Lee Johnson, *The Paintings of Eugène Delacroix: A Critical Catalogue,* 4 vols. (Oxford, 1981–1986), 1: no. 113.

Eugène Delacroix
15 Arab Musicians

NOTES: **1.** Letter to Frédéric Villot, 29 February 1832, *Selected Letters* 1971. / **2.** Letter to Villot, 29 February 1832, *Selected Letters* 1971. / **3.** Johnson 1981–1986, 3: no. 380.

PROVENANCE: Sale, Collection Demidoff, Paris, 13 January 1863; to M. Bouruet-Aubertot; sale, Collection Duval, Paris, 13 June 1872; sale, Collection Faure, Paris, 7 June 1873; sale, Collection Mme R. F., Paris, 17 March 1876; sale, Collection Marmontel, Paris, 1883; sale, Collection Tabourier, Paris, 20–22 June 1898; Galerie de Hauke, New York; Jacques Seligmann and Company; purchased by Bührle in 1953.

EXHIBITIONS: *Exposition Eugène Delacroix;* Ecole des Beaux-Arts, Paris, 1885, no. 303; *Exposition Eugène Delacroix,* Musée du Louvre, Paris, 1930, no. 375; *Delacroix au Maroc,* Orangerie, Paris, 1933, no. 217; *North Africa Interpreted by European Artists,* The Fogg Museum, Cambridge, Mass., 1943, p. 5; *Eugène Delacroix,* Wildenstein and Company, New York, 1944, no. 75; *French Painting from David to Courbet,* The Detroit Institute of Arts, 1950, no. 37; Zurich 1958, no. 113; Paris 1963, no. 232.

LITERATURE: Robaut 1885, no. 630; Hüttinger 1958, no. 113; Serullaz 1963, no. 390; J. Steward, ed., *Eugène Delacroix: Selected Letters, 1813–1863* (London, 1971); Johnson 1981–1986, 3: 191.

Honoré Daumier
16 The Free Performance

NOTES: **1.** Maison 1968, 2:46, 1:206. Maison places the picture in the part of his catalogue raisonné devoted to paintings "with restorations so extensive that they may have decisively altered the appearance of part or the whole of a composition." / **2.** The Maryland Institute, Baltimore (Lucas Collection), on permanent loan to the Walters Art Gallery (Maison 1968, 1:72). / **3.** Quoted in L. Rosenthal, *Daumier* (Paris, n.d.), 99–100: "Aucun mot ne pourrait donner une idée exacte de la diversité de ces physionomies qu'absorbe, qu'allume, qu'excite, qu'affraye, qu'amuse le jeu de la scène. La pose affaissée ou tendu, le jeu des muscles, la distraction des regards, la flamme des prunelles, tout ce qui fait travailler un corps et penser un cerveau est saisi dans son infinie mobilité, fixé avec un art incomparable de l'observation morale et des conditions physiologiques…" Burty continues, "les cadres étroits seront un jour sans prix. On y retrouvera je ne dis pas l'habit de nos contemporains, de nos femmes, de nos enfants, mais leur visage et leur émotion pendant un court moment de la vie vecue" (these narrow frames will one day be priceless. One will find in them, I declare, not the clothes of our contemporaries, of our wives, of our children, but their faces and their emotions during a brief moment of life lived as it is). / **4.** L. Delteil, *Le Peintre-graveur illustré: Honoré Daumier* (Paris, 1925), nos. 2905, 3262, 3266. / **5.** One, a crayon and wash (sale, Palais Galliera, Paris, 30 May 1967, no. 4; Maison 1968, 493), shows three bourgeois spectators leaning eagerly to the left to observe a drama performed beyond the edge of the composition. The other, a small pen and ink drawing (heightened with white; private collection, Basel; Maison 1968, 495), is more plebeian as regards the social status of its subjects, but it similarly depicts them in a tight cluster that presses forward to see a drama conducted off the lower left side of the paper.

PROVENANCE: Durand-Ruel, Paris (until 1900); Collection D. A. Wanklyn, Montreal; Silbermann, New York; purchased by Bührle in 1954 through an American dealer. Maison records a purchase date by Bührle of 1960; see Maison 11-46.

EXHIBITIONS: Zurich 1958, no. 122; *De Géricault à Matisse, Chefs-d'œuvre français des collections suisses,* Petit Palais, Paris, 1959, no. 38.

LITERATURE: E. Klossowski, *Daumier* (Munich, 1908), 92, pl. 43a; A. Fontainas, *La Peinture de Daumier* (Paris, 1923), ill.; Raymond Escholier, *Daumier* (Paris, 1923), 151, A. 1930, pl. 17; ed. 1938, opp. 158; M. Sadleir, *Daumier* (London, 1924), pl. 13; E. Fuchs, *Der Maler Daumier* (Munich, 1927), no. 137; J. Lassaigne, *Daumier* (Paris, 1938), pl. 139; ed. 1947, pl. 139; B. Fleischmann, *Honoré Daumier: Gemälde und Graphik* (Vienna, 1937), pl. 35; M. Sachs, *Honoré Daumier* (Paris, 1935; French ed., Vienna, 1937), pl. 35; M. Fischer, *Daumier* (Bern, 1950), pl. 44; J. Cassou, *Daumier* (Lausanne, 1949), pl. 44; Jean Adhémar, *Honoré Daumier* (Paris, 1954), pl. 25; N. Kalitina, *Honoré Daumier* (Moscow, 1955), pl. 171; K. E. Maison, *H. Daumier, Catalogue raisonné,* 2 vols. (London, 1968), 1:205, 2:46, pl. 197.

Gustave Courbet
17 Portrait of a Hunter

NOTES: **1.** "Realist Manifesto," in Nochlin, ed., 1966, 33. / **2.** Fernier 1977–1978, no. 71, and Jullian 1977, 204, vs. London 1953, no. 6, and Reidemeister 1986, no. 24. / **3.** Fernier 1977–1978, London 1953, and Jullian 1977.

PROVENANCE: Collection Luquet, Paris; Collection G. Potel, Lille (1899); Collection Léon Salavin, Paris (1953); purchased by Bührle in 1955.

EXHIBITIONS: *Moustache: Portraits d'hommes du XVIᵉ siècle à nos jours,* Marcel Rochas, Paris, 1949–1950, no. 17; *Chefs-d'œuvre des collections parisiennes,* Musée Carnavalet, Paris, 1952–1953, no. 21; *Gustave Courbet, 1819–1877,* Marlborough Gallery, London, 1953, no. 6; Zurich 1958, no. 316.

LITERATURE: Charles Léger, *Courbet* (Paris, 1929), 49; *Gustave Courbet, 1819–1877* [exh. cat., Marlborough Gallery] (London, 1953), no. 6; Benedict Nicolson, "Courbet at the Marlborough Gallery," *The Burlington Magazine* 95 (July 1953), 249; Eduard Hüttinger, *Sammlung Emil G. Bührle* [exh. cat., Kunsthaus] (Zurich, 1958), no. 316; Linda Nochlin, ed., *Realism and Tradition in Art, 1848–1900* (Englewood Cliffs, N. J., 1966); Timothy J. Clark, *Image of the People* (Princeton, N. J., 1973); René Jullian, "Courbet et la Hollande," *Eine Festschrift für Fritz Baumgart zm 75. Geburtstag* (Berlin, 1977), 204; Robert Fernier, *La Vie et l'œuvre de Gustave Courbet: Catalogue raisonné,* 2 vols. (Lausanne and Paris, 1977–1978), 1: no. 71; Pierre Courthion, *L'Opera completa di Courbet* (Milan, 1985), no. 65; Leopold Reidemeister, in *Foundation Emil G. Bührle Collection,* 2d ed. (Zurich and Munich, 1986), no. 24.

Gustave Courbet
18 The Houses of the Château of Ornans

NOTES: **1.** "Recueil," in Nochlin, ed., 1966, 46. / **2.** See Stuckey 1971–1973 and Herding 1975.

PROVENANCE: Sale, Collection Luquet, Paris, 30–31 March 1968; Galerie Bernheim jeune, Paris (1904); Collection Baron Denys Cochin; Collection Hébrard; Collection Prince de Wagram; Galerie Durand-Ruel; Knoedler and Company, New York; sale, Collection Rockefeller, New York, 24 March 1938; Paul Rosenberg Gallery, New York; Collection J. Stillman; purchased by Bührle in 1952.

EXHIBITIONS: *Exposition des œuvres de M. G. Courbet,* Rond-Point du Pont de l'Alma, Paris, 1867, no. 126; Salon d'Automne, Paris, 1906; *Masterpieces of French Art,* The Art Institute of Chicago, 1941, no. 27; *Loan Exhibition of Paintings by Gustave Courbet,* Rosenberg Gallery, New York, 1956, no. 4; Zurich 1958, no. 130; Edinburgh and London 1961, no. 7.

LITERATURE: Georges Riat, *Gustave Courbet* (Paris, 1906), 115; Hüttinger 1958, no. 130; Douglas Cooper, *Masterpieces of French Painting from the Bührle Collection* [exh. cat., The National Gallery] (London, 1961), no. 7; Max Buchon, *Recueil de dissertations sur le réalisme* (Neuchâtel, 1856), in Nochlin, ed., 1966, 45–47; Charles Stuckey, "Gustave Courbet's *Chateaux d'Ornans,*" *The Minneapolis Institute of Arts Bulletin* 60 (1971–1973): 27–37; Klaus Herding, "Egalität und Autorität in Courbets Landschaftsmalerei," *Städel-Jahrbuch* 5 (1975): 159–199; *Gustave Courbet, 1819–1877* [exh. cat., Grand Palais] (Paris, 1977–1978), 106; Fernier 1977–1978, 1: no. 175; Anne Wagner, "Courbet's Landscapes and Their Market," *Art History* 4 (December 1981): 410–431; Courthion 1985, no. 170.

Camille Pissarro
19 Road from Versailles to Louveciennes

NOTES: **1.** Janine Bailly-Herzberg, ed., *Correspondence de Camille Pissarro* (Paris, 1980), 62. / **2.** Pissarro and Venturi 1939, 76; the Maryland painting is not listed in Pissarro and Venturi. / **3.** Pissarro and Venturi 1939, 71–80.

PROVENANCE: Collection Camille Pissarro, Paris; sale, Collection Camille Pissarro, Galerie Georges Petit, Paris, 3 December 1928, no. 24; Collection Paul Rosenberg, Paris and New York; purchased by Bührle in 1952 through an American dealer.

EXHIBITIONS: *Retrospective Camille Pissarro,* Galerie Manzi et Joyant, Paris, 1914, no. 7; *Collection de Mme Vve Pissarro,* Galerie Nunes et Fiquet, Paris, 1921, no. 32; *French Art,* Royal Academy of Arts, London, 1932, no. 509; *Sisley and Pissarro,* Knoedler Galleries, London, 1934, no. 13; *Impressionisme,* Palais des Beaux-Arts, Brussels, 1935, no. 59; *French Art of the Nineties,* Institute of Modern Art, Boston, 1943; *Art of the United Nations,* M. H. de Young Memorial Museum, San Francisco, 1945; *Monet and the Beginning of Impressionism,* Currier Art Gallery, Manchester, N. H., 1949; Zurich 1958, no. 190; Berlin 1958, no. 3; Munich 1958–1959, no. 120; *De Géricault à Matisse: Les Chefs-d'œuvre des collections suisses,* Petit Palais, Paris, 1959, no. 106; Edinburgh and London 1961, no. 10; *Die Ile-de-France und ihre Maler,* Ehem. Staatliche Museen, Berlin, 1963, no. 11; Lucerne 1963, no. 19; *Chefs-d'œuvre des collections suisses de Manet à Picasso,* Palais de Beaulieu, Lausanne, 1964, no. 50.

LITERATURE: Georges Lecomte, *Camille Pissarro* (Paris, 1922), 49, ill.; *Les Beaux-Arts* 21 (December 1928), 336; Charles Kunstler, "Camille Pissarro (1830–1903)," *La Renaissance de l'Art français et des Industries de luxe* 12 (December 1928), 501, ill.; "Curioza: La Collection Camille Pissarro," *Le Gaulois artistique* 28 (January 1929), 123–124, ill.; M. Monda, "Revue des ventes de décembre: La Collection C. Pissarro," *Le Figaro artistique* (January 1929), 222, no. 28, ill.; Christian Zervos, *Histoire de l'art contemporain* (Paris, 1938); Ludovic R. Pissarro and Lionello Venturi, *Camille Pissarro: Son Art, son œuvre,* 2 vols. (Paris, 1939), no. 96; Charles Kunstler, *La Maison d'Eragny: A. B. C. artistique et litteraire* 5 (Paris, n. d.), 80, ill.; Hans

Graber, *C. Pissarro, A. Sisley, C. Monet nach eigenen und fremden Zeugnissen* (Basel, 1943), opp. 20, ill.; John Rewald, *History of Impressionism* (New York, 1946), 207, ill. (rev. ed., 1961, p.251); H. Gunther, *Camille Pissarro* (Munich, Vienna, Basel, 1954); John Rewald, *Camille Pissarro* (London, 1956), pl.10; Jean Leymarie, *Französische Malerei, Das 19. Jahrhundert* (Geneva, 1962), 181–182, ill.; John Rewald, *C. Pissarro* (Cologne, 1963), 74–75, ill.; Leopold Reidemeister, *Auf den Spuren des Maler der Ile-de-France* (Berlin, 1963), 43, ill.; René Wehrli, "E. G. Bührle, Zurich, Malerei des 19. Jahrhunderts," *Berühmte private Kunstsammlungen,* ed. Douglas Cooper (Oldenburg, 1963), 220, 223, ill.; Maria and Godfrey Blunden, *Journal de l'Impressionnisme* (Geneva, 1970), 86; *Seurat et le neo-impressionnisme: Le Grands Maîtres de la Peinture moderne,* ed. T. Nishimura (Japan, 1972), pl.1; Christopher Lloyd, *Pissarro* (Oxford, 1979), ill.

Camille Pissarro
20 The Road from Osny to Pontoise—Hoar Frost

NOTES: **1.** Richard R. Brettell, *Pissarro and Pontoise: The Painter in a Landscape* (Ann Arbor, 1988), esp. 70–74. / **2.** Pissarro and Venturi 1939, inv. 169. / **3.** Pissarro and Venturi 1939, 220, 203.

PROVENANCE: Collection Georges Viau, Paris (by 1905); sale, Paris, Galerie Durand-Ruel, 4 March 1907, no. 47; Collection Marquise de Ganay, Paris; purchased by Bührle in 1953 through a French dealer.

EXHIBITIONS: Galerie Blot, Paris, 1907, no. 5; *Werke der französischen Malerei und Grafik des 19. Jahrhunderts,* Folkwang Museum (Villa Hugel), Essen, 1954, no. 73; Zurich 1958, no. 192; Berlin 1958, no. 19; Munich 1958–1959, no. 122.

LITERATURE: Pissarro and Venturi 1939, no. 208.

Edouard Manet
21 Oloron-Sainte-Marie

NOTES: **1.** Françoise Cachin, Charles S. Moffett, and Juliet Bareau, *Manet 1832–1883* [exh. cat., Galeries nationales du Grand Palais, Paris] (New York, 1983), 523. / **2.** Tabarant 1947, 184. / **3.** Tabarant 1947, 184: "Quatre toiles, dont trois n'allèrent pas au dela de l'esquisse. Celle qui fut achevée a été cataloguée par nous: *Sur une galérie à colonnes, à Oloron.*" / **4.** Tabarant 1947, 185. / **5.** Worcester 1941, 28, no. 2; Cachin, Moffett, and Bareau 1983, 284, 296, 298.

PROVENANCE: Sold by Manet to Gauthier-Lathuille, Paris, 29 July 1881, for 200 francs; Mme Joliot, née Gauthier-Lathuille, Paris; Hector Brame, Paris, by 1931; Paul Brame, Paris and New York; Jacques Seligmann and Company, Inc., New York; Paul Brame, Paris and New York; purchased by Bührle in 1949 from a Swiss dealer.

EXHIBITIONS: *Rétrospective Edouard Manet,* Biennale, Venice, 1934, no. 7; *"La Flèche d'Or," French XIXth Century Art,* Arthur Tooth and Sons, London, 1937, no. 27; *The Art of the Third Republic: French Painting 1870–1940,* Worcester Art Museum, Mass., 1941, no. 2; *A Loan Exhibition of Manet for the Benefit of the New York Infirmary,* Wildenstein and Company, New York, 1948, no. 19; *Europäische Kunst des 13.–20. Jahrhunderts,* Kunsthaus, Zurich, 1950, no. 25; Zurich 1958, no. 141; Berlin 1958, no. 12; Munich 1958–1959, no. 93.

LITERATURE: Marie-Louise Bataille, "Manet beim 'Père Lathuille,'" *Kunst und Künstler* 28, no. 5 (February 1930): 206, ill. (as *Blick aus dem Fenster eines Hotels in Oloron-Sainte-Marie*); Adolphe Tabarant, *Manet: Histoire catalographique* (Paris,

1931), no. 161*bis*; Paul Jamot and Georges Wildenstein, *Manet* (Paris, 1932), 1: no. 188, and 2: fig. 373; Adolphe Tabarant, *Manet et ses œuvres,* 4th ed. (Paris, 1947), 184–185, no. 167, fig. 167; Maurice Bex, *Manet* (New York, 1948), 12, 14, pl. 56; Marcello Venturi and Sandra Orienti, *L'opera pittorica di Manet* (Milan, 1967), no. 142, ill.; Denis Rouart and Sandra Orienti, *Tout l'œuvre peint d'Edouard Manet* (Paris, 1970), no. 142; Denis Rouart and Daniel Wildenstein, *Edouard Manet: Catalogue raisonné,* vol. 1: *Peintures* (Geneva, 1975), 17, 23, no. 163, ill.; Sandra Orienti, *Edouard Manet: Werkverzeichnis* (Frankfurt am Main, Berlin, and Vienna, 1981), 1: no. 137, ill.; Leopold Reidemeister, in *Foundation Emil G. Bührle Collection,* 2d ed. (Zurich and Munich, 1986), no. 29, ill., with occasional errors in the provenance and exhibition history dating from the Zurich exhibition of 1958, the result of confusions between this and Jamot and Wildenstein 1932, no. 187.

Edouard Manet
22 The Port of Bordeaux

NOTES: **1.** Tabarant 1947, 186. / **2.** Rouart and Wildenstein 1975, 2: no. 234. / **3.** Tabarant 1947, 186. / **4.** Cachin, Moffett, and Bareau 1983, 512 and 523. / **5.** As quoted in George Heard Hamilton, *Manet and His Critics* (New Haven, 1954), 146.

PROVENANCE: Sold by Manet to Paul Durand-Ruel, Paris, December 1871; Théodore Duret, Paris, by 1884; sale, *Catalogue des Tableaux et Pastels composant la collection de M. Théodore Duret,* Galerie Georges Petit, Paris, 19 March 1894, no. 21, to Durand-Ruel, Paris, for 6300 francs; Jean-Baptiste Faure, Paris; F.-R. von Mendelssohn-Bartholdy, Berlin, by 1906; Francesco von Mendelssohn, Berlin; Eleonora von Mendelssohn, Berlin, until at least 1932; Paul Rosenberg, Paris and New York; purchased by Bührle in 1950.

EXHIBITIONS: *Exposition des œuvres de Edouard Manet,* Ecole nationale des beaux-arts, Paris, 1884, no. 59; Galerie Paul Cassirer, Berlin, 1906, no. 10; *Tableaux et aquarelles de Manet appartenant à la collection Faure,* Durand-Ruel, Paris, 1906, no. 13; *Exhibition of Paintings by Manet from the Faure Collection,* Sulley Galleries, London, 1906, no. 11; *Impressionisten,* Galerie Paul Cassirer, Berlin, 1925; *Manet,* Galerie Thannhauser, Berlin, 1927, no. 141; *Ausstellung Edouard Manet 1832–1883,* Galerie Matthiesen, Berlin 1928, no. 27; *Exposition Manet 1832–1883,* Musée de l'Orangerie, Paris, 1932, no. 46; *Masterpieces of Art,* New York World's Fair, 1940, no. 284; Zurich 1950, no. 25; *Het Franse Landschap von Poussin tot Cézanne,* Rijksmuseum, Amsterdam, 1951, no. 72; *Europäische Meister 1790–1910,* Kunstmuseum, Winterthur, 1955, no. 132; Zurich 1958, no. 142; Berlin 1958, no. 11; Munich 1958–1959, no. 94; *De Géricault à Matisse: Chefs-d'œuvre français des collections suisses,* Petit Palais, Paris, 1959, no. 78; Edinburgh and London 1961, no. 13 (as *Bordeaux: the Harbour*); Lucerne 1963, no. 11; *Chefs-d'œuvre des collections suisses de Manet à Picasso,* Palais de Beaulieu, Lausanne, 1964, no. 33.

LITERATURE: Edmond Bazire, *Manet* (Paris, 1884), 71, 138, ill. (engraving by Guérard); Antonin Proust, "Edouard Manet inédit," *La Revue blanche* (15 February 1897): 178; *Catalogue de la Collection Faure* (Paris, 1902), no. 35; Théodore Duret, *Histoire de Edouard Manet et de ses œuvres* (Paris, 1902), no. 138; Hugo von Tschudi, *Edouard Manet* (Berlin, 1902), 34; Théodore Duret, *Manet and the French Impressionists,* trans. J. E. Crawford Flitch (London and Philadelphia, 1910), 60, 76, no. 138 (erroneously as in the collection of Edouard Arnhold, Berlin); Louis Hourticq, *Edouard Manet* (Philadelphia and London, 1912), 51–52, pl. 26; Julius Meier-Graefe, *Edouard Manet* (Munich, 1912), 160, fig. 75; Théodore Duret, *Histoire de Edouard Manet et de son œuvre,* 2d and 4th ed.

(Paris, 1919 and 1926), 94, 136, 222–223, no. 138, pl. 20; Emil Waldmann, *Edouard Manet* (Berlin, 1923), 62, 65, ill.; Karl Sch[effler], "Impressionisten bei Paul Cassirer," *Kunst und Künstler* 24, no. 2 (November 1925): 72; Etienne Moreau-Nélaton, *Manet raconté par lui-même* (Paris, 1926), 1:128–129, 132–133, fig. 145, and 2:111, 114–115, 117, fig. 345 (installation photograph of Paris 1884 exhibition); Paul Jamot, "Etudes sur Manet (deuxième article)," *Gazette des Beaux-Arts,* ser. 5, 50, no. 778 (June 1927): 382; Tabarant 1931, 14, 222, no. 163; Paul Colin, *Edouard Manet* (Paris, 1932), 178, pl. 35; Jamot and Wildenstein 1932, 1:14, 88, 89, 112, no. 196, and 2: fig. 312; Lionello Venturi, *Les Archives de l'Impressionnisme* (Paris and New York, 1939), 2:191–192, no. 138; Gotthard Jedlicka, *Edouard Manet* (Zurich, 1941), 114–116, ill.; Tabarant 1947, 186, 187, 195, 317, 491, 512, no. 172, ill.; Bex 1948, 15, pl. 55; Jean-Louis Vaudoyer, *E. Manet* (Paris, 1955), no. 31, ill.; François Daulte, "Le Chef-d'œuvre d'une vie: La Collection Bührle," *Connaissance des arts,* no. 52 (15 June 1956): 30, ill.; Max Huggler, "Die Sammlung Bührle im Zürcher Kunsthaus," *Das Werk* 45, no. 10 (October 1958): 369; René Elvin, "Collector Extraordinary: The Bührle Collection and the New Zurich Kunsthaus," *The Studio,* no. 797 (August–September 1959): 54; Denys Sutton, "The Bührle Collection," *The Connoisseur* 143, no. 577 (May 1959): 146; René Wehrli, "Emil G. Bührle: French Nineteenth-Century Painting," in *Great Private Collections,* ed. Douglas Cooper (New York, 1963), 218, 219, ill. (also photographed in room in the Bührle house); Venturi and Orienti 1967, no. 146, pl. 28–29; Merete Bodelsen, "Early Impressionist Sales 1874–1894 in the Light of Some Unpublished 'Procès-verbaux,'" *The Burlington Magazine* 110, no. 783 (June 1968): 344–345; Rouart and Orienti 1970, no. 146; Rouart and Wildenstein 1975, 1:17, no. 164, ill.; Orienti 1981, 1: no. 141, ill.

Edouard Manet
23 La Sultane

NOTES: **1.** Duret 1902, no. 214. *La Sultane* is called *Jeune Femme en Costume Oriental* and grouped with works ascribed to the years 1875–1877. / **2.** Moreau-Nélaton 1926, 1:134 (as *Une Sultane*). See also Jamot and Wildenstein 1932, 2:12 (as *La Sultane*); and Rouart and Wildenstein 1975, 2. / **3.** Colin 1932, 38. / **4.** Emile Littré, *Dictionnaire de la langue française,* vol. 4 (Paris, 1878). / **5.** T. J. Clark, *The Painting of Modern Life: Paris in the Art of Manet and His Followers* (Princeton, 1984), 144–146.

PROVENANCE: Adrien Marx, Paris; ceded to his nephew, Claude Roger Marx, Paris, in 1892; *Catalogue des Tableaux, Pastels, Dessins, Aquarelles... faisant partie de la collection Roger Marx,* Galerie Manzi-Joyant, Paris, 11 May 1914, no. 60, sold to Paul Cassirer for 74.000; Durand-Ruel, Paris; Paul Cassirer, Berlin; Max Silberberg, Breslau; purchased by Bührle in 1952 from an American dealer.

EXHIBITIONS: Carnegie Institute, Pittsburgh, 1924, no. 19; Berlin, 1928, no. 35; *Manet,* Bernheim-Jeune, Paris, 1928, no. 24; *Great French Masters of the XIXth Century,* Durand-Ruel, New York, 1934, no. 31; Person Art Gallery, North Carolina, 1941; *Masterpieces by Manet,* Paul Rosenberg, New York, 1946–1947, no. 6; Zurich 1958, no. 140; Munich 1958–1959, no. 92 (as *Junge Frau im orientalischen Kostüm: "La Sultane"*); Edinburgh and London 1961, no. 14.

LITERATURE: Inventory of Manet's studio recorded in a notebook, 1871 (as *La Sultane,* est. value of 5000 francs) (see Moreau-Nélaton 1926, 1:133–134); Duret 1902, 1910, 1919, 1926, no. 214; Meier-Graefe 1912, 239–240, fig. 140; Otto Grautoff, "Auktionsnachrichten: Paris," *Kunst und Künstler* 12, no. 10 (July 1914): 557, ill.; Moreau-Nélaton 1926, 1:133–135, fig. 154; Karl Scheffler, "Die Sammlung Max Silberberg," *Kunst und Künstler* 30, no. 1 (October 1931): 14, ill.; Tabarant 1931, no. 240; Colin 1932, 38; Jamot and Wildenstein 1932, 1:89, no. 200, and 2: pl. 52; Rey 1938, no. 74, ill.; Tabarant 1947, 289, no. 253, ill.; Huggler 1958, 369; Sutton 1959, 143; Wehrli 1963, 219; Anne Coffin Hanson, *Edouard Manet 1832–1883* [exh. cat., Philadelphia Museum of Art] (Philadelphia, 1966), 73; Venturi and Orienti 1967, no. 214, ill.; Joel Isaacson, *Manet and Spain: Prints and Drawings* [exh. cat., Museum of Art, University of Michigan] (Ann Arbor, 1969), 35; Rouart and Orienti 1970, no. 216; Rouart and Wildenstein 1975, 1:18, no. 175, ill.; Anne Coffin Hanson, *Manet and the Modern Tradition* (New Haven and London, 1977), 88; Hans Luthy, "The E.G. Bührle Foundation," *Apollo* 110 (October 1979): 326; Orienti 1981, 2: no. 212, ill.; Donald A. Rosenthal, *Orientalism: The Near East in French Painting, 1800–1880* [exh. cat., Memorial Art Gallery, University of Rochester] (Rochester, 1982), 143, fig. 142; Françoise Cachin, Charles S. Moffett, and Juliet Bareau, *Manet 1832–1883* [exh. cat., Galeries nationales du Grand Palais, Paris] (New York, 1983), 191; Reidemeister 1986, no. 31, ill.

Edouard Manet
24 The Swallows

NOTES: **1.** Although Manet sold *The Swallows* to the collector Albert Hecht in September 1873, it was still in his studio in December. An article published under the byline "Fervacques" in the 25 December 1873 issue of *Le Figaro* tells of a visit to Manet's studio, mentioning a picture described as "l'ébauche de deux femmes assises en plein champ, en vue du village" (reprinted in Moreau-Nélaton, 1926, 2:8–10). / **2.** As quoted in Hamilton 1954, 184. For the full text of the article, see Mallarmé, "The Painting Jury of 1874 and Manet," reprinted in T. A. Gronberg, *Manet: A Retrospective* (New York, 1988), 132–134. / **3.** As cited in Moreau-Nélaton 1926, 2:12–13; and Rouart and Wildenstein 1975, 1:19: "une boutique dont la porte ne s'ouvre qu'aux fabricants diplomés, aux produit garantis purs de 'tout mélange.'" / **4.** As cited in Moreau-Nélaton 1926, 2:21; and Rouart and Wildenstein 1975, 1:19: "M. Manet est de ceux qui pretendent qu'on peut, en peinture, et qu'on doit se contenter de l'*impression*. Nous avons vu, de ces *impressionnistes*, une exposition naguère au boulevard des Capucines, chez Nadar. C'est purement déconcertant."

PROVENANCE: Sold by the artist to Albert Hecht, Paris, September 1873; Mme Hecht, Paris, until at least 1948; Wildenstein and Company, Paris; purchased by Bührle in 1953 from a French dealer.

EXHIBITIONS: Paris 1884, no. 63; Paris 1932, no. 52; *Masters of French 19th Century Painting*, New Burlington Galleries, London, 1936, no. 39; Zurich 1958, no. 145 (as *"Les Hirondelles" / Sommertag bei Berck-sur-Mer*); Berlin 1958, no. 14; Munich 1958–1959, no. 97; Edinburgh and London 1961, no. 15.

LITERATURE: Stéphane Mallarmé, "Le Jury de Peinture pour 1874 et Monsieur Manet," *La Renaissance littéraire et artistique* (12 April 1874), 155–157; Philippe Burty, "Le Salon de 1874," *La République française* (9 June 1874); Bazire 1884, 71; Duret 1902, 102, no. 150; Théodore Duret, "Edouard Manet et les Impressionnistes," *Histoire du Paysage en France* (Paris, 1908), 308; Duret 1910, 1919, and 1926, no. 150; Moreau-Nélaton 1926, 2:5–6, 8, 9, 11, 12, figs. 172, 345 (installation photograph of Paris 1884 exhibition); Tabarant 1931, no. 189; Jamot and Wildenstein 1932, 1:91, no. 230, and 2: pl. 374; Henri Mondor, *La Vie de Mallarmé* (Paris, 1941–1942), 355–357; Tabarant 1947, 216, 237, 241, 243–244, 491, no. 199, fig. 199; George Heard Hamilton, *Manet and His Critics* (New Haven and London, 1954), 172, 175, 181–184, 265, fig. 24; Sutton 1959, 143; Hanson 1966, 19, 32; Venturi and Orienti 1967, no. 169, ill. (with installation photograph of Paris 1884 exhibition); Rouart and Orienti 1970, no. 169, ill.; Rouart and Wildenstein 1975, 18, 19, no. 190, ill.; Orienti 1981, 1: no. 165, ill.; Reff 1982, 162; Cachin, Moffett, and Bareau 1983, 32, 345, 363, 514; Reidemeister 1986, no. 32, ill.; Robert L. Herbert, *Impressionism: Art, Leisure, and Parisian Society* (New Haven and London, 1988), 276–278, pl. 282.

Edouard Manet
25 The Rue Mosnier with Flags

NOTES: **1.** Reff 1982, 236. / **2.** Tabarant 1947, 319; Reff 1982, 238. / **3.** Collins 1975, 710; Reff 1982, 236. / **4.** Reff 1982, 238. / **5.** Collins 1975, 709–713. / **6.** Clark 1984, 24. / **7.** Reff 1982, 236.

PROVENANCE: Inventory of Manet's studio, Paris 1883; sale, *Catalogue de Tableaux, Pastels, Etudes, Dessins, Gravures par Edouard Manet et dépendant de sa succession*, Hôtel Drouot, Paris, 4–5 February 1884, no. 56 (as *Rue pavoisée, esquisse*), to Bérend, Paris, for 150 francs; Hayashi; Portier, Paris; Eugène Blot, Paris; sale, *Catalogue de Tableaux, Aquarelles, Pastels et Dessins… composant la collection de M.E. Blot*, Hôtel Drouot, Paris, 9–10 May 1900, no. 108, (as *Les Drapeaux*), to Dr. Viau on behalf of Blot for 3500 francs; Cassirer, Berlin; Max Slevogt, Berlin; Galerie Thannhauser, Berlin; purchased by Bührle in 1937 through Galerie Rosengart, Lucerne.

EXHIBITIONS: Bruno Cassirer, Berlin, 1930; *Ausländische Kunst in Zürich*, Kunsthaus, Zurich, 1943, no. 595; *Impressionisten*, Kunsthalle, Basel, 1949, no. 64; Zurich 1950, no. 25; Zurich 1958, no. 147; Berlin 1958, no. 16; Munich 1958–1959, no. 98; Lucerne 1963, no. 14, ill.

LITERATURE: Duret 1902, 1910, 1919, and 1926, no. 242; Tschudi 1902, 41, ill.; Hourticq 1912, 78; Meier-Graefe 1912, 260–261; Waldmann 1923, 67–68; Moreau-Nélaton 1926, 2:46; Karl Scheffler, "Liebermann- und Slevogt-Premiere im Verlag Bruno Cassirer," *Kunst und Künstler* 28, no. 6 (March 1930): 251, 252, ill. (as *Rue de Berne*); Tabarant 1931, no. 281; Jamot and Wildenstein 1932, 1: no. 290, and 2: pl. 329; Julius Meier-Graefe, "Le Centenaire de Manet," *Formes* (April 1932): 253; Eugène Blot, *Histoire d'une collection de tableaux modernes: 50 ans de peinture (de 1882 à 1932)* (Paris, [1934]), 41; Paul Colin, *Edouard Manet*, 2d ed. (Paris, 1937), 79; Jedlicka 1941, 277; Walter Kern, *Galerie und Sammler*, no. 7 (1943): 152; Tabarant 1947, 323–326, no. 294 (as *La Rue Mosnier pavoisée [Les Drapeaux]*, esquisse); Huggler 1958, 369 (as *Rue de Berne*); Sutton 1959, 143, fig. 6; Wehrli 1963, 216, 219; Hanson 1966, 157; Venturi and Orienti 1967, no. 248C, pl. 44; Bodelsen 1968, no. 56; Rouart and Orienti 1970, no. 249c; John Rewald, *The History of Impressionism*, 4th rev. ed. (New York, 1973), 419; Bradford Collins, "Manet's 'Rue Mosnier Decked with Flags' and the Flâneur Concept," *The Burlington Magazine* 177, no. 872 (November 1975), 709–714; Rouart and Wildenstein 1975, 27, no. 271, ill.; Orienti 1981, 2: no. 246c, ill.; Theodore Reff, *Manet and Modern Paris* [exh. cat., National Gallery of Art] (Washington, D.C., 1982), 236–240, fig. 118 (as first of two street scenes painted on 30 June 1878); Cachin, Moffett, and Bareau 1983, 396–404; T. J. Clark, *The Painting of Modern Life: Paris in the Art of Manet and His Followers* (Princeton, 1984), 24, 273 n. 3; Ronda Kasl, "Edouard Manet's 'Rue Mosnier': 'Le pauvre a-t-il une patrie?'" *Art Journal* 45, no. 1 (spring 1985): 49–58; Dennis Farr, "Edouard Manet's *La Rue Mosnier aux Drapeaux*," in *Essays in Honor of Paul Mellon, Collector and Benefactor*, ed. John Wilmerding (Washington, D.C., 1986), 97–109, fig. 2; Herbert 1988, 30–32, pl. 34; Jane Mayo Ross, "Within the 'Zone of Silence': Monet and Manet in 1878," *Art History* 11, no. 3 (September, 1988), 372–407.

Edouard Manet
26 The Great Horned Owl

NOTES: **1.** Tabarant 1947, 420, items 80–85; Rouart and Wildenstein 1975, 27. / **2.** Tabarant 1947, 419. / **3.** Reidemeister 1986, no. 36. / **4.** As cited in Hamilton 1954, 94. See also Emile Zola, "Une Nouvelle Manière en peinture: Edouard Manet," in *L'Artiste: Revue du XIXe siècle* (1 January 1867): 52; and Emile Zola, *Ed. Manet: Etude biographique et critique* (Paris, 1867), 25. / **5.** Emile Zola, "Paris Letter," as cited in Gronberg 1988, 164.

PROVENANCE: Inventory of Manet's estate, 1883 (no. 83); *Catalogue de Tableaux, Pastels, Etudes, Dessins, Gravures par Edouard Manet et dépendant de sa succession*, Hôtel Drouot, Paris, 4–5 February 1884, no. 88, sold to M. de la Narde, Paris, for 380 francs; L.-H. Devillez, Brussels; private collection, Brussels; sale, Galerie Giroux, Brussels, 27 November 1948, no. 39; Galerie Seligmann, Paris; Christophe Bernoulli, Basel; purchased by Bührle in 1955 from a Swiss dealer.

EXHIBITIONS: Paris 1884, no. 110 (as *Grandduc, panneau décoratif*); *Vincent van Gogh en zijn Tidgenooten*, Stedelijk Museum, Amsterdam, 1930, no. 209; *Chefs-d'œuvre de la Curiosité du Monde*, Musée des arts décoratifs, Paris, 1954, no. 27; *Vier Eeuwen Stilleven in Frankrijk*, Museum Boymans, Rotterdam, 1954, no. 89; Zurich 1958, no. 151 (as *"Le grand Duc" / Jagdtrophäen-Panneau: Toter Uhu*); Edinburgh and London 1961, no. 18 (as *A Dead Eagle Owl*).

LITERATURE: Duret 1902, 1910, 1919, and 1926, no. 278; Tabarant 1931, no. 362; Jamot and Wildenstein 1932, 1: no. 463, and 2: fig. 424; Tabarant 1947, 419–420, 491, no. 387, ill.; Venturi and Orienti 1967, no. 352B, ill.; Bodelsen 1968, no. 88; Rouart and Orienti 1970, no. 356b; Rouart and Wildenstein 1975, 27, no. 377, ill.; Orienti 1981, 2: no. 348B, ill.; Reidemeister 1986, no. 36, ill.

Edouard Manet
27 The Suicide

NOTES: **1.** Tabarant 1947, 399. / **2.** Monneret 1978, 1:99–100. / **3.** London and Edinburgh 1961, no. 17. / **4.** Tabarant 1947, 411: "ne fut qu'un incident de palette." / **5.** Emile Zola in *Vente Cabaner*, Hôtel Drouot (Paris, 1881), as cited in Tabarant 1947, 411–412: "et la verité est qu'il meurt de son art. . . . Vingt ans de notre enfer de Paris, nuits enfièvrées, de secousses et de privations de toutes sortes, l'ont jeté ou il est. . . ."

PROVENANCE: Given by the artist to sale on behalf of François Cabaner, Hôtel Drouot, Paris, 14 May 1881, no. 22, sold for 65 francs; Durand-Ruel, Paris; Auguste Pellerin, Paris; Bernheim-Jeune, Paris, by 1910; Baron François de Hatvany, Budapest, in 1910; Drs. Fritz and Peter Nathan, Zurich; purchased by Bührle in 1948.

EXHIBITIONS: *Les Manet de la Collection Pellerin*, Galerie Bernheim-Jeune, Paris, 1910, no. 9; *Edouard Manet (Aus der Sammlung Pellerin)*, Moderne Galerie, Munich, 1910, no. 20; *Œuvre d'art socialisées*, Budapest, 1919, no. V/14; *Honderd Jaar Fransche Kunst*, Stedelijk Museum, Amsterdam, 1938, no. 150; *La Peinture française au XIXe siècle*, Musée du Prince Paul, Belgrade, 1939, no. 76; *Œuvres choisies du XIXe siècle*, Galerie Max Kaganovitch, Paris, 1950, no. 21; Zurich 1950; *Werke der französischen Malerei und Grafik des 19. Jahrhunderts*, Villa Hügel, Essen, 1954, no. 61; Zurich 1958, no. 150; Berlin 1958, no. 15; Munich 1958–1959, no. 99; Edinburgh and London 1961, no. 17; *50 Jahre Kunsthandelsverband der Schweiz: Jubiläumsausstellung mit Werken des*

15.–20. Jahrhunderts aus öffentlichem und privatem Besitz, Kunsthaus, Zurich, 1973, no. 40.

LITERATURE: Duret 1902, 1910, 1919, and 1926, no. 215; Meier-Graefe 1912, pl. 153; Tabarant 1931, no. 353; Colin 1932, 181, pl. 91; Jamot and Wildenstein 1932, 1:101, no. 271, and 2: pl. 332; Rey 1938, no. 109, pl. 109; Jedlicka 1941, 192, ill.; Tabarant 1947, 411–412, no. 379, ill.; "Die Sammlung Emil Bührle in Zürich," *Das Kunstwerk* 7, no. 6 (1953): 27; Wehrli 1963, 219; Eugène Gerlötei, "L'Ancienne collection François de Hatvany," *Gazette des beaux-arts,* ser. 6, 67, no. 1168–1169 (May–June 1966): 362, 364, 369, 371, fig. 10; Hanson 1966, 34; Venturi and Orienti 1967, no. 344, ill.; Rouart and Orienti 1970, no. 348; Linda Nochlin, *Realism* (Harmondsworth, Baltimore, and Victoria, 1971), 73–75, 255, fig. 35; George Mauner, *Manet Peintre-Philosophe: A Study of the Painter's Themes* (University Park, Pa., and London, 1975), 111, 142–143, fig. 87; Rouart and Wildenstein 1975, 23, no. 258, ill.; Sophie Monneret, *L'Impressionnisme et son époque* (Paris, 1978), 1:100, Orienti 1981, 2: no. 340, ill.; Reff 1982, 26–27, fig. 14; Reidemeister 1986, no. 33, ill.; Alena Marchwinsky, "The Romantic Suicide and the Artists," *Gazette des beaux-arts,* ser. 6, 109, no. 1417 (February 1987): 73–74, fig. 5.

Edouard Manet
28 Roses and Tulips in a Vase

NOTES: **1.** Tabarant 1947, 460. / **2.** Gordon and Forge 1986, 4. / **3.** Ecole nationale des beaux-arts, *Exposition des œuvres de Edouard Manet* (Paris, 1884), no. 115; see also Rouart and Wildenstein 1975, no. 428. / **4.** *Exposition,* 1884, no. 116; Rouart and Wildenstein 1975, 1: no. 429. / **5.** John Richardson, *Edouard Manet: Paintings and Drawings* (London, 1958), 30; see also Tabarant 1931, 416–417; and Gronberg 1988, 290. / **6.** Tabarant 1947, 466: "Il y avait toujours eu beaucoup de fleurs dans les ateliers de Manet, mais jamais il n'y en eut tant que rue d'Amsterdam à l'aube du printemps de 1883, amis et amies en faisant déposer dans la loge d'Aristide [concierge] quand ils ne les apportaient pas eux-mêmes. Méry Laurent lui en envoyaient par Elis, sa femme de chambre. Avec quelle joie le malade accueillait ces messagères d'un renouveau qu'il attendait avec tant de confiance! Il eut voulu les peindre toutes; il en peindrait tout au mous quelques-unes."

PROVENANCE: Louis de Fourcade; sale, Hôtel Drouot, Paris, 29 March 1917, no. 49, to Galerie Rosenberg, Paris, for FF 20.000; Walther Halvorsen, Oslo, by 1926 until at least 1931; Herbert Colman, London; Galerie Fischer, Lucerne; purchased by Bührle in 1943.

EXHIBITIONS: *Art français du XIXᵉ siècle,* Galerie Paul Rosenberg, Paris, 1917, no. 36; *French Paintings of the Nineteenth Century: Ingres to Cézanne,* Alex. Reid & Lefevre, Ltd., London, 1933, no. 24; *Ingres to van Gogh,* Galerie Rosenberg, London, 1937, no. 18; Zurich 1950, no. 25; *La Nature Morte de l'Antiquité à Nos Jours,* Orangerie des Tuileries, Paris, 1952, no. 91, pl. 36; Winterthur 1955, no. 134; Zurich 1958, no. 153, pl. 8; Berlin 1958, no. 28; Munich 1958–1959, no. 100, pl. 9; Paris 1959, no. 82, pl. 20; Edinburgh and London 1961, no. 19, ill.

LITERATURE: Duret 1919 and 1926, supplement, no. 11; Moreau-Nélaton 1926, 2:93, fig. 302; Tabarant 1931, no. 404; Jamot and Wildenstein 1932, 1: no. 504, and 2: pl. 398; Tabarant 1947, 462, no. 436, fig. 436; Huggler 1958, 369; Wehrli 1963, 219, ill.; Venturi and Orienti 1967, no. 411F, ill.; Rouart and Orienti 1970, no. 417f; Rouart and Wildenstein 1975, no. 422, ill.; Luthy 1979, pl. 28; Orienti 1981, 2: no. 411f, ill.; Kathleen Adler, *Manet* (Oxford, 1986), 194, fig. 181; Robert Gordon and Andrew Forge, *The Last Flowers of Manet* (New York, 1986), 40, ill.

Edgar Degas
29 Madame Camus at the Piano

NOTES: **1.** Degas later told Walter Sickert that the music was depicted so accurately that an expert was able to identify it as Beethoven's. See Walter Sickert, "Degas," *The Burlington Magazine* 31, (1917): 186, in Reff 1976, 124. / **2.** Jeanne Fevre, *Mon Oncle Degas,* ed. Pierre Borel (Geneva, 1949), 98; Boggs, 1962, 26.

PROVENANCE: Degas studio; *Catalogue des Tableaux, Pastels et Dessins par Edgar Degas et provenant de son atelier,* Galerie Georges Petit, Paris, 6–8 May 1918 (first sale), no. 111, sold for 32,000; Alphonse Kann, Saint-Germain-en-Laye, by 1924 until at least 1937; purchased by Bührle in 1951 from a private French collection.

EXHIBITIONS: *Exposition au profit des Laboratoires,* Galerie Les Arts, Paris, 1923, no. 181; *Exposition Degas,* Galerie Georges Petit, 1924, no. 34; *Exposition d'œuvres importantes de Grands Maîtres du Dix-Neuvième Siècle,* Galerie Paul Rosenberg, Paris, 1931, no. 25; *Degas: Portraitiste, Sculpteur,* Musée de l'Orangerie, Paris, 1931, 19, no. 48; *Chefs d'œuvre de l'art français,* Palais National des Arts, 1937, no. 300; *Degas,* Kunstmuseum, Bern, 1951, no. 13, Zurich 1958, no. 155; Berlin 1958, no. 5; Munich 1958–1959, no. 38; *De Géricault à Matisse: Chefs-d'œuvre français des collections suisses,* Petit Palais, Paris, 1959, no. 42.

LITERATURE: Arsène Alexandre, "Essai sur Monsieur Degas," *Les Arts,* no. 166 (1918): 12; Paul Lafond, *Degas* (Paris, 1919), 2:12 (erroneously described as exhibited at the Salon of 1869); Paul Jamot, *Degas* (Paris, 1924), 50–51; Paul-André Lemoisne, "Artistes contemporains: Edgar Degas, à propos d'une exposition recente," *La Revue de l'Art* 46, no. 257 (June 1924): 24; Arsène Alexandre, "Degas: Nouveaux aperçus," *L'Art et les Artistes* (February 1935): 150; Paul-André Lemoisne, *Degas et son œuvre* (Paris, 1946), 1:56, 58, 62, and 2: no. 207, ill.; Reginald Howard Wilenski, *Modern French Painters,* 3d ed. (London, 1947), 330; "Die Sammlung Emil Bührle in Zürich," *Das Kunstwerk* 7, no. 6 (1953): 27, ill.; G. Schmidt, "La Suisse et la peinture française des XIXᵉ et XXᵉ siècles," *Revue économique franco-suisse* (December 1954): ill.; François Daulte, "Le Chef-d'œuvre d'une vie: La Collection Bührle," *Connaissance des arts,* no. 52 (15 June 1956): ill.; Pierre Cabanne, *Edgar Degas* (Paris, 1957), 24, 96, 109; Max Huggler, "Die Sammlung Bührle im Zürcher Kunsthaus," *Das Werk* 45, no. 10 (October 1958): 371; René Elvin, "Collector Extraordinary: The Bührle Collection and the New Zürich Kunsthaus," *The Studio* 158, no. 797 (August–September 1959): 54; André Chamson and François Daulte, *De Géricault à Matisse: Chefs-d'œuvre d'art français des collections suisses* [exh. cat., Petit Palais] (Paris, 1959), ill.; Denys Sutton, "The Bührle Collection," *The Connoisseur* 143, no. 577 (May 1959): 145, 146, fig. 7; Jean Sutherland Boggs, *Portraits by Degas* (Berkeley and Los Angeles, 1962), 26, 31, 59, 111, pl. 65; René Wehrli, "Emil G. Bührle: French Nineteenth-Century Painting," in *Great Private Collections,* ed. Douglas Cooper (New York, 1963), 220; Franco Russoli, *L'Opera completa di Degas* (Milan, 1970), no. 245, ill.; Shuji Takashina, *Degas* (Tokyo, 1971), 119, pl. 18; John Rewald, *The History of Impressionism,* 4th rev. ed. (New York, 1973), 237 n. 41; Theodore Reff, *Degas: The Artist's Mind* (New York, 1976), 124; Norma Broude, "Degas's 'Misogyny,'" *Art Bulletin* 59, no. 1 (March 1977): 101; Hans Luthy, "The E. G. Bührle Foundation," *Apollo* 110 (October 1979): 326; Antoine Terrasse, *Edgar Degas I: Werkverzeichnis,* trans. Nora Jensen and Rudolph Kimmig (Frankfurt and Berlin, 1980), no. 146, ill.; Eugénie de Keyser, *Degas: Réalité et Métaphore* (Louvain-la-Neuve, 1981), 50, 94, 97; Leopold Reidemeister, in *Foundation Emil G. Bührle Collection,* 2d ed. (Zurich and Munich, 1986), no. 43, ill.

(erroneously says that after first Degas sale the painting passed to Olivier Senn, Paris, and was included in third Degas sale); Denys Sutton, *Edgar Degas: Life and Work* (New York, 1986), 73, 74, fig. 56; Jean Sutherland Boggs, in *Degas* [exh. cat., Galeries nationales du Grand Palais, Paris] (New York, 1988), 155.

Edgar Degas
30 Study for "Madame Camus at the Piano" (Left Hand)

NOTE: **1.** See the *Catalogue des Tableaux, Pastels et Dessins par Edgar Degas et provenant de son atelier,* Galerie Georges Petit, Paris, 1919, no. 152/2; and Lemoisne 208–210, 212.

PROVENANCE: Degas studio; sale, *Catalogue des Tableaux, Pastels et Dessins par Edgar Degas et provenant de son atelier,* Galerie Georges Petit, Paris, 11–13 December 1918 (second sale), no. 243–1°, ill.; Alphonse Kann, Saint-Germain-en-Laye; purchased by Bührle in 1951 from a private French dealer.

EXHIBITIONS: Paris 1931, no. 122 (listed under the same number with Lemoisne 212); Bern 1951, no. 90; Zurich 1958, no. 157; Munich 1958–1959, no. 40.

LITERATURE: Lemoisne 1946, 2: no. 211, ill.; Huggler 1958, 371; Russoli 1970, no. 245; Reidemeister 1986, no. 45, ill.

Edgar Degas
31 Study for "Madame Camus at the Piano" (Right Hand)

PROVENANCE: Degas studio; sale, *Catalogue des Tableaux, Pastels et Dessins par Edgar Degas et provenant de son atelier,* Galerie Georges Petit, Paris, 11–13 December 1918 (second sale), no. 183; Alphonse Kann, Saint-Germain-en-Laye; Galerie Nunès et Fiquet, Paris; purchased by Bührle in 1951 from a private French dealer.

EXHIBITIONS: Paris 1931, no. 121; Bern 1951, no. 89; Zurich 1958, no. 156; Munich 1958–1959, no. 39.

LITERATURE: Huggler 1958, 371; Philippe Brame and Theodore Reff, *Degas et son œuvre: A Supplement* (New York and London, 1984), no. 50, ill.; Reidemeister 1986, no. 44, ill. (erroneously listed as included in Lemoisne 1946, nos. 211 and 212).

Edgar Degas
32 Count Lepic and His Daughters

PROVENANCE: Vicomte Ludovic Napoléon Lepic, Paris; Paul Brame, Paris; Paul Rosenberg, Paris; purchased by Bührle in 1952 from a American private collector.

EXHIBITIONS: *Works by Edgar Degas,* Cleveland Museum of Art, 1947, no. 16; *Loan Exhibition of 21 Masterpieces by 7 Great Masters,* Paul Rosenberg and Company, New York, 1948, no. 7; Zurich 1958, no. 158; Berlin 1958, no. 20; Munich 1958–1959, no. 41; Paris 1959, no. 43; Edinburgh and London 1961, no. 22; *Chefs-d'œuvre des collections suisses, de Matisse à Picasso,* Palais de Beaulieu, Lausanne, 1964, no. 5.

LITERATURE: Lemoisne 1946, 2: no. 272, ill.; Cabanne 1957, 111; Huggler 1958, 371; Raymond Cogniat, *Das Jahrhundert der Impressionisten* (Cologne and Milan, [1959]), ill.; Boggs 1962, 93 n. 16, 120; Wehrli 1963, 220; Russoli 1970, no. 259, ill.; Luthy 1979, 325, pl. 29; Terrasse 1980, no. 157, ill.; Reidemeister 1986, no. 46, ill.; Sutton 1986, 91, fig. 77.

Edgar Degas
33 Ballet Class

NOTE: **I.** Lemoisne 1946, nos. 479 and 588.

PROVENANCE: Degas studio; sale, *Catalogue des Tableaux, Pastels et Dessins par Edgar Degas et provenant de son atelier,* Galerie Georges Petit, Paris, 6–8 May 1918 (first sale), no. 70, sold to [illegible] for 56,000, according to an annotated copy of the sale catalogue in the library of the National Gallery of Art, Washington; Robert Treat Paine II, Boston; sale, C.S. Wadsworth Trust, New York; Jacques Seligmann & Co., New York; purchased by Bührle in 1951 from Jacques Seligmann & Co.

EXHIBITIONS: Cleveland 1947, no. 24; Bern 1951, no. 33; *Werke der französischen Malerei und Grafik des 19. Jahrhundert,* Folkwang Museum (Villa Hügel), Essen, 1954, no. 31; *Europäische Meister 1790–1910,* Kunstmuseum, Winterthur, 1955, no. 66; Zurich 1958, no. 161; Bern 1958, no. 29; Munich 1958–1959, no. 43; Lucerne 1963, no. 16.

LITERATURE: Lillian Browse, *Degas Dancers* (London, [1949]), no. 83, pl. 83 (erroneously as in the collection of Sam. Salz); Lemoisne 1946, 2: no. 587, ill.; Reginald Howard Wilensky, *Modern French Painters,* 3d ed. (London, 1947), 332; Cabanne 1957, 108; Russoli 1970, no. 759, ill.; Terrasse 1980, no. 352, ill.; Boggs 1988, 336 (as a variant of *La leçon de danse,* Lemoisne 1946, no. 479, in the collection of the Philadelphia Museum of Art).

Henri Fantin-Latour
34 Self-Portrait

NOTES: **I.** *Exposition de l'œuvre de Fantin-Latour* [exh. cat., Palais de l'école nationale des beaux-arts] (Paris, 1906), quoted in Druick and Hoog 1983, 71. / **2.** *Explication,* 1861, no. 1059. / **3.** Druick and Hoog 1983, 66. Fantin contradicted this realist view by painting imaginative subjects. / **4.** Druick and Hoog 1983, 66. / **5.** Musée du Louvre, inv. no. 1747.

PROVENANCE: Collection M.G. Viau, Paris; purchased by Bührle in 1954.

EXHIBITIONS: Salon of 1861, Paris, no. 1059; *Exposition centennale de l'art français de 1800–1889,* Exposition Universelle, Paris, 1900, no. 283; *L'Œuvre de Fantin-Latour,* Palais de l'école nationale des beaux-arts, Paris, 1906, no. 10; *Inaugural Exposition of French Art,* California Palace of the Legion of Honor, San Francisco, 1924–1925, no. 22; *Cents Portraits d'hommes,* Galerie Charpentier, Paris, 1952, no. 27; Zurich 1958, no. 317.

LITERATURE: *Explication des ouvrages de peinture, sculpture, gravure…,* Salon of 1861 (Paris, 1861), no. 1059; Victoria Fantin-Latour, *Catalogue de l'œuvre complet de Fantin-Latour* (Paris, 1911), no. 167; Eduard Hüttinger, *Sammlung Emil G. Bührle* [exh. cat., Kunsthaus] (Zurich, 1958), no. 317; Douglas Druick and Michel Hoog, *Fantin-Latour* [exh. cat., Grand Palais, National Gallery of Canada] (Ottawa, 1983); Leopold Reidemeister, in *Foundation Emil G. Bührle Collection,* 2d ed. (Zurich and Munich, 1986), no. 37.

Henri Fantin-Latour
35 Climbing Roses and Peaches

NOTES: **I.** Druick and Hoog 1983, 256. / **2.** Blanche 1906, 312.

PROVENANCE: Private collection, Paris; purchased by Bührle in 1954.

EXHIBITIONS: Zurich 1958, no. 137.

LITERATURE: Jacques-Emile Blanche, "Fantin-Latour," *La Revue de Paris* 13 (May 1906), 289–313; Fantin-Latour 1911, no. 679; Hüttinger 1958, no. 137; Michel Faré, *La Nature morte en France,* 2 vols. (Geneva, 1962), 1: 267–274; Michel Hoog, "A propos de l'exposition Fantin-Latour: Les

Fleurs et les poètes," *L'Œil* (December 1982), 54–60; Druick and Hoog 1983.

Alfred Sisley
36 The Road to Saint-Germain at Marly

NOTES: **I.** Daulte 1959, 155. / **2.** Daulte 1959, 18.

PROVENANCE: Collection Paul Rosenberg, Paris and New York; purchased by Bührle in 1952 through an American dealer.

EXHIBITIONS: Zurich 1958, no. 198; Edinburgh and London 1961, no. 27.

LITERATURE: François Daulte, *Alfred Sisley: Catalogue raisonné de l'œuvre peint* (Lausanne, 1959), no. 156.

Alfred Sisley
37 Summer at Bougival

NOTES: **I.** Emile de la Bedollière, *Histoire des environs de nouveau Paris* (Paris, n.d. [early 1860s?]), 85. / **2.** For Bougival, see Daulte 1959, 39, 41, 76, 78, 179; for Port Marly, see Daulte 1959, 21–24, 71, 72. / **3.** Daulte 1959, 226, 228.

PROVENANCE: Collection François Depeaux, Rouen; sale, Hôtel Drouot, Paris, 30 June 1921 no. 67; Collection Levi-de Benzion, Nice and Cairo; purchased by Bührle in 1942 through a Swiss dealer.

EXHIBITIONS: *Impressionisten,* Kunsthalle, Basel, 1949, no. 85; *Europäische Kunst 13.– 20. Jahrhundert,* Kunsthaus, Zurich, 1950, no. 26; *Europäische Meister 1790–1910,* Kunstmuseum, Winterthur, 1955, no. 184; *Alfred Sisley,* Kunstmuseum, Bern, 1958, no. 26; Zurich 1958, no. 199; Berlin 1958, no. 23; Munich 1958–1959, no. 151; Edinburgh and London 1961, no. 29.

LITERATURE: Daulte 1959, no. 227; *Europas schönste Impressionistensammlung, E. G. Bührle/ Zurich* (Das Schönste, 1959), 24, no. 1.

Paul Cézanne
38 The Thaw in L'Estaque

NOTES: **I.** Rewald, *Cézanne: A Biography,* 86. / **2.** Gowing 1988, 166. / **3.** Vollard 1924, 37–38: "Ecoutez un peu, Monsieur Vollard! Pendant la guerre, j'ai beaucoup travaillé sur le motif à l'Estaque. / Je n'ai d'ailleurs aucun événement extraordinaire à vous raconter sur les années 70–71. Je partageais mon temps entre le paysage et l'atelier." / **4.** Vollard 1924, 40: "Seulement, comprenez, Monsieur Vollard, j'avais en ce moment un paysage qui ne venait pas bien. Aussi restai-je à Aix quelque temps encore, à étudier sur le motif."

PROVENANCE: Ambroise Vollard, Paris; consigned with Bernheim-Jeune, Paris (inv. 18558); sold to Auguste Pellerin, Paris, 8 February 1911, for cash and three paintings, two by Cézanne, and *Le Jardin* by Monet (see cat. 47); by inheritance to his son, Jean-Victor Pellerin, Paris; Wildenstein and Company, Paris, London, and New York; Dr. A. Kauffmann, London; purchased by Bührle in 1953.

EXHIBITIONS: *L'Impressionnisme,* Palais des Beaux-Arts, Brussels, 1935, no. 11; *Cézanne,* Musée de l'Orangerie, Paris, 1936, no. 13; *Hondred Jaar Fransche Kunst,* Stedelijk Museum, Amsterdam, 1938, no. 4; *La Peinture française au XIXe siècle,* Museum Prinz Paul, Belgrade, 1939, no. 4; *Exposition du Centenaire de Paul Cézanne,* Palais Saint-Pierre, Lyon, 1939, no. 9; *Homage to Paul Cézanne,* Wildenstein and Company, London, 1939, no. 11; *A Loan Exhibition of Cézanne for the Benefit of the New York Infirmary,* Wildenstein and Company, New York, 1947, no. 4; *Cézanne: Paintings, Watercolors & Drawings,* The Art Institute of Chicago and The Metropolitan Museum of Art, New York, 1952, no. 13 (as *L'Estaque, Melting Snow*); *Cézanne: Peintures, Aquarelles, Dessins,* Hôtel de

Ribbe, Aix, 1952; Zurich 1958, 24, no. 215; Berlin 1958, 48, no. 6; Munich 1958–1959, no. 13; Edinburgh and London 1961, no. 31 (erroneously listed as initially owned by Bernheim-Jeune, Paris); Lucerne 1963, no. 32.

LITERATURE: Ambroise Vollard, *Paul Cézanne* (Paris, 1914), 34, pl. 9 (2d rev. ed., Paris, 1924); Julius Meier-Graefe, *Cézanne und sein Kreis: ein Beitrag zur Entwicklungsgeschichte* (Munich, 1918), 79, ill. (as *Die roten Dächer*); Gustave Coquiot, *Paul Cézanne* (Paris, 1919), 68, 245; Tristan Klingsor, *Cézanne* (Paris, 1923), 16; Georges Rivière, *Le Maître Paul Cézanne* (Paris, 1923), 199 (as *Les Toits rouges*); Ambroise Vollard, *Paul Cézanne: His Life and Art,* trans. Harold L. van Doren (New York, 1923), 47 n. 2 (as *The Red Roof*); Roger Fry, "Le développement de Cézanne," *L'Amour de l'Art* 7 (1926): 396; Roger Fry, *Cézanne: A Study of His Development* (New York, 1927), 22; Kurt Pfister, *Cézanne: Gestalt / Werk / Mythos* (Potsdam, 1927), 5, 13–14, pl. 23 (as *Winterlandschaft*); Eugenio d'Ors, *Paul Cézanne,* trans. Francisco Amunategui (Paris, 1930), 73; Ambroise Vollard, "Souvenirs sur Cézanne," *Cahiers d'Art* (1931): 392; Lionello Venturi, "Paul Cézanne," *L'Arte* 38 (July–September 1935): 305, ill.; René Huyghe, "Cézanne et son œuvre," *L'Amour de l'Art* (May 1936): 167, pl. 41; Maurice Raynal, *Cézanne* (Paris, 1936), 6, 57, 146, pl. 35; Lionello Venturi, *Cézanne: Son Art, son œuvre* (Paris, 1936), 1:16, 24–25, no. 51, and 2: pl. 11; Fritz Novotny, *Cézanne* (Vienna and New York, 1937), 17; John Rewald, "Paul Cézanne: New Documents for the Years 1870–1871," *The Burlington Magazine* 74, no. 433 (April 1939): 164, pl. 1B; Bernard Dorival, *Cézanne,* trans. H.H.A. Thackwaite (New York, 1948), 32–33, 34, 50, 95, 129, 141, pl. 27; Meyer Schapiro, *Paul Cézanne* (New York, 1952), 25–26, 38, ill. (as *L'Estaque, Melting Snow*); François Daulte, "Le Chef-d'œuvre d'une vie: La Collection Bührle," *Connaissance des arts,* no. 52 (15 June 1956), 34, ill. (as *Neige à l'Estaque*); Max Huggler, "Die Sammlung Bührle im Zürcher Kunsthaus," *Das Werk* 45, no. 10 (October 1958): 369, fig. 2; René Elvin, "Collector Extraordinary: The Bührle Collection and the New Zürich Kunsthaus," *The Studio* 158, no. 797 (August–September 1959): 54; René Wehrli, "Emil G. Bührle: French Nineteenth-Century Painting," in *Great Private Collections,* ed. Douglas Cooper (New York, 1963), 221, 224, ill.; Liliane Brion-Guerry, *Cézanne et l'expression de l'espace* (Paris, 1966), 53–55, 56, 62, 196, 197, fig. 10; Sandra Orienti, *L'opera completa di Cézanne* (Milan, 1970), no. 111, ill.; Lilli Fischel, "Von der Bildform der französischen Impressionisten," *Jahrbuch der Berliner Museen* 15 (1973): 106–108; John Rewald, "Some Entries for a New Catalogue Raisonné of Cézanne's Paintings," *Gazette des Beaux-Arts,* ser. 6, 86, no. 1282 (November 1975): 167 (as Bernheim-Jeune inv. 18558, *L'Estaque, effet de neige*); Nicholas Wadley, *Cézanne and His Art* (London, New York, Sydney, and Toronto, 1975), 27, pl. 23; Liliane Brion-Guerry, "The Elusive Goal," in *Cézanne: The Late Work* [exh. cat., The Museum of Modern Art, New York] (New York, 1977), 73–74; Lionello Venturi, *Cézanne,* trans. R. Skira (Geneva, 1978), 54–55, 59, 162, ill.; Judith Wechsler, *The Interpretation of Cézanne* (Ann Arbor, 1981), 64 (as *Snow at L'Estaque*); François Dumont, *Cézanne* [exh. cat., Musée Granet, Aix-en-Provence] (Aix, 1982), 8, 22, 30–31, ill.; Joseph-Emile Muller, *Cézanne,* trans. Jane Brenton (London, 1983), 11 (as *L'Estaque under Snow*); John Rewald, *Cézanne: A Biography* (New York, 1986), 93, ill.; Lawrence Gowing, *Cézanne: The Early Years 1859–1872* [exh. cat., Royal Academy of Arts, London] (New York, 1988), 166, ill., including Sylvie Patin, "The Collectors of Cézanne's Early Works," 60, 65 nn. 54, 56–57 (erroneously listed as probably bought directly from the artist by its first owner, Auguste Pellerin); Mary Tompkins Lewis, *Cézanne's Early Imagery* (Berkeley, Los Angeles, and London, 1989), 196–197, 260 n. 6, pl. 15.

Paul Cézanne
39 The Artist's Wife in an Armchair

NOTES: **1.** Rewald, *Cézanne: A Biography*, 78. / **2.** Rewald, *Cézanne: A Biography*, 268; Rewald, *Cézanne, the Steins and Their Circle*, 38; and Rewald 1989, 72. / **3.** Venturi 1936; 1: no. 369; van Buren 1966, 117–118, 210. / **4.** Rewald 1989, 72, 94. / **5.** Rewald, *Cézanne: A Biography*, 125, continues, "Cézanne rarely painted any other woman, and it must have entailed considerable sacrifice on the part of his lovely and talkative wife to lend herself to the endless sittings he inflicted on her." / **6.** Fernande Olivier, *Picasso et ses amis* (Paris, 1923), 102, as quoted in Rewald 1989, 56. / **7.** Rewald 1989, 72.

PROVENANCE: Ambroise Vollard, Paris; possibly consigned with or sold to Bernheim-Jeune, Paris (no. 13623, *Femme en gris sur fond gris*); sale, Bernheim-Jeune, Paris, 7 July 1904, to Auguste Pellerin; returned to Bernheim-Jeune, 4 February 1911, in exchange for *Valabrègue* (inv. 18551); sale, Bernheim-Jeune to Vollard; Leo and Gertrude Stein, Paris; retained by Gertrude Stein in 1913 when the collection was divided; César M. de Hauke, Paris; purchased by Bührle in 1952 from a French dealer.

EXHIBITIONS: *Salon d'Automne* (Salle Paul Cézanne), Paris, 1904, no. 9 (as *Femme à l'éventail*); Zurich 1958, no. 223; Berlin 1958, no. 52; Munich 1958–1959, no. 18; *De Géricault à Matisse: Chefs-d'œuvre français des collections suisses*, Petit Palais, Paris, 1959, no. 16; Edinburgh and London 1961, no. 32; *Chefs-d'œuvre des collections suisses de Manet à Picasso*, Palais de Beaulieu, Lausanne, 1964, no. 89.

LITERATURE: Vollard 1914, pl. 45; Venturi 1936, 1: no. 369, and 2: pl. 101 (as *La Dame à l'éventail [portrait de Mme Cézanne]*); Huggler 1958, 369; "Europas schönste Impressionistensammlung: E. G. Bührle," *Das Schönste* 1 (1959): 24; Anne H. van Buren, "Madame Cézanne's Fashion and the Dates of Her Portraits," *The Art Quarterly* 29, no. 2 (1966): 117, 120–121, fig. 5; Wayne Andersen, *Cézanne's Portrait Drawings* (Cambridge, Mass., and London, 1970), 26, fig. 23; Orienti 1970, no. 498, pl. 14 (as *La Signora Cézanne con ventaglio*); Rewald 1975, 161, 162, possibly 166 (Bernheim-Jeune inv. 13623, *Femme en gris sur fond gris*); Leopold Reidemeister, in *Foundation Emil G. Bührle Collection*, 2d ed. (Zurich and Munich, 1986), no. 53, ill.; John Rewald, *Cézanne, the Steins and Their Circle* (New York, 1986), 11, 20, 36–38, no. 4, figs. 4, 14 (undated photograph of the Stein apartment), 25, (1922 Man Ray photograph of Gertrude Stein's apartment), and 26 (undated photograph of the Stein apartment) (as *Madame Cézanne with a Fan*); Bob Kirsch, "Paul Cézanne: 'Jeune fille au piano' and Some Portraits of His Wife. An Investigation of the Late 1870s," *Gazette des Beaux-Arts*, ser. 6, 110 (July-August 1987): 21–26; John Rewald, *Cézanne and America: Dealers, Collectors, Artists and Critics 1891–1921* (Princeton, 1989), 55–56, 63, 72, 85 n. 44, 93–94, figs. 46 (1906 photograph of the Stein apartment) and 59, pl. 5 (as *Portrait of the Artist's Wife*).

Paul Cézanne
40 Still Life with Petunias

NOTES: **1.** Venturi 1936, 1: no. 198. / **2.** John Rewald, *Paul Cézanne: The Watercolors* (Boston, 1983), nos. 194, 211, and 212–214. / **3.** Rewald 1983, nos. 217–219. / **4.** Meyer Schapiro, "The Apples of Cézanne: An Essay on the Meaning of Still-Life (1968)," in *Modern Art: 19th & 20th Centuries, Selected Papers* (New York, 1978), 27.

PROVENANCE: Gustave Fayet, Béziers and Igny; E. Druet, Paris; Charles Pacquement, Paris; sale,

Galerie Georges Petit, Paris, 12 December 1932, no. 14; Sascha Guitry, Paris; Paul Rosenberg, New York; purchased by Bührle in 1952.

EXHIBITIONS: *Manet and the Post-Impressionists*, Grafton Galleries, London, 1910–1911, no. 12; *Première Exposition de Collectionneurs au profit de la Société des Amis du Luxembourg*, Paris, 1924, no. 184; *Trente Ans d'art indépendant: Exposition rétrospective*, Salon des Indépendants, Paris, 1926, no. 287; Chicago and New York 1952, no. 22; Zurich 1958, no. 217; Berlin 1958, 48, no. 24; Munich 1958–1959, no. 14; Edinburgh and London 1961, no. 33.

LITERATURE: Louis Hind, *The Post-Impressionists* (London, 1911), ill.; J. Mauny, "The Charles Pacquement Collection," *The Arts* (January 1928): ill.; *Bulletin de l'Art* (January 1933): 51; Venturi 1936, 1: no. 198, and 2: pl. 198; Dorival 1948, 130, no. 42, pl. 42; Huggler 1958, 369; Orienti 1970, no. 221, ill.

Paul Cézanne
41 The Boy in the Red Vest

NOTES: **1.** Gustave Geffroy, *La Vie artistique*, ser. 6 (Paris, 1900), 218: "soutenir la comparaison avec les plus belles figures de la peinture." / **2.** Venturi 1936, 1: no. 680: "Tableau peint, ainsi que les [Bührle] nos. 681–682–683 et 1094, d'après un modèle italien, qui, à en croire la tradition, se nommait Michelangelo Di Rosa." The two watercolors are fully catalogued in Rewald 1983, nos. 375, 376. See also Rewald, "Paintings by Paul Cézanne in the Mellon Collection," 310. / **3.** Rewald 1983, 174. / **4.** Reff 1977, 18. / **5.** Schapiro 1952, 9–10.

PROVENANCE: Marczell de Nemes, Budapest; sale, *Tableaux Modernes M. de Nemes*, Galerie Manzi-Joyant, Paris, 18 July 1913; Dr. G.-F. Reber, Lausanne; purchased by Bührle in 1948 from a Swiss private collection.

EXHIBITIONS: *Exposition Paul Cézanne*, Galerie Vollard, Paris, 1895; *Collection de Nemes*, Musée des Beaux-Arts, Budapest, 1911; *Die Sammlung von Nemes*, Städtische Kunsthalle, Düsseldorf, 1912, no. 117; *Cézanne*, Galerie Paul Cassirer, Berlin, 1921, no. 31; *Internationale Kunstausstellung*, Dresden, 1926, no. 80; *Erste Sonderausstellung*, Galerie Thannhauser, Berlin, 1927, no. 22; *Exposition Cézanne*, Théâtre Pigalle, Paris, 1929, no. 34; *Exposition Cézanne (1839–1906) organisée à l'occasion de son centenaire*, Paul Rosenberg, Paris, 1939, no. 30; *Europäische Kunst des 13.–20. Jahrhunderts*, Kunsthaus, Zurich, 1950, no. 26; Chicago and New York 1952, 65, no. 75; *Europäische Meister 1790–1910*, Kunstmuseum, Winterthur, 1955, no. 32; *Exposition pour commémorer le cinquantenaire de la mort de Cézanne*, Pavillon de Vendôme, Aix-en-Provence, 1956, no. 51; *Paul Cézanne 1839–1906*, Gemeentemuseum den Haag, The Hague, 1956, no. 39; *Paul Cézanne 1839–1906*, Kunsthaus, Zurich, 1956, no. 70; Zurich 1958, 24–25, no. 227; Berlin 1958, 50, no. 53; Munich 1958–1959, no. 22; Paris 1959, no. 20; Edinburgh and London 1961, no. 36; Lausanne 1964, no. 97; *Chefs-d'œuvre des collections suisses de Manet à Picasso*, Musée de l'Orangerie, Paris, 1967, no. 92.

LITERATURE: G. Biermann, "Die Sammlung Marczell de Nemes," *Der Cicerone* (1913): ill.; G. Mourey, "La Collection Marczell de Nemes," *Les Arts*, no. 138 (1913): ill.; Julius Meier-Graefe, *Entwicklungsgeschichte der modernen Kunst* (Munich, 1915), 3: pl. 496; Meier-Graefe 1918, 75 n. 14, 80, ill.; G. J. Wolf, "Die neugeordneten Bayerischen Staatsgalerien," *Die Kunst* (1920): ill.; M. J. Friedländer "Über Paul Cézanne," *Die Kunst* (1922): ill.; Rivière 1923, 216; Julius Meier-Graefe, *Cézanne*, trans. J. Holroyd-Reece (London and New York, 1927), 63, pl. 77; Julius Meier-Graefe, "Die Franzosen in Berlin," *Der Cicerone* (1927): ill.; Pfister 1927, 5, pl. 3; Fritz Novotny, "Paul Cézanne," *Belvedere* (1929): 440–442, pl. 29; Charensol, "La Quin-

zaine artistique: Cézanne à la galerie Pigalle," *L'Art vivant* 6 (15 February 1930): 183, ill.; Ors 1930, 72, 75, pl. 14; *Cézanne*, foreword by Jacques-Emile Blanche, preface by Paul Jamot [exh. cat., Musée de l'Orangerie] (Paris, 1936), 27; Venturi 1936, 1: 61–62, no. 681, and 2: pl. 220; Fritz Novotny, *Cézanne und das Ende der wissenschaftlichen Perspektive* (Vienna, 1938), 76–78, 86–87, 97–99, 126–127, pl. 47; Paul Rosenberg, *Loan Exhibition of Paintings by Cézanne (1839–1906) for the Benefit of Fighting France* [exh. cat., Paul Rosenberg and Company] (New York, 1942), 33; Dorival 1948, 57, 58, 59–60, 69–70, 132, no. 111, ill.; "Die Sammlung Emil Bührle in Zürich," *Das Kunstwerk* 7, no. 6 (1953): 28, ill.; *An Exhibition of Paintings by Cézanne* [exh. cat., Tate Gallery] (London, 1954), nos. 47, 56; Raynal 1954, 9, ill.; Daulte 1956, 34, ill.; John Richardson, "Cézanne at Aix-en-Provence," *The Burlington Magazine* 98, no. 644 (November 1956): 412; Huggler 1958, 369, 370; Elvin 1959, 54, ill.; Denys Sutton, "The Bührle Collection," *The Connoisseur* 143, no. 577 (May 1959): 145, 146, fig. 11; Theodore Reff, "Cézanne, Flaubert, St. Anthony, and the Queen of Sheba," *The Art Bulletin* 44, no. 2 (June 1962): 117 n. 44; Wehrli 1963, 220, ill.; Brion-Guerry 1966, 20–21, 174–175, 177, 179–180, 257 n. 129, pl. 54; François Daulte, "Un Siècle d'art français dans les collections suisses à l'Orangerie des Tuileries," *La Revue du Louvre* 17, no. 3 (1967): 145; Orienti 1970, no. 580, pl. 50; Lilli Fischel, "Von der Bildform der französischen Impressionisten," *Jahrbuch der Berliner Museen* 15 (1973): 111–113, 115–117, pl. 3; "Nouvelles des arts, Tokyo: L'Œuvre de Cézanne et son rayonnement," *L'Œil*, no. 219 (October 1973): 54, ill.; Wadley 1975, 53–54, ill.; Theodore Reff, "Painting and Theory in the Final Decade," in *Cézanne: The Late Work*, 1977, 15, 17–18; Joyce E. Brodsky, "Cézanne and the Image of Confrontation," *Gazette des Beaux-Arts*, ser. 6, 92, no. 1316 (September 1978): 85–86, 86 n. 3; Venturi 1978, 121, 163, ill.; Hans Luthy, "The E. G. Bührle Foundation," *Apollo* 110 (October 1979): 326, pl. 30; Dumont 1982, 25, 41, ill.; Muller 1983, 27–28, 37, pl. 38; John Rewald, *Paul Cézanne: The Watercolors, A Catalogue Raisonné* (Boston, 1983), 174–175; Reidemeister 1986, no. 55, ill.; John Rewald, "Paintings by Paul Cézanne in the Mellon Collection," in *Essays In Honor of Paul Mellon: Collector and Benefactor*, ed. John Wilmerding (Washington, 1986), 310–313.

Paul Cézanne
42 Vase of Flowers and Apples

NOTES: **1.** Rewald 1983, no. 204. / **2.** Rewald 1983, no. 372. / **3.** Rewald 1983, no. 373. / **4.** Schapiro 1952, 86. / **5.** Pickvance 1986, 56. / **6.** Schapiro 1978, 25.

PROVENANCE: Cornelis Hoogendijk, Amsterdam, until 1911; Hoogendijk heirs, Amsterdam, until 1920; sold to Paul Rosenberg, Paris; Henri-Jean Laroche, Paris, by 1929; Jacques Laroche, Paris; Otto L. Spaeth, New York; Daniel Wildenstein, New York; purchased by Bührle in 1956.

EXHIBITIONS: Rijksmuseum, Amsterdam, 1907–1911, long-term loan; Paris 1929, no. 32; *Cézanne*, Galerie Druet, Paris, 1933, no. 1; Paris 1939, no. 16; *Cézanne*, Rosenberg & Helft, Ltd., London, 1939, no. 10; *A Loan Exhibition of Paintings by Cézanne (1839–1906) for the Benefit of Fighting France*, Paul Rosenberg & Company, New York, 1942, 16, no. 12; *French Masterpieces*, Paul Rosenberg & Company, New York, 1945; *Paintings by Paul Cézanne*, Cincinnati Art Museum, 1947, no. 5; New York 1947, no. 26 (as *Vase de Fleurs et Oranges*); *French Still Life from Chardin to Cézanne*, A. Seligmann-Helft Galleries, New York, 1947, no. 6; *19th Century Influence in French Painting*, Guild Hall of East Hampton, New York, n.d., no. 9; *Loan Exhibition: Magic of Flowers in Painting*, Wildenstein and Company, New York, 1954, no. 7 (as *Vase of Flowers*); *The Spaeth Collection,* Columbus Gallery of Fine Arts, Ohio, 1955, no. 7; Zurich 1958, no. 225; Berlin 1958, no. 50; Munich 1958–1959, no. 20; Edinburgh and London 1961, no. 35; Lucerne 1963, no. 33.

LITERATURE: Charensol 1930, 183, ill., Ors 1930, 66, pl. 18; Venturi 1936, 1: no. 513, and 2: pl. 157 (as *Vase de fleurs et pommes*); "From French Tables," *Art News* 46, no. 9, pt. 1 (November 1947): 39; Dorival 1948, 55, no. 93, pl. 93; Huggler 1958, 369; Meyer Schapiro, "The Apples of Cézanne: An Essay on the Meaning of Still-Life," *Art News Annual* 34 (1968): 34–53, reprinted in Meyer Schapiro, *Modern Art: 19th & 20th Centuries, Selected Papers* (New York, 1978), 1–38, esp. 12–15, 25–33; Orienti 1970, no. 492, ill. (as *Vaso e due mele*); Venturi 1978, 104, 163, ill. (as in a private collection in Paris); Muller 1983, 36, pl. 19; Ronald Pickvance, *Cézanne* [exh. cat., Isetan Museum of Art] (Tokyo, 1986), 56.

Paul Cézanne
43 Self-Portrait with Palette

NOTES: **1.** Schapiro 1952, 11. / **2.** Schapiro 1952, 64. / **3.** Letter to Joachim Gasquet dated 30 April 1896, in Paul Cézanne, *Letters,* ed. John Rewald, trans. Seymour Hacker, rev. ed. (New York, 1984), 248. / **4.** Venturi 1936, 1: no. 516; Venturi 1978, 102, 163; Reidemeister 1986, 146; Rewald 1959, pl. 5; and Rewald, *Cézanne: A Biography,* 190. / **5.** Adrien Chappuis, *Dessins de Cézanne* (Lausanne, 1957), no. 30 (dated 1884); Adrien Chappuis, *The Drawings of Paul Cézanne: A Catalogue Raisonné* (Greenwich, 1973), 1: no. 614 (dated 1880–1882); and Andersen 1970, 34, 65, no. 19.

PROVENANCE: Paul Cézanne (son of the artist) and his wife, Renée Rivière Cézanne, Paris; purchased by Bührle in 1953 from a private Swiss collection.

EXHIBITIONS: *Impressionisten,* Secession, Berlin, 1903, no. 55; possibly *Cézanne,* Galerie Bernheim-Jeune, Paris, 1920; Paris 1929, no. 2 (as *Portrait de Cézanne à son chevalet, par lui-même*); *French Painters of the 19th Century, from Ingres to Cézanne,* Reid and Lefèvre Gallery, London, 1933, no. 4; *Exposition du Dix-Neuf-Cent,* Galerie Braun, Paris, 1934, no. 26; Brussels 1935, no. 5; *Exposition du portrait français de 1400 à 1900,* Galerie Seligmann, Paris, 1936, no. 100; *Paul Cézanne,* Kunsthalle, Basel, 1936, no. 44 (as *Selbstbildnis vor der Staffelei*); *Cézanne,* Detroit Institute of Arts, 1937; *The Post-Impressionists,* Bignou, New York, 1937, no. 1; *Cézanne,* Reid and Lefèvre Gallery, London, 1937, no. 17; Amsterdam 1938, no. 30; *D'Ingres à Cézanne,* Palais Municipale, Lyon, 1938–1939, no. 2; *Centenaire du maître indépendant Paul Cézanne,* Salon des Indépendants, Paris, 1939, no. 13; Zurich 1958, no. 226; Munich 1958–1959, no. 21; Edinburgh and London 1961, no. 34.

LITERATURE: Emil Heilbut, "Die Ausstellung der Berliner Secession," *Kunst und Künstler* 1, no. 8 (1903): 308–309, ill.; Emile Bernard, "Erinnerungen an Paul Cézanne," *Kunst und Künstler* 6, no. 10–12 (June-August 1908): ill.; Meier-Graefe 1918, 79, ill.; M. Deri, *Die Malerei im 19. Jahrhundert* (Berlin, 1919), pl. 46; Ambroise Vollard, *Paul Cézanne,* 2d ed. (Paris, 1919), 180; Joachim Gasquet, "Ce qu'il m'a dit," *L'Amour de l'Art* 1 (December 1920): ill.; Rivière 1923, 216 (as *Portrait de Cézanne par lui-même* or *L'Homme à la Palette*); Meier-Graefe 1927, 46; Ors 1930, 62; Faure 1936, ill.; Venturi 1936, 1: no. 516, and 2: pl. 159 (as *Cézanne à la palette,* described as unfinished); Novotny 1937, 8, pl. 49; Novotny 1938, 118–119 n. 114; Dorival 1948, 57, 132, 150, pl. 104; Schapiro 1952, 15, 29, 64, ill.; Huggler 1958, 369–370; Elvin 1959, 54; John Rewald, *Cézanne, Geffroy et Gasquet, suivi de souvenirs sur Cézanne de Louis Aurenches et de lettres inédites* (Paris, 1959), fig. 5;

Paul Cézanne
44 Mont Sainte-Victoire

NOTES: **1.** Rewald 1977, 95. / **2.** Since establishing a chronology for the late work has proven exceptionally difficult, most authors have followed Venturi 1936, 1: no. 820. / **3.** Gowing 1977, 67–68. / **4.** Reff 1977, 27.

PROVENANCE: Ambroise Vollard, Paris; William Rockhill Nelson, Kansas City; Galerie Rosengart, Lucerne; purchased by Bührle in 1937.

EXHIBITIONS: Paris 1929, no. 41; Basel 1936, no. 57; Lyon 1939, no. 39; *Ausländische Kunst in Zürich,* Kunsthaus, Zurich, 1943, no. 540; Zurich 1950, 26; *P. Cézanne— 28 Malerier,* Kunstnerforbundet, Oslo, 1954, no. 28; Zurich 1958, 25, no. 232; Munich 1958–1959, no. 25; Edinburgh and London 1961, no. 37; Lucerne 1963, no. 35.

LITERATURE: Venturi 1935, 413, pl. 30; Faure 1936, pl. 55; Venturi 1936, 1: 64–65, no. 802, and 2: pl. 265; Novotny 1937, 8, 10, 19–20, 21, pl. 83; Novotny 1938, 10–11, no. 96; Dorival 1948, 78, no. 141, pl. 141; Jedlicka 1948, pl. 44; Raynal 1954, 116, 119, ill. 119; Sutton 1959, 146; Wehrli 1963, 216, 221; Brion-Guerry 1966, 247–249 n. 77; Orienti 1970, no. 764, ill.; Wadley 1975, 70–77, pl. 71; Lawrence Gowing, "The Logic of Organized Sensations," Theodore Reff, "Painting and Theory in the Final Decade," and John Rewald, "The Last Motifs at Aix," in *Cézanne: The Late Work,* 1977, 67–68, 27–29, 83–106, and pl. 123; Brodsky 1978, 85; Norman Turner, "Subjective Curvature in Late Cézanne," *The Art Bulletin* 63, no. 4 (December 1981): 666–667, 669, fig. 5; Wechsler 1981, 50; Silverman 1982, 373–374; John Wetenhall, "Cézanne's 'Mont Sainte-Victoire» Seen from Les Lauves." *Pantheon* 40, no. 1 (January–March 1982): 45–51.

Claude Monet
45 Camille Monet with Dog

PROVENANCE: Michel Monet, Giverny; Wildenstein and Company, New York; Col. and Mrs. Robert W. Reford, Montreal, 1939; François Daulte, Lausanne; purchased by Bührle in 1953.

EXHIBITIONS: *Claude Monet: Exposition rétrospective,* Musèe de l'Orangerie, Paris, 1931, 17, no. 7; *Monet de 1865 à 1888,* Galerie Durand-Ruel, Paris, 1935, no. 3; *A Loan Exhibition of Paintings by Claude Monet,* Wildenstein and Company, New York, 1945, no. 5; Zurich 1958, no. 1782; Berlin 1958, no. 7; Munich 1958–1959, no. 110; *De Géricault à Matisse: Chefs-d'œuvre français des collections suisses,* Petit Palais, Paris, 1959, no. 94; Edinburgh and London 1961, no. 39; Lucerne 1963, no. 27.

LITERATURE: Maurice Malingue, *Claude Monet* (Monaco, 1943), 25, no. 40, ill.; "Die Sammlung Emil Bührle in Zürich," *Das Kunstwerk* 7, no. 6 (1953): 28, ill.; François Daulte, "Le Chef-d'œuvre d'une vie: La Collection Bührle," *Connaissance des arts,* no. 52 (15 June 1956): 3, ill.; The Arts Council of Great Britain, *An Exhibition of Paintings: Claude Monet* [exh. cat., Royal Scottish Academy, Edinburgh] (London, 1957), 41; Léon Degand and Denis Rouart, *Claude Monet,* trans. James Emmons

(Geneva, 1958), 35, ill.; René Wehrli, "Emil G. Bührle: French Nineteenth-Century Painting," in *Great Private Collections,* ed. Douglas Cooper (New York, 1963), 219; Oscar Reuterswärd, *Monet* (Moscow, 1965), no. 6, pl. 6; Daniel Wildenstein, *Monet: Impressions* (Lausanne, 1967), ill.; Luigina Rossi Bortolatto, L'opera completa di Claude Monet *1870–1889* (Milan, 1972), no. 13, ill.; John Rewald, *The History of Impressionism,* 4th rev. ed. (New York, 1973), ill.; Daniel Wildenstein, *Claude Monet: Biographie et catalogue raisonné,* vol. 1, *1840–1881, Peintures* (Lausanne and Paris, 1974), 31–32, no. 64, ill.; Joel Isaacson, *Observation and Reflection: Claude Monet* (Oxford, 1978), 208; Hans Luthy, "The E. G. Bührle Foundation," *Apollo* 110 (October 1979): 325, pl. 27; Yvon Taillandier, *Monet,* trans. A. P. H. Hamilton (New York, 1982), 86–87, ill.; Charles Stuckey, "Monet's Art and the Act of Vision," in *Aspects of Monet: A Symposium on the Artist's Life and Times,* ed. John Rewald and Frances Weitzenhoffer (New York, 1984), 116, ill.; *The Impressionist Revolution,* ed. Bruce Bernard (Boston, 1986), 19, ill.

Claude Monet
46 The Dinner

NOTE: **1.** Reff 1976, 222.

PROVENANCE: Bought from Monet by Durand-Ruel, February 1873; Depeaux, Rouen, sale, Georges Petit, Paris, 31 May–1 June 1906, no. 19; Bernheim-Jeune, Paris (possibly bought at Depeaux sale); Julius Stern, Berlin; Hugo Nathan, Frankfurt am Main, by 1913; Mme Nathan, Basel, c. 1938; Städelsches Kunstinstitut, Frankfurt am Main; Galerie Aktuaryus, Zurich; purchased by Bührle in 1944.

EXHIBITIONS: Possibly *Le Peintre Claude Monet,* Galerie La Vie Moderne, Paris, 1880, no. 16; *Frankfurter Kunstschätze,* Kunstverein, Frankfurt am Main, 1913, no. 59; *Claude Monet 1840–1926: Gedächtnis-Ausstellung,* Galerien Thannhauser, Berlin, 1928, no. 4 (as *Abendessen bei Sisley*); *Impressionisten,* Kunsthalle, Basel, 1949, no. 76; *Claude Monet 1840–1926,* Kunsthaus, Zurich, 1952, no. 24 (as *Déjeuner chez Sisley*); *Claude Monet,* Gemeentemuseum, The Hague, 1952, no. 12 (as *Familie Sisley aan tafel*); *Claude Monet,* Galerie Wildenstein, Paris, 1952, no. 12 (as *Le déjeuner de la famille Sisley*); *Claude Monet 1840–1926,* Marlborough Fine Art Limited, London, 1954, no. 1, ill. (as *Le Déjeuner de la famille Sisley*); Edinburgh and London 1957, 10, no. 14 (as *The Evening Meal,* or *Le Déjeuner chez les Sisley,* or *Le Repas,* identifying the male figure as Sisley and the locale as the Sisley home on rue de la Paix, Paris); Zurich 1958, no. 179 (as *Abendessen bei Sisley*); Berlin 1958, no. 8 (as *Abendessen bei Sisley*); Munich 1958–1959, no. 111 (as *Abendessen bei Sisley*); Edinburgh and London 1961, no. 40 (as painted at the Sisley apartment in the Rue de la Paix, identifying the child as Pierre Sisley, born in 1867).

LITERATURE: Vittorio Pica, *Gl'Impressionisti Francesi* (Bergamo, 1908), ill.; Georg Swarzenski, "Die Sammlung Hugo Nathan in Frankfurt a. M.," *Kunst und Künstler* 15 (December 1916): 112–114, ill. (as *Mittagessen bei Sisley*); Marc Elder, *Chez Claude Monet à Giverny* (Paris, 1924), pl. 13; "Schweiz. Monatsschrift, Zürich," *DU,* no. 5 (1945), ill.; Oscar Reuterswärd, *Monet* (Stockholm, 1948), ill.; Victor Griessmaier, *Impressionismus* (Vienna, 1956), pl. 7; Wehrli 1963, 219; H. Hamm, "Der Mensch als Impression: Zu den figürlichen Bildern Claude Monets," *Die Kunst und das schöne Heim* 64, no. 9 (June 1966): 366 (as *Tischgesellschaft*); John Rewald, "Notes sur deux tableaux de Claude Monet," *Gazette des Beaux-Arts,* ser. 6, 70 (October 1967): 245–248, fig. 1 (as depicting the Monet family); Bortolatto 1972, no. 58, ill. (as *Cena presso Sisley*); Kermit Swiler Champa, *Studies in Early Impressionism* (New Haven and London, 1973),

25–26, 29–31, fig. 38; Rewald 1973, ill.; Wildenstein 1974, 41, 112 n. 848, no. 129, 425–426, letter 44, ill.; Theodore Reff, *Degas: The Artist's Mind* (New York, 1976), 222–223, fig. 148 (as *The Dinner*); Isaacson 1978, 17, no. 15, pl. 15 (as *Dinner*, identifying the near figure, with back shown, as Camille); Pascal Bonafoux, *The Impressionists: Portraits and Confidences* (New York and Geneva, 1986), 190, ill. (as *The Sisley Family at Dinner*); Leopold Reidemeister, in *Foundation Emil G. Bührle Collection,* 2d ed. (Zurich and Munich, 1986), no. 69, ill. (as *Abendessen bei Sisley*); Lorenz Eitner, *An Outline of 19th Century European Painting: From David Through Cézanne* (New York, 1987), 1:351.

Claude Monet
47 Camille Monet, Son, and Nurse in Garden

PROVENANCE: Possibly bought from Monet by Jean-Baptiste Faure, Paris, 1874; Auguste Pellerin, Paris; traded to Bernheim-Jeune, Paris, 8 February 1911, in partial exchange for Cézanne, *L'Estaque (effect of snow)* (Venturi 1936, no. 51; see cat. 38); Ambroise Vollard, Paris; Bruno Cassirer, Berlin; Mrs. Cassirer, Oxford; Dr. Kauffmann, London; purchased by Bührle in 1948.

EXHIBITIONS: *Nineteenth Century French Paintings*, National Gallery, London, 1944(?), no. 43; Zurich 1952, no. 29; The Hague 1952, no. 25; Paris 1952, no. 23; *Claude Monet 1840–1926*, Marlborough Fine Art Limited, London, 1954, no. 8; *Europäische Meister 1790–1910*, Kunstmuseum, Winterthur, 1955, no. 147; Zurich 1958, no. 181; Berlin 1958, no. 25; Munich 1958–1959, no. 112; Edinburgh and London 1961, no. 42; Lucerne 1963, no. 28.

LITERATURE: Reuterswärd 1948, ill.; Arts Council 1957, 46; Wehrli 1963, ill.; Rodolphe Walter, "Les Maisons de Claude Monet à Argenteuil," *Gazette des Beaux-Arts,* ser. 6, 68 (December 1966): 336, fig. 6; Bortolatto 1972, no. 85, ill.; Rewald 1973, ill.; Wildenstein 1974, 65, no. 280, ill.; John Rewald, "Some Entries for a New Catalogue Raisonné of Cézanne's Paintings," *Gazette des Beaux-Arts,* ser. 6, 86, no. 1282 (November 1975): 166–167; Alice Bellony-Rewald, *The Lost World of the Impressionists* (London, 1976), ill.; Isaacson 1978, 20, 205; Paul Hayes Tucker, *Monet at Argenteuil* (New Haven and London, 1982), 135, 137, 138–139, pl. 25; Robert Gordon and Andrew Forge, *Monet* (New York, 1983), 85, 88–89, ill.

Claude Monet
48 Poppies near Vétheuil

PROVENANCE: Possibly bought from Monet by Cantin, November 1879, one of six canvases; Mme Cantin; sale, Hôtel Drouot, Paris, 19 April 1895, no. 50, to Durand-Ruel, Paris; Bernheim-Jeune, Paris, 1898; Paul Cassirer, Berlin; Julius Stern, Berlin, by 1914; sale, Paul Cassirer, Berlin, 22 May 1916, no. 70; J. Atern, Berlin; G. Hauswaldt, Magdeburg; Dr. Emden, Ascona; Nathan, Zurich; purchased by Bührle in 1941.

EXHIBITIONS: *Erste Ausstellung der Freien Sezession*, Berlin, 1914; *Ausländische Kunst in Zürich*, Kunsthaus, Zurich, 1943, no. 613; Basel 1949, no. 147; *Het Franse Landschap van Poussin tot Cézanne*, Rijksmuseum, Amsterdam, 1951, no. 83; Zurich 1952, no. 51 (as *Mohnfeld bei Vétheuil*); Paris 1952, no. 39 (as *La Cueillette des coquelicots*); Zurich 1958, no. 183; Berlin 1958, no. 30; Munich 1958–1959, no. 114; Edinburgh and London 1961, no. 20b; *Die Ile de France und ihre Maler*, Schloss Charlottenburg, Berlin, 1963, no. 42.

LITERATURE: Adolf Hölzel, "Über künstlerische

Ausdrucksmittel und deren Verhältnis zu Natur und Bild, III," *Die Kunst* 11 (December 1904): 129, ill.; Erich Hancke, "Die erste Ausstellung der Freien Sezession," *Kunst und Künstler* 9 (June 1914): ill. (as *Landschaft mit rotem Mohnfeld*); Doris Wild, *Moderne Malerei: ihre Entwicklung seit dem Impressionismus, 1880–1950* (Zurich, 1950), 21, pl. 3; Daulte 1956, 33; Leopold Reidemeister, *Auf den Spuren der Maler der Ile de France* (Berlin, 1963), 118, ill.; Wehrli 1963, 216, 219; Bortolatto 1972, no. 155, pl. 28; Wildenstein 1974, 95, no. 536, ill.; Reidemeister 1986, no. 70, ill.

Auguste Renoir
49 Portrait of the Painter Alfred Sisley

NOTES: **1.** Distel, in Arts Council 1985, 189. / **2.** Distel, in Arts Council 1985, 182. / **3.** Distel, in Arts Council 1985, 183; Kermit Champa, *Studies in Early Impressionism* (London and New Haven, 1973), 35. / **4.** John Rewald, *The History of Impressionism,* 4th rev. ed. (New York, 1973), 76. / **5.** Edgar Degas, notebook 112 (1869), Bibliothèque Nationale, Paris, as quoted in Linda Nochlin, *Impressionism and Post-Impressionism 1874–1904: Sources and Documents* (Englewood Cliffs, N. J., 1966), 62.

PROVENANCE: Alfred Sisley, Paris and Moret-sur-Loing; by inheritance to his daughter, Jeanne Sisley; Henry Lapauze, Paris; Mme Charles Pomaret, Paris, by 1937 until 1955; sold to César de Hauke, 4 June 1955; Paul Brame and César de Hauke, Paris; purchased by Bührle in 1955.

EXHIBITIONS: *L'Atelier de Sisley,* Galerie Bernheim-Jeune, Paris, 1907, no. 1; *Portraits d'hommes,* Galerie Bernheim-Jeune, Paris, 1907–1908, no. 106; *Exposition centennale de l'art français,* Saint Petersburg (Leningrad), 1912, no. 539; *Alfred Sisley,* Galerie Georges Petit, Paris, 1917, no. A; *Art français du XIXᵉ siècle,* Galerie Paul Rosenberg, Paris, 1917, no. 51; *Exposition au profit des mutilés de la guerre,* Galerie Paul Rosenberg, Paris, 1917; *Exposition au profit des Laboratoires,* rue de la Ville-l'Evèque, Paris, 1923; *Exposition Renoir 1841–1919,* Musée de l'Orangerie, Paris, 1933, no. 5; *Chefs-d'œuvre de l'art français,* Palais National des Arts, Paris, 1937, no. 392; *Renoir, portraitiste,* Galerie Bernheim-Jeune, Paris, 1938, no. 10; *Alfred Sisley,* Kunstmuseum, Bern, 1958, no. 99; Zurich 1958, no. 166; Berlin 1958, no. 9; Munich 1958–1959, no. 129; Edinburgh and London 1961, no. 47.

LITERATURE: Julius Meier-Graefe, *Auguste Renoir* (Munich, 1911), ill. (2d ed., Munich, 1920); Théodore Duret, *Renoir* (Paris, 1924), 72; Gustave Coquiot, *Renoir* (Paris, 1925), 224; Julius Meier-Graefe, *Auguste Renoir* (Leipzig, 1929), 26, 437, no. 10, ill.; Claude Roger-Marx, *Renoir* (Paris, 1933), 185, ill.; Michel Florisoone, *Renoir* (Paris, 1937), ill.; Charles Terrasse, *Cinquante portraits de Renoir* (Paris, 1941); Michel Drucker, *Renoir* (Paris, 1944), 193; Gotthard Jedlicka, *Renoir* (Bern, 1947), pl. 7; André Chamson, *Renoir* (Lausanne, 1949), pl. 7; M. Robida, *Le Salon Charpentier et les impressionnistes* (Paris, 1958), pl. 21; François Daulte, *Alfred Sisley* (Lausanne, 1959), fig. 4; B. Reifenberg, *Das Ehepaar Sisley* (Stuttgart, 1959), pl. 5; Denys Sutton, "The Bührle Collection," *The Connoisseur* 143, no. 577 (May 1959): 146; François Daulte, *Auguste Renoir: Catalogue raisonné de l'œuvre peint,* vol. 1, *Figures 1860–1890* (Lausanne, 1971), no. 37, ill.; Elda Fezzi, *L'opera completa di Renoir nel periodo impressionista 1869–1883* (Milan, 1972), no. 24, ill.; *Guida alla pittura di Renoir,* introduction by Sophie Monneret (Milan, 1980), no. 23; Anne Distel, in Arts Council of Great Britain, *Renoir* [exh. cat., Hayward Gallery] (London, 1985), 189; Leopold Reidemeister, in *Foundation Emil G. Bührle Collection,* 2d ed. (Zurich and Munich, 1986), no. 61, ill.; Horst Keller, *Auguste Renoir* (Munich, 1987), 32, pl. 25.

Auguste Renoir
50 Harvesters

NOTES: **1.** Richard R. Brettell, "The Fields of France," in *A Day in the Country: Impressionism and the French Landscape* (Los Angeles, 1985), *243.* / **2.** Louis Leroy, "L'Exposition des Impressionnistes," *Le Charivari* (25 April 1874), quoted in Rewald 1973, 322–323. / **3.** Ernest Chesnau, "A côté du Salon: II. Le plein air, Exposition du boulevard des Capucines," *Paris-Journal* (7 May 1874), quoted in Adhémar and Gache 1974, 269. / **4.** Marc de Montifaud, "Exposition du boulevard des Capucines," *L'Artiste* (1 May 1874), quoted in Adhémar and Gache 1974, 266.

PROVENANCE: Possibly sold by Renoir, *Tableaux et Aquarelles par Claude Monet, Berthe Morisot, A. Renoir, A. Sisley,* Hôtel Drouot, Paris, 24 March 1875, no. 47, procès verbal no. 59 *(Paysage d'été* [Renoir, 60×73]), to Gabriel Thomas, Paris, for 105 francs; Mme Carmona, Paris; sale, *Vente de tableaux modernes,* Hôtel Drouot, Paris, 30 March 1938, no. 27; Galerie Dr. Fritz Nathan, Zurich; purchased by Bührle in 1951.

EXHIBITIONS: *Première Exposition,* Société anonyme des artistes peintres, sculpteurs, graveurs, etc., Paris, 1874, no. 144 (as *Moissonneurs*); Zurich 1958, no. 167 (as *Landschaft [Kornernte]*); Berlin 1958, no. 26; Munich 1958–1959, no. 130, Edinburgh and London 1961, no. 48; Lucerne 1963, no. 21.

LITERATURE: Max Huggler, "Die Sammlung Bührle im Zürcher Kunsthaus," *Das Werk* 45, no. 10 (October 1958): 369; René Wehrli, "Emil G. Bührle: French Nineteenth-Century Painting," in *Great Private Collections,* ed. Douglas Cooper (New York, 1963), 220; Phoebe Pool, *Impressionism* (New York and Washington, 1967), 116; Merete Bodelsen, "Early Impressionist Sales 1874–94 in the Light of Some Unpublished 'Procès verbaux,'" *The Burlington Magazine* 110, no. 783 (June 1968): 336, possibly p. v. 59; Fezzi 1972, no. 100, ill.; John Rewald, *The History of Impressionism,* 4th rev. ed. (New York, 1973), 322–323, ill.; Hélène Adhémar and Sylvie Gache, "L'Exposition de 1874 chez Nadar (rétrospective documentaire)," in *Centenaire de l'impressionnisme* [exh. cat., Galeries nationales du Grand Palais] (Paris, 1974), 250–252, 260, 266, 269; Keith Wheldon, *Renoir and His Art* (London, New York, Sydney, and Toronto, 1975), 58; Anthea Callen, *Renoir* (London, 1978), 50–51, no. 28, ill.; *Guida,* 1980, no. 99; Arts Council 1985, 197, 202; Cynthia P. Schneider, "Renoir: Le Peintre de Figures comme Paysagiste," *Apollo* 122 (July 1985): 56 n. 3; Charles S. Moffett, in *The New Painting: Impressionism 1874–1886* [exh. cat., National Gallery of Art, Washington, and the Fine Arts Museums of San Francisco] (San Francisco, 1986), 122; *Renoir: A Retrospective,* ed. Nicholas Wadley (New York, 1987), pl. 25 (as *Harvest Time*).

Auguste Renoir
51 Young Woman in a Feathered Hat

NOTES: **1.** Sutton 1963, 392–394; Distel, in Arts Council 1985, 217; and Craig Hartley in Cambridge 1989, 163. / **2.** Sutton 1963, 394. / **3.** Edinburgh and London 1961, no. 49; Joel Isaacson, *The Crisis of Impressionism* [exh. cat., The University of Michigan Museum of Art] (Ann Arbor, 1979), 34; Joel Isaacson, "Impressionism and Journalistic Illustration," *Arts Magazine* 56, no. 10 (June 1982): 107. / **4.** Edmond Duranty, "The New Painting," Paris, 1876, as quoted in Moffett 1985, 43–44.

PROVENANCE: Durand-Ruel, Paris, until 1906; Carl Wolde, Bremen, purchased via Julius Meier-Graefe; Dr. Fritz Nathan, Zurich; purchased by Bührle in 1950.

EXHIBITIONS: *Europäische Kunst des 13.– 20. Jahrhunderts,* Kunsthaus, Zurich, 1950, 27; *La Moda in cinque secoli di pittura,* Palazzo Madama,

Turin, 1951, no. 222; Zurich 1958, no. 168; Berlin 1958, no. 27; Munich 1958–1959, no. 131; Edinburgh and London 1961, no. 49; Lucerne 1963, no. 22.

LITERATURE: Emil Waldmann, "Bremer Privatsammlungen," *Kunst und Künstler* 17 (1919): 180, ill.; Théodore Duret, *Histoire des peintres impressionnistes* (Paris, 1939), ill.; Douglas Cooper, *Catalogue of the Courtauld Collection* (London, 1953), III, no. 55; *Impressionnistes de la collection Courtauld de Londres* [exh. cat., Musée de l'Orangerie] (Paris, 1955), no. 42; François Fosca, *Renoir* (Paris, 1961), ill.; Denys Sutton, "An Unpublished Sketch by Renoir," *Apollo* 77 (May 1963): 392–394, fig. 3; Daulte 1971, no. 324, ill. (as *Etude pour "La Place Clichy"*); Fezzi 1972, no. 404, ill.; *Guida,* 1980, no. 406; Arts Council 1985, 217; *Treasures from the Fitzwilliam* [exh. cat., National Gallery of Art, Washington] (Cambridge, 1989), 163.

Auguste Renoir
52 Portrait of Mademoiselle Irène Cahen d'Anvers

NOTES: **1.** Paul Cézanne, *Correspondence,* ed. John Rewald (Paris, 1978), 193–194, as quoted in Arts Council 1985, 300. / **2.** Théodore Duret, *Renoir* (Paris, 1924), 61–62; Arts Council 1985, 224. / **3.** Daulte 1971, no. 338. / **4.** Isaacson 1979, 30. / **5.** Théodore Duret, as cited and translated in White 1984, 132: "Dès l'abord nous lui reconnaissons la faculté de peindre la femme dans toute sa grâce et sa délicatesse, ce qui l'a conduit tout particulièrement à exceller dans le portrait. Ce don du charme, l'artiste l'a manifesté dès le début dans sa plénitude, et c'est dans ses qualités de peintre et de coloriste que nous vous avons à observer le progrès et le développement." See also Drucker 1944, 177.

PROVENANCE: Commissioned by Mme Cahen d'Anvers, Paris; by inheritance to comtesse Irène de Sampieri, née Cahen d'Anvers; Léon Reinach, Paris; collection of Hermann Göring, 1941; Walter Feuz, Clarens; purchased by Bührle in 1949.

EXHIBITIONS: *Exposition Renoir,* Galerie Durand-Ruel, Paris, 1883, no. 6; Paris 1933, no. 57; Paris 1938, no. 13; *Les Cents Chefs-d'œuvre de l'art français,* Musée du Louvre, Paris, 1945; *Les Chefs-d'œuvre des collections privées françaises retrouvés en Allemagne,* Musée de l'Orangerie, Paris, 1946, no. 41; Zurich 1958, no. 169; Berlin 1958, no. 31; Munich 1958–1959, no. 132; Edinburgh and London 1961, no. 50 (London only).

LITERATURE: H. Michaux, "Visages de jeunes filles," *Verve* 2, no. 5–6 (1939): 85, pl. 4; Drucker 1944, 185, no. 59, pl. 59; Reginald Howard Wilenski, *Modern French Painters,* 3d ed. (London, 1947), 340; René Elvin, "Collector Extraordinary: The Bührle Collection and the New Zurich Kunsthaus," *The Studio* 158, no. 797 (August–September 1959): 54; M. Robida, *Renoir: Enfants* (Lausanne, 1959), ill.; Sutton 1959, 146; Fosca 1961, ill.; Wehrli 1963, 220; Michel Drucker, *Renoir* (Paris, 1967), pl. 14; *Renoir* (Collection Génies et Réalités) (Paris, 1970), ill.; Daulte 1971, 410, no. 338, ill.; Fezzi 1972, no. 428, pl. 55; Hans Lüthy, "The E. G. Bührle Foundation," *Apollo* 110 (October 1979): 326; *Guida,* 1980, no. 424; Joel Isaacson, *The Crisis of Impressionism 1878–1882* [exh. cat., The University of Michigan Museum of Art] (Ann Arbor, 1980), 32; Barbara Ehrlich White, *Renoir: His Life, Art, and Letters* (New York, 1984), 102, ill.; Arts Council 1985, 224, 300; Reidemeister 1986, no. 62, ill.; Keller 1987, pl. 60.

Paul Gauguin
53 Mette Gauguin

NOTES: **1.** There are no paintings dated 1878 in the catalogue raisonné (Wildenstein 1964). / **2.** See Christopher Gray, *Sculpture and Ceramics of Paul Gauguin* (Baltimore, 1963), no. 1. / **3.** Cachin, 1968, 43. / **4.** For example, Wildenstein 1964, nos. 39, 47, 209. / **5.** Wildenstein 1964, nos. 39, and Charles F. Stuckey, in *The Art of Paul Gauguin* [exh. cat., National Gallery of Art] (Washington, D.C., 1988), no. 4.

PROVENANCE: M. Peter Krag, Norwegian general consul to Paris; Nobel Roede, Oslo, by 1926; private collection, Oslo; purchased for Bührle Foundation in 1964 from a Swiss dealer.

EXHIBITIONS: *Foreningen Fransk Kunst: Paul Gauguin,* Nasjonalgalleriet, Oslo, 1926, no. 64.

LITERATURE: Georges Wildenstein, *Gauguin,* ed. Raymond Cogniat and Daniel Wildenstein (Paris, 1964), no. 26; Françoise Cachin, *Gauguin* (Paris, 1968), 43; Leopold Reidemeister, in *Foundation Emil G. Bührle Collection,* 2d ed. (Zurich and Munich, 1986), no. 78.

Paul Gauguin
54 Pape moe

NOTES: **1.** Paul Gauguin, "Noa Noa," Musée du Louvre, Département des Arts Graphiques, 87–88. / **2.** Nicholas Wadley, ed., *Noa Noa, Gauguin's Tahiti* (London, 1985), 32. / **3.** One of these watercolors, dated 1894, is uncatalogued. For the other works, see John Rewald, *Gauguin Drawings* (New York and London, 1958), no. 53; Richard S. Field, *Paul Gauguin: Monotypes* [exh. cat., Philadelphia Museum of Art] (Philadelphia, 1973), no. 13; and Christopher Gray, *Sculpture and Ceramics of Paul Gauguin* (Baltimore, 1963), no. 107. / **4.** Stuckey in Washington 1988, 287. / **5.** On this relationship, see Field 1977, 198–193. / **6.** Bengt Danielsson, *Gauguin in the South Seas* (New York, 1966), 134.

PROVENANCE: *Vente de tableaux et dessins par Paul Gauguin,* Hôtel Drouot, Paris, 18 February 1895, no. 9; purchased for 500 francs by Ambroise Vollard, Paris; private collection, France; private collection, New York; private collection, Switzerland; Wildenstein and Company, Paris; purchased by Bührle in 1953.

EXHIBITIONS: *Exposition d'œuvres récentes de Paul Gauguin,* Galerie Durand-Ruel, Paris, 1893, no. 4; Zurich 1958, no. 248; Lucerne 1963, no. 36; *The Art of Paul Gauguin,* National Gallery of Art, Washington; The Art Institute of Chicago; Musée d'Orsay, Paris, 1988–1989, no. 157 (shown in Paris only).

LITERATURE: Charles Morice, *Gauguin* (Paris, 1919), 178–179; Jean de Rotonchamp [Louis Brouillon], *Paul Gauguin* (Weimar, 1925), 137 and 154; Richard S. Field, "Plagiaire ou créateur?" in *Gauguin* (Paris, 1960), 165–166; Wildenstein 1964, no. 498; Richard S. Field, *Paul Gauguin: The Paintings of the First Trip to Tahiti* (New York and London, 1977), 189–193; Naomi Maurer, "The Pursuit of Spiritual Knowledge: The Philosophical Meaning and Origins of Symbolist Theory and Its Expression in the Art of Redon, van Gogh, and Gauguin" (Ph. D. diss., University of Chicago, 1985), 1005–1010; Yann le Pichon, *Sur les Traces de Gauguin* (Paris, 1986), 170–171; Charles F. Stuckey, in *The Art of Paul Gauguin* [exh. cat., National Gallery of Art] (Washington, D.C., 1988), nos. 157, 286–287.

Paul Gauguin
55 Still Life with Sunflowers on an Armchair

NOTES: **1.** Letter to Vollard, January 1900, in John Rewald, ed., *Paul Gauguin: Letters to Am-broise Vollard and André Fontainas,* trans. G. Mack (San Francisco, 1943), 32. / **2.** Wildenstein 1964, nos. 603, 604, 606. / **3.** Wildenstein 1964, no. 49. Gauguin also used this motif in no. 46 (1880) and no. 404 (1890). / **4.** J. B. de la Faille, *The Works of Vincent van Gogh: His Paintings and Drawings* (New York, 1970), no. F 498, *Vincent's Chair with His Pipe,* and F 499, *Gauguin's Armchair, Candle and Books.* This similarity was pointed out in *Masterpieces of French Painting from the Bührle Collection* [exh. cat., National Gallery] (London, 1961), no. 52. / **5.** Gauguin also painted sunflowers in *Tropical Nude with Sunflowers* or the so-called *Femme Caraïbe* (Wildenstein 1964, no. 330). For the most recent note on that picture, see Charles F. Stuckey, unpublished supplement to Washington 1988, for The Art Institute of Chicago, 3.

PROVENANCE: Ambroise Vollard, Paris; Leo and Getrude Stein, Paris, by c. 1905; Halvorsen, Copenhagen; Galerien Thannhauser, Berlin; Josef Stransky, New York, by 1931; Wildenstein and Company, New York, from 1936 until at least 1937; Sam Salz; Félix Wildenstein by 1944; Oscar Homolka, Hollywood or New York, by 1946; purchased by Bührle from a dealer in Zurich in 1952.

EXHIBITIONS: *Paul Gauguin,* Galerien Thannhauser, Berlin, 1928, no. 72; *Collection of Modern Art lent by Josef Stransky of New York,* Worcester Art Museum, Mass., 1933–1916 (no catalogue); *Paul Gauguin 1848–1903: A Retrospective Loan Exhibition,* Wildenstein and Company, New York, 1936, no. 43; *Paul Gauguin,* The Fogg Art Museum, Cambridge, Mass., 1936, no. 42; *Paul Gauguin: A Retrospective Exhibition of His Paintings,* The Baltimore Museum of Art, 1936, no. 28; *The Collection of a Collector: Modern French Paintings from Ingres to Matisse,* Wildenstein and Company, London, 1936, no. 24; *La Vie ardente de Paul Gauguin,* Gazette des Beaux-Arts, Paris, 1936, no. 110; *The Development of Flower Painting from the Seventeenth Century to the Present,* City Art Museum, St. Louis, 1937, no. 37; *Masters of Painting and Printmaking,* Portland Art Museum, Oreg., 1941; *Nineteenth Century French Painting,* Virginia Museum of Fine Arts, Richmond, 1944, no. 36; *Paul Gauguin,* Wildenstein and Company, New York, 1946, no. 38; *Werke der französischen Malerei und Graphik des 19. Jahrhunderts,* Folkwang Museum, Essen, 1954, no. 43; *Europäische Meister 1790–1910,* Kunstmuseum, Winterthur, 1955, no. 91; *Gauguin: An Exhibition of Paintings, Engravings, and Sculpture,* The Royal Scottish Academy, Edinburgh, and the Tate Gallery, London, 1955, no. 60; *Paul Gauguin,* Kunstnerforbundet, Oslo, 1955; Zurich 1958, no. 251; Berlin 1958, no. 43, Munich 1958–1959, no. 61; *Paul Gauguin,* Österreichische Galerie im oberen Belvedere, Vienna, 1960, no. 46; Edinburgh and London 1961, no. 52.

LITERATURE: Ralph Flinn, "The Private Collection of Josef Stransky," *Art News* 29 (16 March 1931), 107, ill.; Wildenstein 1964, no. 602; Reidemeister 1986, no. 81.

Paul Gauguin
56 Idyll in Tahiti

NOTES: **1.** See Françoise Cachin in *Gauguin* [exh. cat., Musée d'Orsay] (Paris, 1989), no. 231bis. The Jongkind in question appeared in album of the Arosa Collection in the 1870s. For a reproduction of the painting, see Victorine Hefting, *Jongkind, sa vie son œuvre* (Paris, 1975), no. 208. / **2.** Wildenstein 1964, no. 587. / **3.** Bengt Danielsson, "Gauguin's Tahitian Titles," *Burlington Magazine* 109, no. 760 (April 1967), 233, no. 76.

PROVENANCE: A. Fontaine, chief of labor ministry, Paris; Georges Bernheim, Paris; Edwin M. Otterbourg, New York; Vandyck Gallery, Washington, D.C.; purchased by the Phillips Memorial Art Gallery, Washington, D.C., in 1925 [cited with permission of the Phillips Collection, Washington, D.C.,

TPC Archives]; traded to Newhouse Gallery, New York, in December 1936; purchased by Bührle in 1952 from an English dealer.

EXHIBITIONS: *A Survey of French Painting from Chardin to Derain*, Phillips Memorial Art Gallery, Washington, D.C., 1928; *Art Is International*, Phillips Memorial Art Gallery, Washington, D.C., 1928–1929; *Sources of Modern Art*, Phillips Memorial Art Gallery, Washington, D.C., 1930, no. 13; *French Painting from Manet to Derain*, Phillips Memorial Art Gallery, Washington D.C., 1931, no. 81 [these exhibitions cited with permission of the Phillips Collection, Washington, D.C., TPC Archives]; exhibited at M. Knoedler and Company, New York, December 1934; *One Hundred Years of French Painting, 1820–1920*, The William Rockhill Nelson Gallery of Art and the Mary Atkins Museum of Fine Arts, Kansas City, 1935, no. 26; New York 1936, no. 44; Cambridge, Mass. 1936, no. 43; Zurich 1958, no. 250 (as *Tahiti—Strandlandschaft mit Mädchen und Hütten*); Munich 1958–1959, no. 60.

LITERATURE: Wildenstein 1964, no. 598; *The Phillips Collection in the Making: 1920–1930* [exh. cat., The Phillips Collection and the Smithsonian Institution Traveling Exhibition Service] (Washington, D.C., 1979–1981), 93; le Pichon 1986, 226–227; Reidemeister 1986, no. 80.

Paul Gauguin
57 Still Life with Fruit, Basket, and Knife

NOTES: **1.** Richard Brettell in Washington 1988, no. 255. / **2.** Lionello Venturi, *Cézanne, son art, son œuvre* (Paris, 1936), no. 341. / **3.** A. Joly-Segalen, *Lettres de Paul Gauguin à Georges-Daniel de Monfreid* (Paris, 1918), 247. / **4.** Joly-Segalen 1918, 315.

PROVENANCE: Druet, Paris; Dr. Max Meirowski, Berlin; Wildenstein and Company, New York; Wildenstein and Company, Paris; purchased by Bührle in 1953.

EXHIBITIONS: On loan to the Musée d'Art et d'Histoire, Geneva, 1948; *De Watteau à Cézanne*, Musée d'Art et d'Histoire, Geneva, 1951, no. 73; Zurich 1958, no. 252; Berlin 1958, no. 42; Munich 1958–1959, no. 62; *De Géricault à Matisse: Chefs-d'œuvre français des collections suisses*, Petit Palais, Paris, 1959, no. 58; Lucerne, 1963, no. 37.

LITERATURE: Wildenstein 1964, no. 607.

Vincent van Gogh
58 The Bridge at Asnières

NOTES: **1.** Vincent van Gogh, *The Complete Letters of Vincent van Gogh*, 2d ed. (Greenwich, 1959), 2:513, no. 459a. / **2.** *Letters*, 3:425, no. W1, summer or fall of 1887. / **3.** Welsh-Ovcharov 1976, 169. / **4.** Welsh-Ovcharov 1976, 189. / **5.** Willem van Gulik and Fred Orton, *Japanese Prints Collected by Vincent van Gogh* [exh. cat., Rijksmuseum Vincent van Gogh] (Amsterdam, 1978). / **6.** Rewald 1978, 56–57. / **7.** Rewald 1978, 58.

PROVENANCE: Collection of the Prince of Wagram, Paris; Galerie Druet, Paris, 1908; P. Goujon, Paris, 1911; Bernheim-Jeune, Paris; Madame L. Reinach-Goujon, Paris; purchased by Bührle in 1951 from an English private collection.

EXHIBITIONS: Grafton Galleries, London, 1910, no. 126; *Van Gogh*, Stedelijk Museum, Amsterdam, 1930, no. 12; *Vincent van Gogh*, Kunsthaus, Zurich, 1954 (hors du catalogue); *Vincent van Gogh, Leben und Schaffen*, Villa Hügel, Essen, 1957, no. 245; Zurich 1958, no. 237; Berlin 1958, no. 38; Munich 1958–1959, no. 68; *Van Gogh*, Musée Jacquemart André, Paris, 1960, no. 33; Edinburgh and London 1961, no. 57.

LITERATURE: J.-B. de la Faille, *Vincent van Gogh* (Paris and Brussels, 1928), no. 301; L. Gold-

scheider and W. Uhde, *Vincent van Gogh* (Vienna, 1936), pl. 13; W. Weisbach, *Vincent van Gogh: Kunst und Schicksal* (Basel, 1951), 2:30–31, ill.; John Rewald, *Von van Gogh zu Gauguin* (Munich, Vienna, and Basel, 1957), 60, ill.; John Rewald, *Post-Impressionism: From van Gogh to Gauguin*, 3d rev. ed. (New York, 1978), 56, 58, ill.; *Leven and scheppen in Beeld: Documentaire tentoonstelling Vincent van Gogh* [exh. cat., Stedelijk Museum] (Amsterdam, 1958), 201, 202, ill. (with photograph of bridge); Marc Edo Tralbaut, *Eine Bildbiographie* (Munich, 1958), 70–71, ill.; F. Elger, *Van Gogh: Life and Work* (Munich and Zurich, 1959), pl. 85; Leopold Reidemeister, *Auf den Spuren der Maler der Ile-de-France* (Berlin, 1963), 116, ill.; Leopold Reidemeister, *Die Ile-de-France und ihre Maler* (Berlin, 1963), no. 39; P. Leprohon, *Tel fut Van Gogh* (Paris, 1964), 409–411; *La Vie du Rail* (9 February 1964), 22–23, ill.; Marc Edo Tralbaut, *Vincent van Gogh* (Lausanne, 1969), 211, ill.; Marc Edo Tralbaut, *Vincent van Gogh* (New York, 1969), 210, 211, ill. (with photograph of van Gogh and Bernard seated at a table on the quai); J.-B. de la Faille, *The Works of Vincent van Gogh: His Paintings and Drawings* (Amsterdam, 1970), no. F301; Paolo Lecaldano, *L'Opera pittorica completa di van Gogh* (Milan, 1970), 1: no. 386, pl. 45; Bogomila Welsh-Ovcharov, *Vincent van Gogh: His Paris Period* (Utrecht, 1976), 169, 189; Jan Hulsker, *The Complete Van Gogh: Paintings, Drawings, Sketches* (Amsterdam and New York, 1977/1980), 292, 298, no. 1327, ill.; Bogomila Welsh-Ovcharov, *Vincent van Gogh and the Birth of Cloisonism* (Toronto, 1981); A. M. Hammacher and Renilde Hammacher, *Van Gogh: A Documentary Biography* (New York, 1982), 146–147; Bogomila Welsh-Ovcharov, *Van Gogh à Paris* [exh. cat., Musée d'Orsay] (Paris, 1988).

Vincent van Gogh
59 Apricot Trees in Blossom

NOTES: **1.** *Letters*, 2:545, no. 477, c. 13 April 1888. / **2.** Pickvance 1984, 47. / **3.** Hulsker 1977/1980, 310. / **4.** de la Faille 1970, 235, no. 556; *Letters*, 2:541, no. 474; see also Pickvance 1984, 262. / **5.** *Letters*, 2:536, no. 471. / **6.** de la Faille 1970, 192, no. F406. / **7.** de la Faille 1970, 264, no. F671. / **8.** de la Faille 1970, 188, no. F394; see also *Letters*, 2:538, no. 472, 30 March 1888.

PROVENANCE: Collection of Paul Dahlmann, Le Rainey; N. Eisenloeffel Art Gallery, Amsterdam; Unger and Van Mens Art Gallery, Rotterdam, c. 1922; A. van Hoboken, Vienna; Oscar Federer, Mährisch-Ostrau; Walter Feilchenfeldt, Zurich; Georges Renand, Paris; private collection, Switzerland; purchased by Bührle in 1940 from a Swiss private collection.

EXHIBITIONS: *Ausländische Kunst in Zürich*, Kunsthaus, Zurich, 1943, no. 715; *Ausstellung der Holland-Hilfe*, Galerie M. Schulthess, Basel, 1945; *Van Gogh*, Kunsthalle, Basel, 1947; *Europäische Kunst des 13.–20. Jahrhunderts*, Kunsthaus, Zurich, 1950, no. 28; Zurich 1958, no. 240; Edinburgh and London, 1961, no. 58.

LITERATURE: de la Faille 1928, no. 556; J.-B. de la Faille, *Vincent van Gogh* (Paris, 1939), no. 579; E. Briner, *Vincent van Gogh: Sechs farbige Wiedergaben seiner Werke* (Zurich, 1947), 13, pl. 1; M. Valsecchi, *Van Gogh* (Milan, 1952), pl. 11; *Sammlung Emil G. Bührle* [exh. cat., Kunsthaus] (Zurich, 1958), 137, no. 240; de la Faille 1970, no. 556; Lecaldano 1971, 2: no. 476; Hulsker 1977/1980, 310, 314, no. 1383; Ronald Pickvance, *Van Gogh in Arles* [exh. cat., The Metropolitan Museum of Art] (New York, 1984), 47.

Vincent van Gogh
60 The Sower

NOTES: **1.** *Letters*, 3:96, no. 558a. Hulsker, 1973, 167, dates the letter to c. 21 November 1888, whereas Pickvance 1984, 218, dates it to c. 25 November 1888. / **2.** Pickvance 1984, 219–220; Hulsker 1980, 374. / **3.** Rijksmuseum Kröller-Müller, Otterlo (F422); Rijksmuseum Vincent van Gogh, Amsterdam (F1441); private collection, Switzerland (F494); location unknown (F1442); The Armand Hammer Collection, Los Angeles (F575a); Collection of Mrs. L. Jäggli-Hahnloser, Winterthur, Switzerland (F494). / **4.** *Letters*, 1:203–204, no. 135, 7 September 1880. / **5.** de la Faille 1970, 320, 323, and 324: F856, F857, F858, F862, F865, and F866a. / **6.** *Letters*, 1:505, no. 221. / **7.** The drawings are F1539 verso, F1550, F1551, F1592 verso, F1603 recto and verso, F1618, F1639 verso, F1645 recto and verso. The paintings are *The Sower* (after Lerat's etching of Millet's Sower), October 1889, Rijksmuseum Kröller-Müller, Otterlo (F689); and *The Sower* (after Millet), January–February 1890, Collection of Stavros S. Niarchos (F690). / **8.** *Letters*, 1: no. 101, 12 June 1877. / **9.** Meyer Schapiro, *Vincent van Gogh* New York, 1950), 80; Reidemeister 1986, 212; and Jan Hulsker 1977/1980, 372, 374. / **10.** Reidemeister 1986, 212, notes a connection between the two compositions but indicates that van Gogh probably could not have known *The Vision after the Sermon*. But Gauguin sent a sketch of his painting to van Gogh in a letter c. 22 September 1888 (Vincent van Gogh Foundation, Rijksmuseum Vincent van Gogh, Amsterdam). / **11.** For an illustration of the drawing in the letter, see Richard R. Brettell, in *The Art of Paul Gauguin* [exh. cat., National Gallery of Art] (Washington, 1988), 103. / **12.** Pickvance 1984, 130.

PROVENANCE: Johanna van Gogh-Bonger (the artist's sister-in-law), 1890; presented to Frederik van Eeden, Laren, 1891; collection of Mme. van Eeden-van Vloten, Laren; Galerie d'Audretsch, The Hague; sold to Paul Cassirer, Berlin, March 1914; sold to Franz von Mendelssohn, Berlin, 1914; to the heirs of Franz von Mendelssohn, Zurich; Fritz Nathan (dealer), Zurich; purchased by Bührle in 1951.

EXHIBITIONS: *Vincent van Gogh*, Stedelijk Museum, Amsterdam, 1905, no. 112a; *Van Gogh*, Nationalgalerie, Berlin, 1921; Zurich 1954 (hors du catalogue); Zurich 1958, no. 241; Munich 1958–1959, no. 72; Edinburgh and London 1961, no. 59; *Chefs-d'œuvre des collections suisses de Manet à Picasso*, Palais de Beaulieu, Lausanne, 1964, no. 114; *Van Gogh in Arles*, The Metropolitan Museum of Art, New York, 1984, no. 129.

LITERATURE: de la Faille 1928, no. 450; de la Faille 1939, no. 481; W. Sherjon and J. de Gruyter, *Vincent van Gogh's Great Period* (Amsterdam, 1937), 143, no. 114; W. Weisbach, *Vincent van Gogh, Kunst und Schicksal* (Basel, 1951), 2:79; François Daulte, "Le Semeur de van Gogh," *Arts* (14 May 1953): 2, ill.; J. Cassou, *Die Impressionisten und ihre Zeit* (Lucerne, 1953), pl. 66; François Daulte, "Le Chef-d'œuvre d'une vie: La Collection Bührle," in *Connaissance des Arts*, no. 52 (15 June 1956): 35, ill.; Max Huggler, "Die Sammlung Bührle im Zürcher Kunsthaus," in *Das Werk* 45, no. 10 (October 1958): 370; René Elvin, "Collector Extraordinary: The Bührle Collection and the New Zürich Kunsthaus," *The Studio*, no. 797 (August–September 1959), 54; Jan Hulsker in *Maatsaf* (1960), 1:333; René Wehrli, "Emil G. Bührle: French Nineteenth-Century Painting," in *Great Private Collections*, ed. Douglas Cooper (New York, 1963), 218, 221, ill.; H. R. Graetz, *The Symbolic Language of Vincent van Gogh* (New York, Toronto, and London, 1963), 127–128; Jan Bialostocki, *Stil und Ikonographie* (Dresden, 1966), 184; Mark Roskill, *Van Gogh, Gauguin, and the Impressionist Circle* (London, 1970), 147, 152, ill.; de la Faille 1970, no. F 450; Lecaldano 1971, 2: no. 594; Jan Hulsker, *Van Gogh door Van Gogh* (Amsterdam, 1973), 176 (letter 558a); Hulsker 1977/1980, 374–375, no. 1627; Pickvance 1984, 218–220, no. 219, ill.; Leopold Reidemeister, in *Foundation Emil G. Bührle Collection,* 2d ed. (Zurich and Munich, 1986), 212, ill.; Walter Feilchenfeldt, *Vincent van Gogh and Paul Cassirer, Berlin: The Reception of Van Gogh in Germany from 1901 to 1914* (Amsterdam, Rijksmuseum Vincent van Gogh: Cahier Vincent 2, 1988), 95.

Vincent van Gogh
61 Olive Orchard

NOTES: **1.** For a discussion of the development of the olive orchard theme in van Gogh's work of June–December 1889, see Pickvance 1986, 100–103; 158–167. / **2.** *Letters,* 3:220, no. 608, 28 September 1889. / **3.** *Letters,* 3:219, no. 608, 28 September 1889. See Pickvance 1986, 300–301, and Hulsker 1988, 412, no. 1791. Pickvance suggests that the Zurich *Olive Orchard* might be the copy mentioned in the letters and indicates his uncertainty with a question mark; Hulsker states that it is a copy after F 585 (Rijksmuseum Kröller-Müller, Otterlo). Although there is a loose resemblance to the work in Otterlo, the viewpoint is closer to the trees, and the trees and the composition are different. Other replicas and reduced versions, such as the variants (F 615 and F 743) after *Wheat Field with Cypresses* (F 717, cat. 62), are obviously copies, further evidence that the Bührle painting is an independent work of art. / **4.** *Letters,* 3:522–523, no. B 21, c. 22 November 1889 (Pickvance's date). / **5.** *Letters,* 3:158, no. 587, 25 or 26 April 1889 (for the date, see Hulsker, 1973, 177). / **6.** *Letters,* 3:232, no. 614a (for the date, see Pickvance 1986, 292). / **7.** *Letters,* 3:233, no. 615, 26 November 1889 (for the date, see Pickvance 1986, 291). / **8.** *Letters,* 3:158, 232, no. 587 and 614a, 25 or 26 April 1889, and 24–25 May 1890 (for the dates, see Pickvance 1986, 177, 292).

PROVENANCE: Johanna van Gogh-Bonger (the artist's sister-in-law), presumably 1890; Isaac Israëls, The Hague, from at least 1921 until 1935; sale, Isaac Israëls, Amsterdam, 2 April 1935, no. 1; Galerie Thannhauser, Paris; Nieuwenhuizen Segaar Art Gallery, The Hague, from 1936; Galerie Rosengart, Lucerne; purchased by Bührle in 1937.

EXHIBITIONS: *Vincent van Gogh,* Brakl and Thannhauser, Moderne Kunsthandlung, Munich, 1909, no. 38; *Vincent van Gogh,* Kunstverein, Munich, 1910; *Vincent van Gogh,* Ernst Arnold, Kunsthandlung, Breslau/Dresden, 1910; *Vincent van Gogh,* Kunstsalon Gerstenberger, Chemnitz, 1910; *Vincent van Gogh,* Commeter'sche Kunsthandlung, Hamburg, 1911, no. 43; *Vincent van Gogh,* Ernst Arnold, Kunsthandlung, Breslau/Dresden, 1912, no. 32; *Vincent van Gogh* (?), J. H. de Bois, Haarlem, 1913, no. 2; *Exposition Hollandaise, Tableaux, Aquarelles, et Dessins, Anciens et Modernes,* 1921, no. 161; *Tentoonstelling van Kunstwerken uit het bezit van werkende leden van het genootschap Pulchri Studio,* 1924, no. 12; *Hollandische en Fransche schilderkunst der XIXᵉ en XXᵉ eeuw,* E. J. van Wisselingh & Co., Amsterdam, 1932, no. 19; Zurich 1943, no. 716; Basel 1945, no. 16; *Peinture Contemporaine, École de Paris,* Kunsthalle, Bern, 1946, no. 22; Basel 1947, no. 88; Zurich 1950, 28; *Um 1900 – Art Nouveau und Jugendstil,* Kunstgewerbemuseum, Zurich, 1952; Zurich 1958, no. 242; Berlin 1958, no. 45; Munich 1958–1959, no. 73; Lucerne 1963, no. 41.

LITERATURE: de la Faille 1928, no. 711; de la Faille 1939, no. 724; H. P. Bremmer, in *Beeldende Kunst,* 23/4 no. 30; Scherjon and de Gruyter 1937, no. 172, 15, pl. 4; D. Wild, *Moderne Malerei* (Zurich, 1950), pl. 15; Valsecchi 1952, pl. 21; Zurich, 1958, no. 242; de la Faille 1970, no. F 711; Lecaldano 1971, 2: no. 736; Huls-

ker 1977/1980, no. 1791; Ronald Pickvance, *Van Gogh in Saint-Rémy and Auvers* (New York, 1986), 300–301; Feilchenfeldt 1988, 115, no. F 711.

Vincent van Gogh
62 Wheat Field with Cypresses

NOTES: **1.** Pickvance 1986, 133. / **2.** Pickvance 1986, 98. / **3.** Pickvance 1986, 108, 110. / **4.** Private collection (F 743); and National Gallery, London (F 615). See Pickvance 1986, 132–133. / **5.** *Letters,* 3:185, no. 596, 25 June 1889. / **6.** Pickvance 1986, 108. For a discussion of musicality, see H. R. Rookmaaker, *Gauguin and 19th Century Art Theory* (Amsterdam, 1972), 210–220. / **7.** *Letters,* 3:253, no. 625, 2 February 1890. / **8.** *Letters,* 3:425, no. W 1, summer or fall 1887. / **9.** *Letters,* 3:456, no. W 13, 2 July 1889. / **10.** *Letters,* 3:218, no. 607, 19 September 1889.

PROVENANCE: Collection of the Prince of Wagram, Paris; Galerie H. Barbazanges, Paris; sold to Paul Cassirer, Berlin, November 1910; sold by Paul Cassirer to Franz von Mendelssohn, Berlin, November or December 1910; Fritz Nathan, Zurich; purchased by Bührle in 1951.

EXHIBITIONS: *Van Gogh—Matisse,* Kronprinzenpalais, Nationalgalerie, Berlin, 1921; *Vincent van Gogh: Dipinti e disegni,* Palazzo Reale, Milan, 1952, no. 107; Zurich 1958, no. 243; Munich 1958–1959, no. 74; *De Géricault à Matisse: Chefs-d'œuvre d'art français des collections suisses,* Petit Palais, Paris, 1959, no. 68.

LITERATURE: Julius Meier-Graefe, *Vincent van Gogh* (Munich, 1912), 21; A. Dreyfus, "Vincent van Gogh," *Die Kunst* (1914): 99; de la Faille, 1928, no. 717; de la Faille 1939, no. 633; Michel Floorisone, *Van Gogh,* Paris, 1937, 49; Scherjon and de Gruyter 1937, no. 48; Weisbach 1951, 2:178; Valsecchi 1952, pl. 21; Lecaldano 1971, 2: no. 669; Rewald, 1978, 303; Hulsker 1977/1980, 400, 406, no. 1756; Pickvance 1986, 110, 133, 298, 299, ill.

Vincent van Gogh
63 Blossoming Chestnut Branches

NOTES: **1.** *Letters,* 2:529, no. 466, c. 3 March 1888: "two little studies of an almond branch already in blossom in spite of [winter]." / **2.** *Letters,* 3:258, no. 627, c. 20 February 1890: Vincent announced to his mother: "I started immediately to make a picture for him . . . big branches of white almond blossoms against a blue sky." The same day he wrote to his sister Wilhelmina, *Letters,* 3:467, no. W 20, c. 20 February 1890: "some days ago I started painting a big canvas for him, of a blue sky with blossoming branches standing out against it." / **3.** Pickvance 1986, 179. Pickvance also points out that Theo confirmed receipt of the painting on 3 May, but Vincent himself indicates in a letter to his sister that he delivered the painting himself: "I brought along a relatively large picture for Theo and Jo's little boy—which they hung over the piano" (*Letters,* 3:470, no. W 22, 4 June 1890). / **4.** Pickvance 1986, 195–196. The village was especially well-known to artists. Charles-François Daubigny had lived there from 1861 to 1878; Cézanne had worked there from 1872 to 1874, in 1880, and again in 1881; Pissarro and Guillaumin had worked there in the early 1870s; and by 1890 there was a small community of resident painters. / **5.** In June 1890 van Gogh drew a feather-hyacinth in bloom (Rijksmuseum Vincent van Gogh, Amsterdam; F 1612), included sprigs of flowering foxglove in both versions of his portrait of Dr. Gachet (S. Kramarsky Trust Fund, New York, and Musée d'Orsay, Paris; F 753 and 754), executed several still lifes of flowers, and painted *Blossoming Chestnut Branches.* / **6.** *Letters,* 3:575, no. T 39, 30 June 1890.

PROVENANCE: Collection of Dr. Paul Gachet, Auvers-sur-Oise, 1890; Galerie Bernheim-Jeune, Paris; collection of Franz von Mendelssohn, Berlin, by 1914; Dr. Fritz Nathan, St. Gallen; purchased by Bührle in 1951.

EXHIBITIONS: *Vincent van Gogh,* Galerie Paul Cassirer, Berlin, 1914, no. 135; *Vincent van Gogh,* Nationalgalerie, Berlin, 1921; *Das Stilleben in der deutschen und französischen Malerei,* Galerie Matthiesen, Berlin, 1927, no. 122; *Vincent van Gogh,* Galerie Paul Cassirer, Berlin, 1928, no. 92; *Europäische Meister 1790–1910,* Kunstmuseum, Winterthur, 1955, no. 104; Zurich 1958, no. 246; Berlin 1958, no. 48; Munich 1958–1959, no. 77; Paris 1959, no. 69; Edinburgh and London 1961, no. 61.

LITERATURE: G. Biermann, "Das Stilleben in der deutschen und französischen Malerei," in *Der Cicerone* 19 (1927), 151; de la Faille 1928, no. 820; de la Faille 1939, no. 747; Scherjon and de Gruyter 1937, no. 118; G. Schmidt, *Van Gogh* (Bern, 1947), 30, pl. 48; W. de Gruyter and E. Andriesse, *Die Welt von Van Gogh* (The Hague, Brussels, Paris, Milan, Basel, and Tokyo, *1953*), 128, ill.; Valsecchi 1952, pl. 28; André Chamson and François Daulte, "De Géricault à Matisse: Chefs-d'œuvre d'art français des collections suisses," *Art et Style* 50 (1959): ill.; Wehrli 1963, 221; de la Faille 1970, no. F 820; Lecaldano 1971, 2: no. 805; Hulsker 1977/1980, 461–462, no. 2010; Reidemeister 1986, 216–217, ill.; Feilchenfeldt 1988, 1223, 150.

Georges Seurat
64 Study for "Sunday Afternoon on the Island of La Grande Jatte"

NOTES: **1.** de Hauke 1961, 92. / **2.** de Hauke 1961, 162. See also D. Rich, *Seurat and the Evolution of "La Grande Jatte"* (Chicago, 1935), 10. / **3.** Thomson 1985, 116–126. / **4.** Seurat studied at the Municipal Drawing School (1875–1878) and at the Atelier of Henri Lehmann (1878–1879). / **5.** On loan from the Keynes Collection, King's College, Cambridge. See de Hauke 1961, 138. / **6.** de Hauke 1961, 142. / **7.** Dorra and Rewald 1959, nos. 116c and 117a.

PROVENANCE: Collection Edmond Cousturier, Paris; Collection François Cousturier, Paris; Collection Rosenberg, London; purchased by Bührle in 1951.

EXHIBITIONS: *Seurat,* La Revue blanche, Paris, 1900, no. 13; *Retrospective Seurat,* XXI Salon des Indépendants, Paris, 1905, no. 19; *Retrospective Georges Seurat,* Galerie Bernheim-Jeune, Paris, 1908–1909, no. 44; *Seurat et ses amis,* Galerie des Beaux-Arts, Paris, 1933–1934, no. 76; *Georges Seurat,* Galerie Pierre Rosenberg, Paris, 1936, no. 27 (?); *Seurat and His Contemporaries,* Wildenstein Gallery, London, 1937, no. 47; *Seurat: Paintings and Drawings,* The Art Institute of Chicago and The Museum of Modern Art, New York, 1958, no. 95; Zurich 1958, no. 210; Berlin 1958, no. 34.

LITERATURE: Inventaire posthume, no. 109; F. Biedart, *La Revue Glos Plastykow* (Cracow) (March 1934), 85, ill.; François Daulte, "Le Chef-d'œuvre d'une vie: La Collection Bührle," *Connaissance des Arts,* no. 52 (15 June 1956), 30–37; *Festschrift Sammlung Emil G. Bührle* (Zurich, 1958), 124–125, no. 210; Henri Dorra and John Rewald, *Seurat: l'œuvre peint, biographie et catalogue critique* (Paris, 1959), 127, no. 117; César M. de Hauke, *Seurat et son œuvre,* 2 vols. (Paris, 1961), no. 127; M. Ogawa and T. Washiwa, *Seurat* (Japan, 1978), pl. 9; Richard Thomson, *Seurat* (Oxford, 1985), 99.

Georges Seurat
65 Study for "Invitation to the Sideshow"

NOTES: **1.** de Hauke 1961, 187, and 185. / **2.** Gustave Kahn, "Peinture: Exposition des Indépendents," *La Revue indépendente* (April 1888), 161. / **3.** Such haste is also found in the relatively few studies for *The Models.* See Dorra and Rewald 1959, 180a–c; and Thomson 1985, 148. / **4.** Robert L. Herbert, "*La Parade de Cirque* de Seurat et l'esthétique scientifique de Charles Henry," *La Revue de l'Art* 50 (1980), 9–23. / **5.** See Francis Haskell, "The Sad Clown," in *Studies in French 19th-Century Literature and Painting,* ed. Ulrich Finke (Manchester, 1982). / **6.** See Thomson 1985, 152–156.

PROVENANCE: Collection Mme Vildrac, Paris; Collection Loeb, Paris; purchased by Bührle in 1951 through an American dealer.

EXHIBITIONS: *Twenty-four paintings and drawings by Georges-Pierre Seurat,* The Renaissance Society of the University of Chicago, 1935, no. 24; *Cubism and Abstract Art,* The Museum of Modern Art, New York, 1936, no. 260; *The Little Show,* Art Institute, Dayton, 1945, no. 10; *Camille Pissarro,* Wildenstein and Company, New York, 1945, no. 67; *Post-Impressionists and Their Followers,* Palm Beach, Fla., 1949, no. 18; *Seurat: paintings and drawings,* Knoedler Galleries, New York, 1949, no. 21; *15 Impressionists,* New York State University of Syracuse, College of Fine Arts, 1949, no. 27; Biennale, Venice, 1952, cat. S. 389, no. 16; Zurich 1958, no. 36; Berlin 1958, no. 36; Munich 1958–1959, no. 147; Lucerne 1963, no. 46.

LITERATURE: Roger Fry, "Seurat's *La Parade,*" *The Burlington Magazine* (December 1929), 290; Robert J. Goldwater, "Some Aspects of the Development of Seurat's Style," *Art Bulletin* 23, no. 2 (June 1941): 122, 124; ill.; John Rewald, *Seurat* (New York, 1943), 102, pl. 76 (rev. ed., 1948, p. 106, pl. 81); G. Seligmann, *The Drawings of Georges Seurat* (New York, 1947), 17, 19, 23; John Rewald, *Georges Seurat* (Paris, 1948), 108, pl. 81; Jacques de Laprade, *Seurat* (Paris, 1951), 62, ill.; Raymond Cogniat, *Seurat* (n.d.), 30, ill.; Muraro, "Divisionismo," *Emporium* (July 1952): 25, ill.; Daulte, 1956, 30–37; *Festschrift Emil G. Bührle* (Zurich, 1958); 125; Dorra and Rewald 1959, 224, no. 180, ill.; César M. de Hauke, *Seurat: l'œuvre peinte, biographie et catalogue raisonné* (Paris, 1961), no. 186, ill.; Pierre Courthion, *Seurat* (London, 1969), 138, no. 38, ill.; Mark Roskill, *Van Gogh, Gauguin and the Impressionist Circle* (London, 1970), pl. 74; André Chastel and F. Minervino, *Tout l'œuvre peint de Seurat* (Paris, 1973); Ogawa and Washiwa 1978, pl. 26; Thomson 1985, 148, pl. 153.

Henri de Toulouse-Lautrec
66 The Redheaded Girl

NOTES: **1.** F. Gauzi, *Lautrec et Son Temps* (Paris, 1954), 129. Crippled at fifteen by fractures in both legs, Lautrec was barred from the conventional pursuits of his aristocratic upbringing such as riding and shooting. Instead he became increasingly interested in drawing and painting, for which he had shown an early aptitude. He first took informal lessons with Henri Princeteau, a family friend and painter of horses, then beginning in 1882 studied in the ateliers of two successful Salon artists, Léon Bonnat and Fernand Corman. Although Lautrec thus learned the basics of Salon artistic practices, he preferred to work from nature, encouraged by the work of impressionists such as Manet, Degas, Forain, and Renoir. / **2.** Dortu 1971, 346. / **3.** Dortu 1971, 305, 243, 244, 245, and 246. Studies are in the Sterling and Francine Clark Institute, Williamstown, Mass.; Collection Mrs. Mellon Bruce, New York; and Musée d'Albi, recto and verso. / **4.** Dortu 1971, 343, 246. / **5.** G. Mack, *Toulouse-Lautrec*

(New York, 1938), 32. / **6.** Dortu 1971, 124 and 147–150. / **7.** Charles F. Stuckey, "Models and Spectators in the Art of Lautrec," in *Toulouse-Lautrec: Paintings* [exh. cat., The Art Institute of Chicago] (Chicago, 1979), 19–22. / **8.** See *Portrait of a Woman in Yellow* of c. 1450, by Baldovinetti, then attributed to Piero della Francesca (National Gallery, London).

PROVENANCE: Galerie Paul Cassirer, Berlin; Collection Hugo Simon, Berlin; Collection Silberberg; sale, Galerie George Petit, Paris, 9 June 1932, no. 31; Boussard; purchased by Bührle in 1955 from Max Kaganovitch, Paris.

EXHIBITIONS: Zurich 1958, no. 202; Berlin 1958, no. 40; Munich 1958–1959, no. 158; Edinburgh and London 1961, no. 63; Lucerne 1963, no. 44.

LITERATURE: M. G. Dortu, *Toulouse-Lautrec et son œuvre* (New York, 1971), no. P. 353.

Henri de Toulouse-Lautrec
67 The Two Friends

NOTES: **1.** *Unpublished Correspondence of Henri de Toulouse-Lautrec,* ed. Lucien Goldschmidt and Herbert Schimmel (London, 1969), 81, no. 58. / **2.** Dortu 1971, 436–439. / **3.** Michel Georges-Michel, *Les Peintres que j'ai connus* (Paris, 1954), 16. / **4.** Dortu 1971, 598, 601.

PROVENANCE: Collection Koenigs, Haarlem; private collection, England; purchased by Bührle in 1954 through an American dealer.

EXHIBITIONS: *Sezession,* Berlin, 1903; *Van Gogh,* Stedelijk Museum, Amsterdam, 1930, no. 306; Stedelijk Museum, Amsterdam, 1947, no. 24; Kunsthalle, Basel, 1947, no. 117; *Six Masters of Post-Impressionism,* Wildenstein and Company, New York, 1948, no. 33, Zurich 1958, no. 205; *De Géricault à Matisse: Les Chefs-d'œuvre des collections suisses,* Petit Palais, Paris, 1959, no. 130; *Chefs-d'œuvre des collections suisses de Manet à Picasso,* Palais de Beaulieu, Lausanne, 1964, no. 144; *Toulouse-Lautrec,* Kunsthalle, Tübingen, 1987.

LITERATURE: Emil Bührle, "La Vocation du collectionneur," *Arts* 471 (7/13 June 1954); François Daulte, "Le Chef-d'œuvre d'une vie: La Collection Bührle," *Connaissance des Arts,* no. 52 (15 June 1956), 35, ill.; René Wehrli, "E. G. Bührle, Zürich, Malerei des 19. Jahrhunderts," in *Berühmte private Kunstsammlungen,* ed. Douglas Cooper (Oldenberg, 1963), 221; Philippe Huisman and M. G. Dortu, *Lautrec par Lautrec* (Paris, 1964), 129, ill.; G. Caproni, *L'opera completa di Toulouse-Lautrec* (Milan, 1969), no. 410; Dortu 1971, no. P. 602.

Henri de Toulouse-Lautrec
68 Messaline

NOTES: **1.** See *La Modiste* of 1900 (Musée d'Albi) (Dortu 1971, 716). / **2.** Dortu 1971, 4637–4639, 706–708, and 703–705. / **3.** Wolfgang Wittrock, *Toulouse-Lautrec. The Complete Prints,* 2 vols. (London, 1985), no. 330. / **4.** Quoted in Mack 1938, 356, and 356–357.

PROVENANCE: Galerie Bernheim-Jeune, Paris; Galerie Paul Cassirer, Berlin; Collection Levesque, Paris; Collection Dr. Viau, Paris; Galerie Paul Cassirer, Berlin; Collection E. Katzenellenbogen, Berlin; purchased by Bührle in 1951 through a Swiss dealer.

EXHIBITIONS: *Henri de Toulouse-Lautrec,* Galerie Manzi et Joyant, Paris, 1914, no. 37; *Impressionisten,* Galerie Paul Cassirer, Berlin, 1925, no. 59; *French Art,* Royal Academy of Arts, London, 1932, no. 547 (cat. 526); *Französische Meister des 19. Jahrhunderts,* Kunsthaus, Zurich, 1933, no. 98; *Van Delacroix tot Cézanne en Vincent van Gogh,* Museum Boymans-van Beuningen, Rot-

terdam, 1933–1934, no. 80; *Chefs-d'œuvre de l'art français,* Petit Palais, 1937, no. 426; Wildenstein and Company, New York, 1946, no. 34; *French Art from David to Toulouse-Lautrec,* The Metropolitan Museum of Art, New York, 1951, no. 117; *Paris 1900,* Musée Jenisch, Vevey, 1954, no. 110; Zurich 1958, no. 209; Berlin 1958, no. 59; Munich 1958–1959, no. 163; Paris 1959, no. 132.

LITERATURE: Théodore Duret, *Lautrec* (Paris, 1920), 122; Gustave Coquiot, *Lautrec ou quinze ans de mœurs parisiennes, 1885–1900* (Paris, 1921), 144 (Berlin, n.d., pl. 34); Achille Astre, *H. de Toulouse-Lautrec* (Paris, 1925), 91; Maurice Joyant, *Henri de Toulouse-Lautrec* (Paris, 1926–1927), 1:236–237, 299, 2:38; Emile Schaub-Koch, *Psychoanalyse d'un peintre moderne* (Paris, 1935), 203; G. Mack, *Toulouse-Lautrec* (New York, 1938), 214, 356; V. Christoffel, *Meisterwerke der französischen Kunst* (Leipzig, 1939), 136; Frantz Jourdain and Jean Adhémar, *Toulouse-Lautrec* (New York, 1952), 52; M. G. Dortu, *Toulouse-Lautrec* (Paris, 1952), 10; Jacques Lassaigne, *Le Gout de notre temps—Lautrec* (Geneva, 1953), 108; Douglas Cooper, *H. de Toulouse-Lautrec* (London, 1955), 47; Henri Perruchot, *La Vie de Toulouse-Lautrec* (Paris, 1958), 331; Edouard Julien, *Lautrec* (Paris, 1959), 69, 80, ill.; *Europas schönste Impressionistensammlung, E. G. Bührle, Zürich* (Das Schönste, 1959), 23, no. 1, ill.; Werner Hofmann, *Das irdische Paradies, Kunst im 19. Jahrhundert* (Munich, 1960), pl. 97; Raffaelle Carrieri, *Epoca* (18 September 1960), pl. 49; *Genies et Réalités* (Paris, 1962), 233, ill. (detail); Wehrli 1963, 221; *Kindlers Malerei-Lexikon* 5 (Zurich, 1968), 547; Horst Keller, *H. Toulouse-Lautrec* (Cologne, 1968), 73, pl. 12; Caprioni 1969, 518 B, pl. 63; Dortu 1971, no. P. 703.

Wassily Kandinsky
69 The Blue Rider

NOTE: **1.** Quoted in Wassily Kandinsky, *Rückblicke* (Berlin, 1913), 14: "Zu der Zeit der Enttäuschung in der Atelierarbeit und der auswendig gemalten Bilder malte ich besonders viel Landschaften, die mich aber wenig befriedigten, so dass ich nur ganz wenige davon später zu Bildern verarbeitete. ... Ich dachte wenig an Häuser und Bäume, strich mit dem Spachtel farbige Streifen und Flecke auf die Leinwand und liess sie so stark singen, wie ich nur konnte. In mir klang die Moskauer Vorabendstunde, vor meinen Augen war die kräftige, farbensatte, in den Schatten tief donnernde Skala der Münchner Lichtatmosphäre. Nachher, besonders zu Hause, immer eine tiefe Enttäuschung. Meine Farben schienen mir schwach, flach, die ganze Studie eine erfolglose Anstrengung, die Kraft der Natur zu fangen."

PROVENANCE: J. B. Citroen, Amsterdam; Galerie Abels, Cologne; purchased by Bührle in 1955.

EXHIBITIONS: Wiesbaden, 1903; Prague, 1903; St. Petersburg, 1904; Paris, 1904; *Kandinsky Kollektivausstellung,* Berlin 1906, no. 18 (2d ed. of exh. cat., nos. 17, 29); Kunsthalle, Basel, 1945, not listed in catalogue; Stedelijk Museum, Amsterdam, 1947–1948, no. 14; *Der Blaue Reiter,* Haus der Kunst, Munich, 1949, no. 59; *Der Blaue Reiter,* Kunsthalle, Basel, 1950, no. 157; *Der Blaue Reiter,* Curt Valentin Gallery, New York, 1954–1955, no. 11; *Deutsche Malerei,* Volkswagenwerk, Wolfsburg, 1956, no. 75; *Art in Revolt: Germany 1905–1925,* Marlborough Fine Art Ltd., London, 1959, no. 50; *Der Blaue Reiter,* Neue Galerie der Stadt Linz, Linz, and Österreichische Galerie, Vienna, 1961, no. 2; *Kandinsky in München: Begegnungen und Wandlungen, 1896–1914,* Städtische Galerie im Lenbachhaus, Munich, 1982, no. 68; *Der Blaue Reiter,* Kunstmuseum, Bern, 1987, nos. 24, 40.

LITERATURE: Hans K. Roethel and Jean K. Benjamin, *Kandinsky: Catalogue raisonné de l'œuvre peint,* vol. I (*1900–1915*) (Paris, 1982), no. 82.

Pierre Bonnard
70 Races at Longchamp

NOTES: **1.** Maurice Denis, *Nouvelles Théories sur l'art moderne, sur l'art sacré, 1914–1921* (Paris, 1922), 66. / **2.** Dauberville and Dauberville 1965, no. 150.

PROVENANCE: Eugène Blot, Paris; Collection Bernard, Paris 1906; Collection Bernheim-Jeune, Paris; B. Goudchaux, Paris; Collection Schick; private collection, London; A. Kauffmann, London; purchased by Bührle in 1952.

EXHIBITIONS: *Europäische Meister 1790–1910,* Kunstmuseum, Winterthur, 1955, no. 17; *Pierre Bonnard,* Brunswick, 1955, no. 4; Zurich 1958, no. 258; Berlin 1958, no. 60; Munich 1958–1959, no. 1; Edinburgh and London, 1961, no. 65; Lucerne 1963, no. 49.

LITERATURE: Jean Dauberville and Henry Dauberville, *Bonnard: Catalogue raisonné de l'œuvre peint,* vol. I, *1888–1905* (Paris, 1965), no. 75.

Pierre Bonnard
71 The Luncheon

PROVENANCE: Collection Bernheim-Jeune, Paris 1900; Ambroise Vollard, Paris; Collection Bernheim-Jeune, Paris 1903; Alexandre Natanson, Paris 1907; private collection, Sweden; Collection Scheidegger, Zurich; purchased by Bührle in 1946.

EXHIBITIONS: *Französische Kunst,* Kunstforening, Christiania (Oslo), 1906, no. 3; *Pierre Bonnard,* Kunsthaus, Zurich, 1949, no. 11; *Die Maler der Revue Blanche: Toulouse-Lautrec und die Nabis,* Kunsthalle, Bern, 1951, no. 11; *Bonnard, Vuillard et les Nabis,* Musée d'Art Moderne, Paris, 1955, no. 74; Brunswick 1955, no. 6; Zurich 1958, no. 259; Berlin 1958, no. 61; Munich 1958–1959, no. 2; Edinburgh and London 1961, no. 66; *Bonnard,* Kunsthaus, Zurich, 1984–1985, no. 29.

LITERATURE: François Fosca, *Bonnard* (Geneva, 1919), pl. 4; "Bulletin de la vie artistique," Paris (15 August 1923), no. 16, 335; Dauberville and Dauberville 1888–1905, I: no. 216; Antoine Terrasse, *Pierre Bonnard* (Paris, 1967), 56; *Foundation E. G. Bührle Collection,* 2d ed. (Zurich and Munich, 1986), no. 99, ill.

Edouard Vuillard
72 At the Theater

NOTES: **1.** Quoted from Françoise Cachin, *Gauguin* (Paris, 1989), 84: "Que tout œuvre d'art était une transposition, une caricature, l'équivalent passionnée d'une sensation reçue." / **2.** Quoted from Claude Roger-Marx, *Vuillard: His Life and Work* (London, 1946), 23: "Je n'ai jamais été qu'un spectateur."

PROVENANCE: S. Schtschukin, Moscow; Princess Bibesco, London, 1900; Marlborough Fine Art Ltd., London; purchased by Bührle in 1955.

EXHIBITIONS: *Twentieth Century Masters,* Marlborough Fine Art Ltd., London, 1955, no. 66; Zurich 1958, no. 266; Berlin 1958, no. 63; Munich 1958–1959, no. 172; Edinburgh and London 1961, no. 68.

LITERATURE: *Foundation E. G. Bührle Collection,* 2d ed. (Zurich and Munich, 1986), no. 105, ill.

Edouard Vuillard
73 The Visitor

NOTE: **1.** Jean Dauberville and Henry Dauberville, *Bonnard: Catalogue raisonnée de l'œuvre peint,* vol. I (*1888–1905*) (Paris, 1966), no. 218.

PROVENANCE: G. Bernheim de Villers, Paris; The Phillips Memorial Gallery, Washington, D.C.; Gallery Knoedler & Co., New York; purchased by Bührle in 1953.

EXHIBITIONS: *Trends of European Paintings 1880–1930,* The Century Association, New York, 1949, no. 10; Zurich 1958, no. 269; Munich 1958–1959, no. 175.

LITERATURE: Claude Roger-Marx, *Vuillard: His Life and Work* (London, 1946), 46; *Catalogue of the Phillips Collection* (Washington, 1952), 104, pl. 101; C. Schweicher, *Vuillard* (Bern, 1955) pl. 30; Stuart Preston, *Edouard Vuillard* (New York, 1972), 90; *Foundation E. G. Bührle Collection,* 1986, no. 106, ill.

Henri Matisse
74 The Pont Saint-Michel, Paris

NOTES: **1.** Compare two versions of *The Pont Saint-Michel:* formerly Wright Ludington Collection, Santa Barbara, California; and Mrs. William A. M. Burden, New York. / **2.** Quoted from Dominique Fourcade, Henri Matisse, *Ecrits et propos sur l'art (Notes d'un peintre)* (Paris 1972), 45: "Une traduction rapide du paysage ne donne de lui qu'un moment de sa durée. Je préfère, en insistant sur son caractère, m'exposer à perdre le charme et obtenir plus de stabilité."

PROVENANCE: Ambroise Vollard, Paris; Marlborough Fine Arts Ltd., London; purchased by Bührle in 1954.

EXHIBITIONS: Zurich 1958, no. 293; Berlin 1958, no. 65; Munich 1958–1959, no. 103; *Französische Malerei von Delacroix bis Picasso,* Wolfsburg, 1961, no. 94; *Matisse,* Marlborough Gallery, Zurich, 1971.

LITERATURE: Leopold Reidemeister, *Auf den Spuren der Maler der Ile-de-France* (Berlin, 1963), 180; *Kindlers Malerei-Lexikon* (Zurich, 1967), 4:348; Jack D. Flam, *Matisse: The Man and His Art 1896–1918* (Ithaca and London, 1986), no. 80.

Georges Rouault
75 Guy de Charentonay (recto of no. 76)

NOTE: **1.** Georges Rouault, *Sur l'art et sur la vie* (Paris, 1971), 56: "Le dessin est un jet de l'esprit en éveil."

PROVENANCE: Marlborough Fine Art Ltd., London; purchased by Bührle in 1959.

EXHIBITIONS: Lucerne 1963, no. 59.

LITERATURE: Georges Charensol, *Georges Rouault* (Paris, 1926), pl. 16; Isabelle Rouault, *Rouault: Catalogue raisonné de l'œuvre peint* (Monaco, 1988), 2: no. 2568.

Georges Rouault
76 Clown with a Big Drum (verso of no. 75)

NOTES: **1.** Rouault 1971, 171: "J'ai vu clairement que le 'Pitre' c'était moi, c'était nous. ... Cet habit riche et pailleté c'est la vie qui nous le donne, nous sommes tous des pitres plus ou moins, nous portons tous un 'habit pailleté' mais si l'on nous surprend comme j'ai surpris le vieux pitre oh! alors qui osera dire qu'il n'est pas pris jusqu'au fond des entrailles par une incommensurable pitié. Tirer tout son art d'un regard d'une vieille rosse de saltimbanque (homme ou cheval) c'est d'un 'orgueil fou' ou d'une 'humilité parfaite' si l'on est fait pour cela.'" / **2.** Letter to André Suarès from 22 August 1911, *Georges Rouault – André Suarès, Correspondance* (Paris, 1960), 6: "... jusqu'à ce jour ma conscience d'artiste est restée pure ... mais la lutte me semble si ardue et si pénible que je n'engage personne à me suivre."

PROVENANCE: Marlborough Fine Art Ltd., London; purchased by Bührle in 1959.

EXHIBITIONS: Lucerne 1963, no. 59.

LITERATURE: Charensol 1926, pl. 16; Rouault 1988, 2: no. 122.

Maurice de Vlaminck
77 Banks of the Seine at Chatou

NOTES: **1.** Quoted from Marcel Giry, *Der Fauvismus, Ursprünge und Entwicklung* (Freiburg und Neuenburg, 1981), 118. / **2.** Maurice de Vlaminck, *Portraits avant décès* (Paris, 1943), 98: "Seule, la série des couleurs sur la toile avec toute leur puissance et leur résonnance pouvait, en s'orchestrant, traduire l'émotion colorée de ce paysage." / **3.** Vlaminck 1943, 52: "La peinture, je la voulais vivante, émotive, tendre, féroce, naturelle comme la vie."

PROVENANCE: Collection Kaganovitch, Paris; F. Nathan, Sankt Gallen; purchased by Bührle in 1944.

EXHIBITIONS: *Les Fauves,* Kunsthalle, Bern, 1950, no. 118; *Biennale,* Venice, 1950, no. 52; Zurich 1958, no. 271; Berlin 1958, no. 68; Munich 1958–1959, no. 166; Edinburgh and London 1961, no. 72; Lucerne 1963, no. 55.

LITERATURE: Marcel Sauvage, *Vlaminck: sa vie, son message* (Geneva, 1956), no. 35.

Maurice de Vlaminck
78 Still Life with Oranges

NOTES: **1.** Quoted in Françoise Cachin, *Gauguin* (Paris, 1989), 45: "Un grand sentiment peut être traduit immédiatement, rêvez dessus, et cherchez-en la forme la plus simple." / **2.** Vlaminck 1943, 140: "Entre Gauguin et sa peinture, je découvre un désir forcené d'invention, une volonté de créer, à tout prix, un style original. Les brosses en main, il cherche ce qu'il souffre de ne pouvoir trouver en lui-même."

PROVENANCE: Collection Schwabacher, New York; P. Nathan, Zurich; purchased by Bührle in 1954.

EXHIBITIONS: *Dokumenta, Kunst des XX. Jahrhunderts,* Fridericianum, Kassel, 1950, no. 648; Berlin 1958, no. 70; Munich 1958–1959, no. 169; *Triumph der Farbe,* Museum zu Allerheiligen, Schaffhausen, 1959, no. 24; Edinburgh and London 1961, no. 73.

LITERATURE: *Foundation E. G. Bührle Collection,* 2d ed. (Zurich and Munich, 1986), no. 118, ill.

Franz Marc
79 The Dog in Front of the World

NOTES: **1.** Schardt 1936, 92: "Er und seine Frau sassen ausruhend an einem Hang, und ihnen zur Seite sass der Hund Russi. Er sah still und unentwegt in die Landschaft, so dass Marc sagte: ich möchte einmal wissen, was in dem Hund vorgeht, wenn er so dasitzt und die Landschaft ansieht!" / **2.** Franz Marc in *Pan* 2 (March 1912): "Natur ist überall, in uns und ausser uns; es gibt nur etwas, das nicht ganz Natur ist, sondern vielmehr ihre Überwindung und Deutung, und dessen Kraft von einem uns unbekannten Stützpunkt ausgeht: die Kunst. Die Kunst war und ist in ihrem Wesen jederzeit die kühnste Entfernung von der Natur und der Natürlichkeit. Unverständnis und Angst vor ihren neuen Formen verstehen wir – Kritik nicht."

PROVENANCE: Dr. Koehler, Berlin; Baron von Löffelholz, Munich; purchased by Bührle in 1952.

EXHIBITIONS: *Franz Marc,* Kunstsalon Schames, 1912; *Franz Marc: Gedächtnisausstellung,* Neue Sezession, Munich, 1916, no. 164; *Franz Marc: Gedächtnisausstellung,* Nationalgalerie, Berlin, 1922, no. 80; *Franz Marc: Gedächtnisausstellung,* Kestner-Gesellschaft, 1936, no. 162;

Franz Marc, Galerie Nierendorf, Berlin, 1936; *Lehmbruck, Macke, Marc,* Kunsthalle, Bern, 1948, no. 136; *Der Blaue Reiter: München und die Kunst des 20. Jahrhunderts,* Städtische Galerie, Munich, 1949, no. 234; *Der Blaue Reiter,* Kunsthalle, Basel, 1950, no. 205; Goetheschule, Wolfsburg, 1952; Zurich 1958, no. 291.

LITERATURE: Alois J. Schardt, *Franz Marc* (Berlin, 1936), no. 6, 94; Georg Schmidt, *Franz Marc und die deutsche Malerei des 19. und 20. Jahrhunderts* (Berlin, 1957), 9; Klaus Lankheit, *Franz Marc: Katalog der Werke* (DuMont, 1970), no. 170.

Franz Marc
80 Mare with Foals

NOTES: **1.** Wassily Kandinsky, *Das Kunstblatt* 14 (Berlin, 1930), 59: "Beide liebten wir Blau, Marc Pferde, ich Reiter. So kam der Name von selbst." / **2.** Franz Marc, in: Reinhard Piper, *Das Tier in der Kunst* (Munich, 1910), 190: "Ich sehe kein glücklicheres Mittel zur 'Animalisierung' der Kunst, wie ich es nennen möchte, als das Tierbild. Darum greife ich danach. . . . Meine Plastik ist ein tastender Versuch nach derselben Richtung. Das Kreisen des Blutes in den beiden Pferdeköpfen, ausgedrückt durch die mannigfachen Parallelismen und Schwingungen in den Linien. Der Betrachter sollte gar nicht nach dem 'Pferdetyp' fragen können, sondern das innerlich zitternde Tierleben herausfühlen. Ich habe absichtlich getrachtet, den Pferden jedes besondere Rassezeichen zu nehmen."

PROVENANCE: Baron von Löffelholz, Munich; purchased by Bührle in 1953.

EXHIBITIONS: *Der Sturm, Der Blaue Reiter,* Helsingfors, Trondheim, Göteborg, 1914, no. 42?

LITERATURE: Schardt 1936, no. 30; Lankheit 1970, no. 191.

André Derain
81 The Table

NOTE: **1.** Guillaume Apollinaire, *Catalogue André Derain* (Paris 1916): "Derain a passionnément étudié les maîtres. Les copies qu'il en a faites montrent le souci qu'il a eu de les connaître. En même temps, par une audace sans égale, il passait par dessus tout ce que l'art contemporain comptait de plus audacieux pour retrouver avec la simplicité et la fraîcheur, les principes de l'art et les disciplines qui en découlent."

PROVENANCE: Collection Hector Brame S. R. L., Paris; purchased by Bührle in 1952.

EXHIBITIONS: *Les Fauves,* The Museum of Modern Art, New York, 1952, no. 24; Berlin 1958, no. 76; Munich 1958–1959, no. 54; *Triumph der Farbe,* Museum zu Allerheiligen, Schaffhausen, 1959, no. 35; Edinburgh and London, no. 74.

LITERATURE: Georges Hilaire, *Derain* (Geneva, 1959), pl. 31; Denys Sutton, *A. Derain* (Cologne, 1950), 23; *Foundation E. G. Bührle Collection,* 2d ed. (Zurich and Munich, 1986), no. 119, ill.

Pablo Picasso
82 The Italian Girl

NOTE: **1.** Pierre Daix, *Picasso Créateur* (Paris, 1987), 163: "L'Antiquité grouille toute neuve dans ce Montmartre arabe."

PROVENANCE: Mme Wildenstein; G. Kahnweiler, London; purchased by Bührle in 1954.

EXHIBITIONS: Zurich 1958, no. 306; Munich 1958–1959, no. 119; *Pablo Picasso,* Tate Gallery, London, 1960, no. 85; *Chefs-d'œuvre des collections suisses,* Palais de Beaulieu, Lausanne, 1964, no. 234; *Hommage à Picasso,* Grand Palais, Paris, 1966, no. 102; *Pablo Picasso,* Österreichisches Museum, Vienna, 1968, no. 30.

LITERATURE: Christian Zervos, *Pablo Picasso,* vol. 3, *Œuvres de 1917 à 1919* (Paris, 1949), no. 18, pl. 7; Wilhelm Boeck, *Picasso* (Stuttgart, 1955), 171; René Elvin, "The Bührle Collection and the New Zürich Kunsthaus," *The Studio* 158 (1959): no. 797; Reginald H. Wilenski and Roland Penrose, *Picasso: die frühen Jahre* (Berlin, 1961), 14; *Foundation Emil G. Bührle,* 2d ed. (Zurich and Munich, 1986), no. 138, ill.

Georges Braque
83 The Port of L'Estaque

NOTE: **1.** Quoted in Serge Faucherau, *Braque* (Paris, 1987), 8: "La peinture fauve m'avait impressionné par ce qu'elle avait de nouveau et cela me convenait. . . . J'avais vingt-trois ans. . . . Cette peinture physique me plaisait. . . ."

PROVENANCE: Gallery Knoedler, New York; purchased by Bührle in 1956.

EXHIBITIONS: Berlin 1958, no. 77; Munich 1958–1959, no. 8; Edinburgh and London 1961, no. 76; Lucerne 1963, no. 67.

LITERATURE: *Foundation Emil G. Bührle Collection,* 2d ed. (Zurich and Munich, 1986), no. 125, ill.

Georges Braque
84 The Violinist

NOTE: **1.** Auction at Christie's, 15 November 1988, no. 31.

PROVENANCE: Collection D. H. Kahnweiler, Paris; Collection P. Lhote, Paris; Marlborough Fine Art Ltd., London; purchased by Bührle in 1955.

EXHIBITIONS: *Twentieth Century Masters,* Marlborough Fine Arts Ltd., London, 1955, no. 4; *Braque,* The Royal Scottish Academy, Edinburgh, 1956, no. 29; Zurich 1958, no. 299; Munich 1958–1959, no. 7; *De Géricault à Matisse,* Petit Palais, Paris, 1959, no. 13; The Museum of Modern Art, New York, 1989.

LITERATURE: Umbro Apollonio, *Fauves und Kubisten* (Stuttgart, 1959), 51; John Golding, *Cubism* (London, 1959), pl. 40; Jean Leymarie, *Braque* (Geneva, 1961), 52; Marco Valsecchi and Massimo Carra, *L'opera di Braque, 1908–1929* (Milan, 1971), no. 82; Nicole Worms de Romilly, *Braque le cubisme fin 1907–1914: Catalogue raisonné de l'œuvre peint* (Paris, 1982), no. 125; *Foundation E. G. Bührle Collection,* 1986, no. 126, ill.

Oskar Kokoschka
85 Portrait of Emil G. Bührle

NOTE: **1.** Letter from Kokoschka to his wife Olda of 20 December 1951, in *Briefe,* 1986, 3:259.

PROVENANCE: Comissioned by Bührle in 1951/1952.

EXHIBITIONS: *Biennale Internazionale d'Arte di Venezia,* 1952, Venice, no. 97; *Der späte Kokoschka,* Haus Salve Hospes, Brunswick, 1960, no. 23; *Chefs-d'œuvre des collections suisses de Manet à Picasso,* Palais de Beaulieu, Lausanne, 1964; *Oskar Kokoschka,* Kunsthaus, Zurich, 1966, no. 98; *Oskar Kokoschka, Bildnisse von 1907 bis 1970,* Haus der Kunst, Munich, 1971, no. 42.

LITERATURE: D. Wild, *Moderne Kunst in Schweizer Sammlungen* (Baden-Baden, 1954), 18; H. M. Wingler, *Oskar Kokoschka, Das Werk des Malers,* (Salzburg, 1956), no. 374, pl. 129; *DU, Die Kunstzeitschrift,* 10, 1981, 60 (fig. 4); H. Spielmann, ed., *Oskar Kokoschka, Briefe* (Düsseldorf, 1986), 3:258, 259„ 261.